X-mas 94

Rich.

I was flipping
through this book
and read the
acknowledgements and
knew I had to get this
for my agriculture man.

To the greatest!!

Love,
Kra

# CUTTING HILL

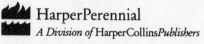 HarperPerennial
*A Division of* HarperCollins*Publishers*

# CUTTING HILL

## A Chronicle of a Family Farm

*by* ALAN PISTORIUS

WITH ILLUSTRATIONS BY KATHLEEN KOLB-FISHER

A portion of this work was originally published in *Vermont* magazine.

A hardcover edition of this book was published in 1990 by Alfred A. Knopf, Inc.
It is here reprinted by arrangement with Alfred A. Knopf, Inc.

First Harper Perennial edition published 1991.

LIBRARY OF CONGRESS CATALOG CARD NUMBER 90-56182

ISBN 0-06-097403-6

91 92 93 94 95 FG 10 9 8 7 6 5 4 3 2 1

FURTHERMORE, TO THE END THAT HIS PEOPLE MAY *not live idle, . . . which being imployed about some one or other worke, [the husbandman] shall dispose of his workes so, as that they may everie one have [its] certaine time, and he shall know at his fingers ends what things is to be done everie moneth and time of the yeare. . . . In May hee shall water the Trees that are newly planted: hee shall sheare his Sheepe, . . . gather great store of Butter, and make much Cheese, geld his Calues, and begin to looke to his Bees. . . . In Iune hee shall make readie his Threshing floore, and cause it to be thorowly cleansed of straw, durt, and dust: he shall cut downe his Medowes, mow his Barley, crop his Vines, thresh his Corne to sow in Seed time. . . .*

*I doe not find the state or place of a Huswife or Dairie-woman to be of lesse care and diligence than the office of her Husband. . . . Countrie Women looke vnto the things necessarie and requisite about Kine, Calues, Hogges, Pigges, Pigeons, Geese, Duckes, Peacockes, Hennes, Fesants, and other sorts of Beasts, as well for the feeding of them as for the milking of them: making of Butter and Cheese: and the keeping of Lard to dresse the labouring men their victuals withall. Yea, furthermore they haue the charge of the Ouen and Cellar . . . of spinning and combing of Wooll to make Cloth to cloath the familie, or ordering of the Kitchin Garden, and keeping of the Fruits, Hearbes, Rootes, and Seeds. . . . I meane also that she must . . . not [be] contentious, full of words, toyish, tatling; nor drowsie-headed.*

From Charles Stevens and John Liebault's
*Maison Rustique, or, The Countrie Farme*, translated
from the French by Richard Surflet and revised
by Gervase Markham, London, 1616

# Contents

# Acknowledgments

A formal bibliography would probably serve little purpose here, but anyone who writes about matters agricultural will read around in the farm literature, and will be indebted in various ways to the books of Louis Bromfield and Jerome Blum and Wendell Berry and Mark Kramer and Robert West Howard and others. He will likely also spend more time than he might care to with the governmental ag literature, from the massive, multivolume *Agriculture in the United States: A Documentary History* to the latest USDA monographs and articles, documents with titles like *Fact Book of United States Agriculture, 1986* and "Financial Well-Being of Farm Operators and Their Households" and *Disaggregated Farm Income by Type of Farm, 1959–82* and "Analysis of Cooperative Over-Order Pricing of Fluid Milk."

People, however, have been more important than print in the process of writing this book, and I am grateful first of all to Dick and Joan Treadway and their extended families, who welcomed me to the farm and allowed me to tag along through thick and thin. I am also indebted to the feed dealers and tool salesmen and veterinarians and milk haulers and barn inspectors and extension agents who helped educate me as they went about their business on the farm. No names of persons or places have been changed in this book.

Editor Jane Garrett was not only "on board" but on hand from the beginning. Indeed, had it not been for her initial sympathetic enthusiasm, this project would never have been undertaken. Kathleen Kolb-Fisher's evocative and empathetic watercolors contribute much to the book's appeal, and have my appreciation.

My thanks, finally, to the several readers inside and outside Knopf who searched the manuscript for problems, and to Robin Conway and Carole Fenn, who put draft after draft of typescript through the computers and printers at QB Fox.

A.P.

# *Preface*

Probably everyone would agree with Stevens and Liebault—the reference is to the epigraph, in case you're lost—that farmers keep busy, that a farm is no place for the "drowsie-headed." Beyond that, it's difficult to imagine finding consensus on any aspect of the subject.

Our understanding of farmers and farming is largely mythic, and the two dominant myths are antithetical. One—it seems to have been compounded of Roman philosophy and pastoral literary tradition—holds that the country is the repository of all virtues, the home of healthy, upright, sober, contemplative men, a moral bulwark against the city, that breeder of profligacy, luxury, ambition, and corruption.

Isaac Newton, Commissioner of Agriculture in Abraham Lincoln's newly established United States Department of Agriculture, stood four-square in this tradition when he declared that in "all ages wise, learned, and good men have gladly turned away from the employments of public life to the pleasures, the consolations, and the quietude of rural pursuits. . . . All their plans of life have a kind of natural culmination in the determination to retire into the country and share with the farmer the healthful and dignified occupation of husbandry." No "truer or more comprehensive line of poetry" was ever penned, the eloquent Newton averred, than this: "God made the country—man made the town."

But in that same year, 1862, the *Annual Report* of Newton's own USDA struck a radically different note: "In passing through a lunatic asylum the visitor is sometimes surprised to learn that the most numerous class of unfortunates are from the farm. . . .

[T]he key to the so frequent cases of insanity and suicide among farmers [is that] their subjects of thought are too few; their life is a ruinous routine; there is a sameness and a tameness about it, a paucity of subjects for contemplation, most dangerous to mental integrity."

If nineteenth-century insane asylums were packed with farmers, it was partly an accident of demographics: the majority of Americans lived on farms. (Lawyers, engineers, stock brokers, and psychologists, of whom there are a lot around, have replaced farmers in today's asylums.) Still, this passage is an expression of our second major farm myth, the city's revenge myth, if you will. It holds that the country is a place where nothing happens outside the round of back-breaking, mind-deadening labor, a "boondocks" wasteland untouched by culture, unsoftened by conversation or manners, home to "hayseeds," "rubes," and cloddish boors.

Either or both of these myths play about in the minds of nonfarm Americans, and play there, in most cases, in an experiential vacuum. Ninety-eight percent of us live off farms now, and for most of us the Thanksgiving or Christmas trip to Grandmother's house is no longer a ride—and certainly not a sleigh ride—over the river and through the woods to the family farm, but a taxi drive from the airport to a condominium in Cleveland or Phoenix. Though the majority of Americans are at most several generations removed from farm stock, few know anything firsthand about farming. Paradoxically, farming, which spreads out across the landscape, is an invisible enterprise, an undercover operation like spying or diamond mining. The lives of farmer and nonfarmer simply don't intersect, except briefly and uninformatively when a tractor-pulled manure spreader impedes automobile progress on a country road or highway.

What most of us know about farming is what we hear on thirty-second television news spots highlighting pigeonholed problems: Crop Failure, Controversial Price Supports, Declining Farm Property Values, Crop Surpluses, Escalating Bank Foreclosures on Farms, all of which—with others—add up to a Farm

Crisis. And while a passing acquaintance with farm *issues* may be of some value, we lack a context to give them meaning. We mourn the Loss of the Family Farm(er) without having much sense of what one is all about. What *is* farm life like these days? Are farmers still (if, indeed, they ever were) different—as both myths assume—from other people? What, exactly, is going on out there in the country?

I'm glad you asked.

# SPRING

# I

I'T'S SPRING!'' SAYS JOAN EXULTINGLY. ''DICK'S fixing fences.'' It is the third day of May, and when spring is mentioned in these parts the response you mostly get is a grumbling "about time." April has been cold and rainy. The third week in particular was bleak and raw, with temperatures below freezing every morning. On the twenty-first a blanket of snow covered the daffodils.

If April was hell—or at least purgatorial—this first warm day of May is simply glorious. It has a soft, summery feel, with quiet breezes; delicate smears of mare's tails ride in a high sky. Clearly spring will come—as it so often does in mid–New England— with a rush this year; the interval between snow shovel and lawn mower will be measured in weeks.

After a hesitant beginning, the greening of this Vermont hill-and-valley country—a topographical "rumple" where the Taconic Mountains to the south slide down to the broad Champlain Valley to the north—is going confidently forward now as Dick Treadway, hatless, gloveless, in dark cords and a light check shirt, sets out to fix fence around ninety-odd acres of mostly rock-ledge mixed woods where his older heifers will soon run. An axe over one shoulder, a roll of shiny electrical-fence wire over the other, hammer and wire cutters secured in a heavy leather linesman's belt around his waist, Dick heads west down the fenceline accompanied by the listless song of a black-and-white warbler (the season's first, a full week late) and by Thorson, a huge-footed, black-muzzled, red-brown Great Dane–mastiff mix.

One farms literally on top of the work of earlier generations of farmers, and nowhere is that more apparent than when one cruises fence. This first west-running section is ancient zigzag rail fence—the "worm" fence of an earlier age—reinforced by old rusted two-strand barbed wire. Age and the combined forces of winter—frost heaving, wind, the weight of snow, falling trees and limbs—conspire against fence; rails tumble, wire sags. Eyeing the fence from a heifer's perspective as he walks along, Dick stops to deal with problems. Fallen rails are lifted into place. A sagging length of barbed wire is pulled taut against the inside of its anchoring post or fenceline tree and secured by an inch-and-a-half staple, whose legs spread when driven by virtue of planed points. If the sag is severe, Dick simply grabs the wire at midpoint with the jaws of his wire cutter and rotates the tool, twisting the wire tight (and leaving a curious conelike excrescence projecting from it).

The neighbor's young black retriever spots the fencing crew across the pasture to the south and makes a bee-line. He arrives all wiggles and jumps and wags and charges. In Thorson's view of life there is no excuse for these enthusiasms. He is appalled, and gravely repudiates the puppy's overtures.

"We had a two-hundred-twenty-pound St. Bernard before. The kids rode him like a pony. He was gentle, but fierce-looking. Strangers didn't fool with him." When the St. Bernard died, the Treadway family got another big dog from a man who had for some reason named him Thorson G. Orson and kept him chained up. Given his liberty on the farm, he had practically run himself to death—uncoordinatedly at first—and, as Dick puts it, nearly "wore out his nose" trailing scents. Thor has matured into an effective watchdog, intimidating in size and voice and mien. (At close range, one finds his soft brown eyes fixed in an expression of sad apology, as if he were chagrined at his own ferocity. Few strangers ever get near enough to notice.) Apparently bored with the fence detail, Thorson strikes off cross-country, the puppy in pursuit, still soliciting sport.

The property line turns north, and the fence here is newish-looking, sturdy barbed wire. "Heifers are pretty good about fence if they're only on one side," Dick says. "If there are heifers on both sides, they try to get together." That was the case here, and, tired of chasing and sorting, Dick and his neighbor got together and put in better fence.

The land drops abruptly to a spring-fed stream, whose bank is littered with light tan wood chips below fresh pileated wood-pecker work. The barbed wire here parallels a stretch of old stump fence, a picturesque form of livestock control rarely encountered now in the countryside. (Rail fences are increasingly scarce on farms as well. The old rails are fed into farmhouse woodstoves, turn up as rustic accents on monied country estates—having been bought at farms or from intermediaries who are likely to have stolen them—or simply rot on the ground.)

Fence cruising gets tougher as the boundary line humps and dips near the base of a steep, ledgy hill. There is no livestock forage here ("Heifers shouldn't get down in here, but you never know"), but the hardhack is flourishing, as well as the occa-sional magnificent red oak, trees ten and even fifteen feet in trunk circumference. Here the fence is "woven wire," a fence of barbless wire whose horizontal strands are tied together with short verticals to form rectangular units. "This fence must have come in back when some Vermont farmers were still running sheep. But how do you suppose they ever got it in here?" Dick wonders, casting an eye over the steep, loose, and wooded hill-side. "Just carrying it in would have been tough enough, but can you imagine trying to unroll it in here?"

The Treadway farm boasts nearly every conceivable sort of fence except what has become most common for livestock con-trol, the single-strand electric fence. What with continually fall-ing limbs, that fence would be useless in these woods. But even in the open cropland to the east, they haven't electrified. "Elec-tric fence is handy if you want to move your pastures around," says Dick. "We don't. Beyond that, electric fence demands con-stant attention, and cows walk through electric just like they do barbed wire. I'm not sure we'd be better off with electric. We fix up what we've got."

In the absence of a handy tree, broken fence is a problem here. Dick lays out a four-inch-diameter downed hardhack, and, anchoring it with a sneakered foot, chops it to length. Unable to drive it into this ledgy ground, he wedges the post in alongside a boulder. Unable to staple into a less-than-firm post, he cuts short lengths from his roll of electrical-fence wire and ties up the fence twisty-fashion.

If one imagines this fence as a piece of linear sculpture, its title would be "Improvisation in Wood and Wire." Wood mostly takes a supporting role, and anything substantial will do. Trees living and dead are pressed into service, as is the occasional downed giant. Posts—red cedar cut on the farm and white cedar from area swamps ("They may cost you a dollar-twenty-five each; you can make some money cutting posts")—fill in the gaps. When posts rot off at ground level, they are left standing in place as oversized supporting "spacers." Wire mostly serves as barrier, but it is pressed into support service as well in the form of guy lines, anchoring both wood and wire.

At one point a double deadfall, crisscrossed, has flattened a stretch of barbed-wire fence. Clearly nobody is going to lift these two mature trees off the fence, and to chop them out would take ages. Dick cuts the strands of wire at the first standing post, fishes them out from under the far side of the deadfall, and reroutes them back over and through the downed trees. But the strands don't reach the post. Dick cuts a length of his new wire for each barbed strand and proceeds to splice. He pokes the end of a piece of new wire through a space between the two twist-around filaments composing the strand of barbed wire, wraps the short end a few turns around the old wire behind a barb, takes a complete turn around the post with the spliced new wire, stretches the strand tight, takes a few turns with the free end around itself, and the fix is complete.

The object here is neither a pretty fence nor even a particularly strong one. It is, rather, to quickly bring the fence back—using available material and a few tools—to a condition adequately substantial to say "barrier" to a heifer. After one piece of makeshift repair melding old wood and rusty wire and new wire, Dick nods approvingly at his work and chuckles. "*Any*body would be proud of that!" (Dick's quiet humor is expressed largely by the eyes, whence a full smile spreads via a double sweep of crow's-feet more than halfway to jaw and ears.)

The skeleton fence crew rustles through parchment-tan dried leaves of elm, beech, maple, and oak, here and there coming upon lovely stands of bloodroot, the showy white flowers cupped by the curious reptile-leather leaves, and of hairy-stemmed white and pale lavender hepatica. The protracted, cheerfully conversational song of a ruby-crowned kinglet sounds oddly out of place coming from the otherwise silent woods up-slope.

"It's pretty secluded back here," says Dick. "We hear coyotes back in here; at least it sounds like they're back here. There're deer in here too. I saw a doe with twins once in that meadow. The fawns were playing—chasing each other like puppies, kicking up their heels like calves." A bold, high ridge called the Pinnacle rises beyond the open meadow to the west. "It's the highest point in the area. They say you can see Lake Champlain from the top; I've never climbed it."

Scattered in the near margin of the neighbor's meadow are a number of recently cut oak stumps, and another forms the corner for a jog in the fence. Of course, fences move around some from decade to decade, and no one knows exactly where the property boundaries are; but this oak stump is on the inside of the wire, suggesting that the tree had belonged to the Treadways. "I asked the people who did the lumbering, and they said neighbors get every other tree in a fenceline. But there's no other mature oak in this fenceline; where's my tree?" He adds without rancor: "Now that it's gone, there's nothing I can do about it."

The fence continues north after the jog, skirting a drier hillside where aspen, sumac, and brambles replace white pine and hardhack. Now walking the boundary of land he rents, Dick discovers a new problem. The owner of this land had recently lumbered off the mature white pine, and had taken down the fence in the process of dumping the saw-logs on the edge of the adjoining meadow. Inexplicably, the ten- and twelve-foot logs remain where dumped, rapidly becoming worthless, and the fence is still down. Dick makes a mental note to call the lumberers and ask them to put the fence to rights.

There's another, and larger, potential problem here. The adjoining longtime farm meadow is at this moment being transformed into an apple orchard. A New Jersey orchardist has bought the spread to set up a son-in-law in the McIntosh-growing business, aiming, as Dick understands it, at an orchard of 50,000 trees. A giant tractor drones ahead in the distance, scraping parallel lines along the hillside while dragging behind a tree planter which sets the four-foot slips in the ground.

"He had thermometers scattered all over here last fall and winter, checking temperatures, looking for cold-drainage patterns. He seems to know what he's doing." Dick will also have to know what he's doing now. Traditionally, farm neighbors share responsibility for fixing fence. But the orchardist will have no livestock, and so the whole responsibility will likely devolve on the Treadways. And should their cows manage to break out and begin to chew on apple trees, the consequences could be serious.

Dick gestures at the sweep of land to the west and north. "Things are changing. This land will never be farmed again. At least, with orchard, it'll stay open land." Some of this land soon to go into apples had long been rented and farmed by the Treadways. "It's pretty wild in there," he says. "Seventy acres of ravines and woods. We lost some heifers in there a few years ago, and it took us two days to find them and chase them out." The fence turns east now, and Dick's memory turns to winter scenes. "The whole family used to come down here for Christmas trees. We'd walk and walk. The kids could always see a better one up ahead."

Working east, the land flattens and opens up into pasture dotted with clumps of white and gray birch. The odd wild strawberry is already in bloom, and the foot-high anthill chimneys are active. A field sparrow tunes up, repeatedly delivering its bouncing-ball monotonic song. A small brook meanders through the pasture, dropping at one point into a lovely deep pool before heading west for the Lemon Fair River, which will carry this water via Otter Creek into Lake Champlain to the northwest. It feels almost hot working up the fence under the sun after the cool work under the ledge hill.

Dick's roll of wire is nearly exhausted, and a check of his watch confirms that he is past due at the barn. He has this afternoon fixed perhaps two of the roughly eight miles of fence he'll walk this week. He strikes south through a grove of hemlock, cuts through to the road, and heads for home.

THE FOLLOWING SATURDAY IS BRIGHT AND sunny but windy out of the north when the whole Treadway family heads out to mend more fence. Dick drives the '79 Jeep Renegade, lurching eastward behind the farmstead along a tractor track through a corn piece and a meadow, with Joan and three of their children—Kevin, Brian, and Rebecca—aboard. Jeffrey, the eldest, brings up the rear, driving one of the farm's two John Deere 4000s, its bucket loader hauling cedar posts, wire, and tools.

"Oh, look!" Joan points, as a red-tailed hawk slips south out of the pasture just over stubby red cedars away from the arriving Jeep; "we're sure a pair nested on the farm last year." The old barbed wire in this stretch of north-south-running fence has deteriorated to the point where it often breaks while being tightened. It will be left in place, and three strands of new wire added. With the free end of the shiny silver barbed wire stapled to a post, Dick and Jeff pick up either end of a pipe inserted through the seventy-eight-pound roll and walk along the fence, unrolling wire as they go. When fifty feet or so of wire lies along the fence, it is cut and strung. The key tool here is the wire stretcher, which looks (and works) something like an extended,

baseless car jack with a hook on one end. Jeff secures the end of
the wire on the straight end of the stretcher, throws the hooked
end around a post at the proper height, and simply ratchets the
strand tight. The rest of the family now secure the strand by
driving staples into the intervening posts. Hitting a headless
staple with a hammer is easy, but driving it straight into an often
less-than-solid post is another matter. "*Hit* it!" urges Jeff, as
Brian whacks and whacks at a staple going every which way
but in.

The new fence goes in a section at a time, with backtracks for
new strands. From time to time Joan does pipe duty with Dick.
In their late thirties, both are probably five-feet-eight. ("Pretty
soon I'll be the shortest one on this farm," moans Dick. "I used
to be taller, but farming is wearing me down.") Dick doesn't, in
fact, look at all "worn," though his golden-brown hair has begun to thin on top, and a hint of a midriff shows on what
otherwise might be a college wrestler's body. Joan is trim in
jeans and a shirt, her blonde hair done up in a blue bandanna,
silver cats hanging from her earlobes.

As the afternoon wears on, some of the crew drift away,
apples and bananas in hand. Thirteen-year-old Kevin—slender,
soft-spoken like his father (and with his father's hair) and mu-
sical like his mother, and who, in partial confirmation of his
father's doleful prediction, will this year become the second-
tallest family member after Jeff—moseys out to put an east-
running rail fence to rights. Brian, still growing out of baby-fat
awkwardness—and with more than a little puckish mischief in
his blue eyes—will be nine next month. He is in a subdue-
the-wilderness phase, and now wanders about thwacking
downed (and some standing) timber with a hatchet, disdainful of
his siblings' predictions of ghastly leg and foot injuries. Rebecca,
at five, is a miniature replica of her mother, spare, adventure-
some, wide-eyed. "And *tough*," adds Joan. "People said with
three older brothers to protect her she'd be a wallflower; boy, were
*they* wrong." (In the framed family portrait hanging on the living
room wall, the faces of Dick, Joan, Jeff, and Kevin beam forth in

all's-right-with-the-world radiance. Brian and Becky, on the other
hand, are concerned with matters at hand. Becky is alert, quiz-
zical, reserving judgment, while Brian's gaze casts unmasked sus-
picion on the entire profession of portrait photography.) Becky
now wanders down to the stream to hunt among the cowslips for
the green frogs she had found earlier in the week.

A reduced crew composed of Dick and Jeff—who, on the shy
side in public, his almond-shaped eyes set at a striking tilt, is at
sixteen already an accomplished farmer and holder of a number
of Future Farmers of America awards—heads east to check the
wire threaded through the rail fence. Joan drops gloves and
hammer and climbs to a bench interrupting the upslope near the
top of a long rise which parallels the eastern border of the
"town" (many states call them townships) of Shoreham. She
leans against the trunk of a large shagbark hickory and admires
the view. "I like to come up here to view my kingdom," she says.
The white pine woods to the north along the ridge is in a corner
of the town of Whiting, and beyond the woods loom the hills of
southern Cornwall. The view to the northwest, beyond an invisible Lake Champlain, encompasses three tiers of upstate New
York's Adirondack Mountains. Off the south end of the pasture,
three turkey vultures tilt like kites in the strong wind. Here and
there in distant fencerows a fuzzy white blob marks a newly
blooming shad. "It's something," Joan says, "to see the heifers
charging down this hill."

The family reassembles at the hemlock-shaded stream at the
head of the rail fence. Shining green and yellow marsh marigold
clumps are thick and resplendent here, and Becky shows off a
large green frog in a small pool. Brian announces his intention to
murder the creature, whereupon Becky assumes a protective
posture and shrieks. Kevin has found a couple of small shelf
lichens growing on a fallen tree, and, confident in the freshly
won knowlege of junior high biology, he quizzes Brian: "So
what is this, fungus or lichen?"

The crew motors back to put in some new posts on the fence
bordering the road below the farmyard, with Kevin and Brian

making a detour for a resupply of snacks. Mindy, the other family dog, follows the boys down the road and joins the family party. Part sheepdog and part "traveling salesman," Mindy sports black and white curly shag—with the odd patch of reddish brown reminiscent of bad hair dye jobs—on a corpulent body. She mostly sticks close to home, where she challenges strangers with a throaty bark that would be more effective if her tail weren't wagging all the while.

New posts—these are red cedar, one end sawn to a rough point—are "planted" via tractor power. Jeff maneuvers the big tractor around boulders and between trees up to the fence. Dick takes a post from the bucket loader, positions it, then uses hand signals to Jeff, who brings the bucket loader over the post and lowers it. When the bucket has set down on the post top, Dick backs out a respectful distance ("These posts occasionally shatter and fly"), and Jeff lowers the boom, driving the give-or-take $7\frac{1}{2}$-foot post in two feet or to bedrock, whichever comes first.

Joan shakes her head at the sight of Jeff working the tractor controls with one hand while manipulating a package of saltines with the other. "My kids live to eat," she says. "It's no wonder our grocery bill is a hundred and fifty bucks a week," Dick adds, to which his wife retorts: "You haven't seen the checkbook recently; it's closer to two hundred."

Brian and Becky dash off to play Robin Hood. Jeff and his father set the needed new posts; Dick, Joan, and Kevin drive staples and tighten wire. Dick points out a strand stapled to the back (or road) side of a post. Wire is always fastened on the inside, or livestock side of posts, so that a leaning or pushing animal will be shoving posts as well as wire and can't pop staples "You're dealing with rookies here," Joan declares; "maybe I should go home and do something domestic."

The afternoon is waning, and the unchecked couple of sections of fence will be left for another day. Dick and Joan put tools, barbed wire, and electrical-fence wire into the bucket loader, and walk up the road. "Time we were in the barn," Dick says.

## 2

THE MORNING OF MAY 13 IS SUNNY AND MOD-
erately warm. The rich notes of a recently arrived northern oriole sound from trees across the road, and somewhere to the
north and south male downy woodpeckers are drumming on
snags, dividing up the farm: drum-roll to the north, drum-roll to
the south; to the north, to the south. A strong wind sweeps out
of the south, whipping the margins of the tire-anchored black
plastic covering the sawdust pile. Dick and a young man named
Aaron are changing hydraulic fluid—capacity ten gallons—in
one of the Deeres, and from time to time they turn their faces
away as a wind swirl loads up on loose sawdust and drives at
them. The forecast calls for rain later on today, and Dick wants
to get a ten-acre piece west of the road—in corn last year—
planted to meadow, a job you can't do on wet ground.

But Dick has manpower problems. Brian suffered an attack of
what appears to be asthma ("He couldn't breathe," Becky vol-
unteers) in the middle of the night, and Joan's day started at the
hospital emergency room at 2:30 A.M. with shots and oxygen.
Brian has a follow-up appointment with a doctor in town this
afternoon, and, his progress unsatisfactory, he will spend tonight back in the hospital. Joan doesn't say much, but is clearly
worried. Dick and Jeff have been sporadic asthma sufferers for
years; now it appears that Brian will make a third.

Joan's unexpected responsibilities have cost Dick a tractor
driver, and Aaron, a family friend and artificial inseminator who
has stopped by to breed a cow, is pressed into service. He will
harrow for Dick this afternoon, and Dick will drive out to his place
some afternoon next week to help with a furniture-moving chore.

Don Treadway, Dick's father, comes down off the open south-facing porch of the old Treadway farmhouse, located between Dick and Joan's house and the barn, to check on preparations. Physically, Don is a heavier version of Dick—in fencer's parlance, a post to Dick's spacer. He favors two-piece work suits in olive green—the color of his eyes, and of the 1966 Dodge 100 pickup sitting, apparently permanently, outside his house—the pants belted under an ample belly. Another well-developed part of Don's anatomy is his funny bone. The "things people do," the ironies and illogicalities manifest in the passing scene tickle him no end, and he comments on them freely. (His humor is typically deadpan, though often betrayed by a guttural chuckle.) He now stares at the five-ton-capacity dry-fertilizer spreader parked and ready for hitching in his driveway and inquires: "You gonna spread that little piece with this? You could use a salt-and-pepper shaker."

The economics of farm transactions are sometimes curious. The bin of this spreader is but half-full for the complete job, and it has been rented from the fertilizer dealer for the $20 per diem figure even though the Treadways have their own spreader. But it's cheaper to do it this way, because they are buying the fertilizer at bulk cost. Should a farmer wish to use his own spreader, the fertilizer would be delivered in bags. The bagging fee, in this case, would be higher than the spreader rental, and they would have to wrestle with the bags as well.

A three-tractor parade sets off north on Cutting Hill Road—luckily meeting no traffic, as the fifteen-foot-wide harrow is the exact width of the road—and progresses west down a steep tractor road and into the plowed and harrowed piece. After some tinkering with a refractory release lever, Don Treadway begins spreading on the west margin, the fertilizer pellets—an 8/32/16 nitrogen/phosphorus/potash mix—fed from the bin onto a spinning pan, which fires them in a spray pattern calibrated for a fifty-foot spread.

Aaron follows the spreader in the Treadways' largest tractor, an Allis-Chalmers 7000, his black dog beside him, working the fertilizer in with the circular blades of the harrow. Meanwhile, Dick attacks a mostly submerged boulder in the center of the field. He drives the lip of the lowered bucket loader under the soil and into the boulder, then pulls the lever to raise the bucket. Under full power, the Deere struggles mightily, the front wheels picking up off the ground, but the boulder, of unknown size, doesn't budge. Approaches from three sides bring the same results. "We just don't have the power," Dick concludes. "Nothing we can do but bury it and plant over it," and, using the bottom of the bucket loader, he drags a layer of soil over the boulder. Harrowing always turns up rocks in this valley clay, and Dick now sweeps up and down the piece, stopping to chuck into the lowered bucket loader rocks football-sized and larger, driving to field's end to dump loads over the fence into what will soon be heifer pasture.

Field preparation goes forward nicely until late morning, when a coupler attaching one of two hydraulic lines from tractor to harrow breaks, and the tractors aren't carrying the tool needed to replace it. Don, meanwhile, has finished spreading, but his Deere is losing oil. "Parts place closes noon tomorrow," Dick points out, "and we have to take that platform off to find out which oil line has broken." That problem will have to wait. Joan arrives in the Renegade to announce lunch, and they've got to get the harrow going and get the grass planted before rain.

After a quick lunch, Aaron leaves in his pickup; five farms await insemination services this afternoon. Dick wants to get back to work, but the vet calls to say he will arrive in half an hour to check three cows for pregnancy and two for heat, and to vaccinate the heifers for the highly contagious fly-carried pinkeye. Joan has left with Brian for the doctor visit, and Dick feels obliged to be present when the vet arrives. He sits on a bucket in the barn and waits. "Hurry up and wait. This is the part of farming that gets me down."

An hour later the vet and his helper drive up. The vet dons a plastic glove that extends to his armpit and checks the target cows. He picks up the tail with the bare hand, works the other into the cow, corkscrewing the arm and pulling out feces as he goes, then, full in, pauses to feel for a calf or to check the condition of the cow's ovaries, Dick noting the results on a chart. Vaccination is a quick job. The vet loads his gun—it looks rather like and triggers like a small caulk gun—and walks behind a row of stanchioned heifers, jabbing the needle behind a projecting hip bone and triggering in a dose. The needled animal plunges and kicks, but soon calms down.

When the vet leaves, Dick hitches his seeder to a small International Harvester and creeps down the road, the racket of the dragged seeder rollers obliterating the cowbell-like chimes of the rear-wheel chain links sliding over the tire lugs. Back in the field, Don is at work finishing the harrowing and picking up rocks, and Dick loads the two hoppers of his seeder with a bacteria-inoculated mix of 120 pounds of alfalfa and 30 pounds each of trefoil and climax timothy. "This is a shotgun approach," Dick remarks. "Alfalfa doesn't like wet feet; we hope the timothy will fill in the low spots."

Dick starts up the west field margin, jerking a release rope with his left hand to start the feeding. The seed is fed out of the hoppers between two shields to drop between the two twelve-foot-long rollers, which amount to oversized rolling pins decorated with rotary rows of blunt teeth. The roller ahead of the seed-drop packs the seedbed, while the second disturbs the ground just enough to achieve a shallow plant. "These rollers break up dry clay real nice," says Dick; "you get a good-looking field when you're done seeding." The key word here is "dry." In wet soil, the spaces between rows of teeth in the trailing roller quickly pack with mud, which promptly picks up the seed you have just dropped. If the rain beats him now, Dick will have to wait through a whole drying cycle before he can plant again.

Gradually, the slow, steady twelve-foot sweeps take the little International Harvester 544 toward the center of the new meadow, away from the unplowed field margins where young hard maple and white pine are coming in to shade out the wild strawberries and small, light violet-blue violets. The hardhack, leaning over the fences into the light, sport furry catkins, and a whole troop of early tachinid flies clusters about the tiny yellow-green flowers of an early-blooming currant. The preferred feeding posture of these flies is upside down, so that their bristly yellow "rump" patches glow like muted headlamps out of the bush. Here and there along the field margin a clump of old corncobs indicates where a gray squirrel or raccoon had feasted on leftovers from last fall's harvest.

Tractor operators live in a moving pod of insistent noise compounded of tractor-engine drone and equipment clank. They worked this morning unaware of the chipping sparrow's trill from the nearby fencerow or of the *tea-CHER tea-CHER tea-CHER* song of the ovenbird back in the woods, just as Dick is now oblivious to the occasional snap and crash of limbs breaking off snags in the strengthening southerly wind. What he *is* aware of is the progressive darkening of the western sky, and at 4 P.M. a single crack of lightning and a distant roll of thunder signal rain. Dick stops to load his hoppers ("Gee, I wish I had that hour I spent waiting for the vet"), and continues to seed in a light but steady rain from the only cabless tractor (chosen for the job because of its lightness) on the farm.

Jeff and his grandfather drive up in the Jeep to see if Dick needs cover. He declines for the time being, and Don takes advantage of the wait to bring Jeff up to date on an accident of some time ago about which the state police are now issuing subpoenas to those who had arrived first at the crash scene. It seems two local miscreants were cruising a pickup while under the influence. They somehow left the road and bounced off a tree or two and rolled the pickup a couple of times. First witnesses on the scene found the two lying in the road near the overturned truck rubbing sore bodies and arguing about who had been driving. "Nobody else around," Don chuckles, "but they wa'nt neither one of them driving!"

After half an hour the rain backs off to a sporadic sprinkle, and the soil has not become wet enough to clog the seeder's rollers. The job will be completed before dark. Given the 350-

odd-acre scope of the Treadway farm, this piece of new meadow may well seem salt-and-pepper-shaker size, but the cost of seeding it to grass has been substantial. Earlier in the week the lime truck had spread two tons per acre at $20 a ton to increase the alkalinity of the soil. The half-bin of fertilizer has cost nearly $300, the 180 pounds of mixed seed nearly $500. So that preparing and seeding a ten-acre plot to grass has cost—adding something for the fuel (mostly diesel, but the International Harvester runs on gas) expended during all those tractor hours—something over $1,300.

"Hopefully we'll get a couple of good cuttings of hay off this piece for five years," says Dick. "Of course, ice sheeting or a low-snow winter could wipe out this grass next year, and we wouldn't even get the seed-money back."

3

IT IS MID-MAY. THE FENCES HAVE BEEN FIXED, the heifers vaccinated; it's time to turn them out to pasture. But a scheduling problem has arisen. When indispensable "hired" help consists of school-aged boys, and when the milking routine consumes both pre- and post-school daylight hours, this sort of job must be done on the weekend. Sunday morning had been designated, but that happens to be First Communion Sunday, and the priest at the Leicester Catholic Church particularly wants Joan, his regular organist, to do the service.

Work planned for Saturday morning is put aside, and Dick and his two older boys gather at the younger heifer pens at the south end of the barn, where tagging will be the first order of business. Calves receive their official identification numbers in the form of small metal ear tags shortly after birth. These tags

cannot, however, be read unless the animal is caught, and for
ready identification purposes young heifers get "barn numbers"
before their first release to pasture. Barn numbers are marked by
hand on a pair of large, brightly colored plastic tags, and neighbor farmers often coordinate color choice to facilitate sorting
when animals break fences. One of each pair of the Treadways'
yellow barn tags can be read from the front of the animal (useful
when "graining" cows), the other from the rear (particularly
handy when milk testing).

Kevin, the operation's tag-loader and record-keeper, sits on a
pail and goes to work. Having wrapped the two self-adhesive
"wings" of a plastic package of insecticide—advertised to control horn flies and face flies—around the stem end of the larger
ear tag, and having used thumb pressure to break the insecticide-
containing capsules within, he loads the tagger. The tagging tool
looks like an outsized paper punch, except that the blunt-ended
punching rod is replaced by a needle-sharp spike. Kevin threads
the hollow-rod base of the larger ear tag over the spike, slips the
base of the other tag into a clip in the tool's other jaw, and
announces that he is ready for action.

The first pen contains four heifers, weighing between 700 and
750 pounds each. They provide the action, and Jeff is the cata-
lyst. He climbs into the pen with a looped rope, which he tries
to slip over the head of a heifer. Roping the first heifer is relatively easy, but she has never before been subjected to any kind
of restraint, and she doesn't like it a bit. Her panic—manifested
by kicks and plunges and rushes—is instantly communicated
to her pen-mates, and now 3,000 pounds of young Holsteins
are charging around the pen, Jeff flying about on the end of
a rope.

"Ride 'em cowboy!" hollers Kevin, and indeed the spectacle
looks like a cross between rodeo and mud wrestling, except that
what the heifers and Jeff are slipping and sliding in isn't mud.
Dick joins the fray, and together they drag the roped animal to
a corner post, around which they take a turn of the rope to
secure it. Jeff finds the metal ear tag and reads out a long num-

ber, which Kevin notes on a sheet of paper opposite the barn number on the loaded tags.

Jeff now takes a headlock on the terrified heifer, and Dick centers the tagger between ridges radiating up the inside surface of the animal's ear. "Ready?" he inquires. Jeff tightens his grip, Dick grunts as he squeezes with both hands, driving the spike through the ear and popping the larger tag's nipple through a hole in the other, and the tool is already releasing as the hindquarters of the tagged heifer plunge in distress. "There's a delicate moment there," Dick says. "The tagger is spring-loaded, and the spike pulls out as soon as you release the handles. But it takes a second to seat the tags, and if the heifer jerks her head during that second, she'll tear her ear."

The newly tagged heifer calms down immediately, is unroped and released. The crew inquires, not without pique: "Now that wasn't so bad, was it?" But cows, regardless of age, simply do not reassure, and each succeeding rope-and-drag is played out in a context of mayhem. When the rodeo show moves across the barn to a second pen, Jeff finds one heifer particularly refractory, or perhaps only especially strong. It *will* not be dragged to a corner post, and on one plunge toward the rear of the pen Jeff loses his footing on the dung-slippery floor and falls to his knees, disappearing from view in the bovine melee. "Shit!" he yells angrily, and "That's what you're in," retorts his mother, who has just returned from the hospital with Brian.

Eventually all the young heifers carry barn numbers. The animals in the second pen mill about some; those in the first stand and stare, wondering what's next. Their canary yellow tags have reddened with blood, but most heifer ears heal without complications.

The family pauses to catch breath and inquire after Brian. But the morning is wearing on, and pastures new await the heifers. The older animals, destined for the open woods west of the road, are up first. Having closed off the south end of the barn, Dick reads barn numbers from a prepared list, and Jeff opens twelve stanchions. "Come on," he urges, "it's spring; this is what you've been waiting for all winter." If they have entertained any such yearnings during the long months in the barn, the heifers have forgotten them now. Most decline even to leave their stanchions; Jeff prods them out with that familiar tool of cattle auctions, the cane. Several stumble in the gutter and go down to their knees. All soon find themselves in the barn's broad central aisle, a straight run out the north end where Don stands on the low rise behind his house to direct them down his driveway to the road, which is guarded by Kevin ("Last year they stampeded down the hill and headed for three towns") near the open gate inviting them to lush pasture.

A few of the animals do head out of the barn, but most have no intention of leaving their accustomed home. Some mill about in the central aisle, while others plunge back into the line of stanchioned cows, getting stuck between stanchions, and others, which seem to be headed out of the barn, veer off into one of the perimeter aisles and run for the south end of the barn. Joan or Dick or Jeff breaks after them, trying to get ahead of the runaway, turn her, and drive her back north. This job is a bit dicey: the outside aisles are narrow, and these nearly full-sized and panicked heifers can smash a person against the wall or a projecting water cup.

A few animals have now left the barn, but a stubborn clot has formed in the doorway, and more heifers muscling up from behind fill the passageway, overturning a wheelbarrow and smashing the plywood slab record-keeping table that had perched upon it. Finally, eleven animals are driven from the barn. Number twelve, meanwhile, has fetched up short where the gutter swings across the north end of the barn. This fifteen-inch-wide, eight-inch-deep trench might as well be a moat full of crocodiles. She has set her front legs and stares at the gutter in abject horror. Shoves, shouts, cane blows rained on her hindquarters do not move her, nor does the bucket of grain Joan shows her from the other side of the gutter. Now they turn the animal and walk her well down the aisle, head her back north, and urge her forward, attempting to run her over the obstacle.

But the heifer holds her speed to an amble, and skids to a halt before the mesmerizing gutter.

Finally they leave number twelve, lest the others should out-maneuver Don and Kevin and scatter. Together the family drives strays out of Don's garden and backyard, and herds the lot down the driveway, across the road, and into their summer quarters. The gate shut, Joan and Dick and the older boys return to deal with number twelve. They secure a rope around her neck, and Dick and Jeff crouch behind the beast, a shoulder to both haunches, as if they were rear fenders on a stuck car. While Joan and Kevin lean and strain at the rope, Dick says "One, two, *three!*" and a concerted shove from behind initiates a reluctant lunge that brings the 1,000-pound animal well clear of the horrid gulf, and she joins her companions across the road.

Young heifers are, if possible, even less predictable when released. Some kick up their heels and scatter; others have to be forcibly ejected from their pens, the only home they've known. The Treadways now barricade the north end of the barn and swing open the south end gate. This lot of ten young heifers proves to be of the conservative variety: they prefer to stay put, thank you. Green grass and sunlight have no appeal for them. They charge about the barn, hiding among the milk cows, fleeing up the side aisles, charging between stanchions.

These heifers will summer in the open pasture beyond the corn pieces east of the homestead, and they must be driven a half-mile south and east to reach it. Once they have been driven from the barn, Joan paces ahead toward the first fence showing a grain bucket and singing: "Here, girls, girls, girls." But for once the girls aren't interested in grain. They find themselves in a wondrously new and wide world, with soft, lumpy ground and hard bedrock outcrops and growing vegetation, all of which invite curious investigation. "Keep 'em moving," Dick shouts, and he and Jeff and Kevin bring up the rear, swatting animals with stick, cane, and, in Kevin's case, a length of hollow plastic pipe, whose blows resound impressively down the valley. ("That's my number two son, the sadistic one," comments Joan.)

The three lead animals are driven through the first gate, and a guard is posted while the other drivers retreat to help bring along the malingerers. The *weep-weep* notes of a great crested flycatcher in the wooded road margin mix with approaching shouts and thwacks as more heifers are driven up through the fence. A quick count shows that one animal is missing. Dick returns to the barn and discovers her nestled between two stanchioned cows. Hallooed by his father, he also discovers that the older heifers are standing around in the road. (Has a wind-thrown snag broken the fence somewhere in the last few days, or have they found a low place and jumped out?) Dick and Don open the gate and drive eleven animals back into pasture. Has the twelfth headed for parts unknown, or is it simply out of sight in the woods?

Dick returns escorting the last of the young heifers, and the mini cattle drive goes forward in fits and starts, punctuated by irked shouts ("Get out!" "Go on!") and crisp thwacks. Thorson dashes here and there in grand dramaturgical style, but he has never got the hang of herding. A kingbird splutters up the fencerow as the drive swings east, heading down to a marshy stream. "One year this creek was high," Dick recalls, "and the heifers were afraid to cross; it was two weeks before we got them over to pasture."

Half of this spring's young heifers find the stream irresistible. They stand up to their knees in mud and water nosing cowslip clumps, and seem prepared to stay. "*Move* 'em," Dick hollers, and Joan wades in to urge them out. A second group of animals, never before having seen soil wet or dry, knows exactly what use to make of a dry cut near the base of a steep hillock. They crowd up, drop to their front knees, and rub their heads vigorously in the dry clay. Joan has her heifers moving now, and two blunder into what looks like an impossible route, up a small ravine which tops out with a steep rockface, up which they struggle slipping and sliding, driving with the rear legs while "walking" on the front knees.

The morning is shot when the ten young black-and-whites are driven through a gate into their dandelion-studded summer pasture, welcomed by the double trill of a Savannah sparrow and two salt blocks, which Don has hauled over by tractor. Joan and the boys drop to the ground under a small hawthorn tree. Jeff, pretending to be terminally bushed, declares: "I want four thousand slushies." "You have to clean out the calf pens first," says Dick.

Kevin climbs into the Deere to ride back with his grandfather, and the rest of the family head cross-lots for the homestead, Dick and Joan walking hand in hand. They arrive to find the older heifers conveniently gathered near the gate across from the older Treadway house. The family pauses to count, and are relieved to find all twelve animals present. Don, watching the tableau unseen from below his porch, grins and chuckles. "From now till snow falls," he says, "every time you see heifers, you count. It's one of the things that help keep farmers crazy."

The family scatter for chores and home to lunch. Joan has to finish lettering an oversized menu, the top item of which reads: Hot Dogs—$1. She will be selling food out of the Chuckwagon this afternoon at Shoreham's annual charity Apple Blossom Days celebration, featuring a five-mile road race, a celebration which will, this tardy spring, precede by several days the spectacular display of bloom on Shoreham's and neighboring Cornwall's orchards. Those who work for the event get to eat free, and Joan is taking the kids along as assistants. "The town," she says, "doesn't know what it's let itself in for."

4

THE LAST NIGHT IN MAY NEVER QUITE MANages darkness. The second full moon of the month—an official "blue moon"—hangs in the south-southwest of a clear and windless sky, the stars few and high. By 4 A.M., when the earliest birds begin to tune up, a pale pink hue barred by dark horizontal cloud smudges marks the northeastern horizon. The squeaky chatter of a barn swallow is followed by the crowing of a rooster from the next place north, and then the first of the neighborhood robins begins its tireless warbling.

The plaintive, slurred whistle of a wood pewee sounds from the woodlot across the road, and to the east the first half-hearted notes of a song sparrow compete with the loose-banjo-string *gunk* of a green frog. The soft *cucucu* of a black-billed cuckoo sounds from the woods, and the otherworldly whiffling of vibrating outer tail feathers locates a snipe in courtship flight somewhere overhead. At 4:15, the prolonged and urgent whistle of a train advertises (to what audience?) its passage to the east. Then a surprise. From the meadow fringe beyond the woodlot comes the unmistakable two-part whistle of a bobwhite, a bird well north of expected range, whose confident and cheery whistle declares a territory he will never need to defend and seeks a mate he will almost certainly never find.

By 4:30, song is piling on top of song. The familiar rattling trill of a chipping sparrow competes with the first cardinal notes, both of which are drowned by the insistent cawing of a crow. The two-level trill of a Savannah sparrow—the first meadow species in voice—mixes with the *peer* and rattle notes of a red-winged blackbird and the plaintive lament of a mourning dove. A ruby-throated hummingbird buzzes up the road, and a phoebe begins the day-long work of iterating its name.

By 4:45, the barn is adding starling screech and pigeon coo to the chorus, and a field sparrow is singing from a pasture to the east, but meadowlark, kingbird, great crested flycatcher, northern oriole, and other local birds have not yet found voice at 4:55 when Dick and Joan emerge from their house to find the lines of cloud smudges on the northeastern horizon turned a theatrical rose and the increasingly lightened sky illuminating the darkened earth just sufficiently to pick out a disembodied sea of yellow spots—the heads of newly blooming celandines—crowding the far side of the road and continuing as far as one can see into the woodlot.

Jeff joins his parents, and he and Dick hike south down the pasture to call the cows, leaving Joan in the barn to scatter sawdust—more of the absorbent stuff is used as part of the barn-cleaning routine in winter, when the cows bed down in the barn—down the central aisle from a large wheelbarrow.

The early arrivals, including Fluffy ("She always wants to be first in the barn") appear at the south barn gate, and wait quietly. More cows come up, halt in line, and wait, like queuers at a movie theater. A large black cow stares at a small black cat; the cat returns the indignity. A larger yellow tiger cat appears and rubs against Joan's leg. The Humane Society had placed this cat with several families, but he had always been returned, pronounced troublesome. "I think they call us as a last resort," laughs Joan. "But Freddy is a good cat; he hasn't been a problem at all."

Dick and Jeff are in sight now, and, having roped off the north end of the barn, Joan admits the cows, which slowly pace down the central aisle, individuals breaking off left or right to a stanchion. The Treadway cows aren't trained to take a particular stanchion, but most have preferences, at least for one side and/or one section of the barn. It will take about fifteen minutes for all sixty-odd milkers to find places, Dick and Jeff walking up the side aisles shoving the triangular pipe stanchions closed behind the cows' heads.

Meanwhile, Joan pushes through a swinging door at the northwest corner of the barn to enter the milkroom, where the six milking machines—assemblages of plastic hoses hung from the hook ends of rod supports like queer octopi hung on upside-down gaffs—are suspended over a tub. She gives them a quick disinfectant rinse, then inserts a coiled-wire-supported two-foot-long heavy paper filter in the end of the milk pipe, which she then locks into the top of the bulk tank. It's 5:30, and time to milk.

Often it is Kevin who prepares the cows, but he is sleeping in this morning, and Jeff takes his place, pulling a child's wagon to the center aisle at the north end of the barn. From the wagon he takes a brown paper towel, wets it with an iodine udder wash, disinfects the four teats of the first cow, and throws the towel into the gutter behind the cow, which signals that the animal has been readied for milking. Finally, he "strips" the teats, forcing out a stream of milk from each, which both checks for teat blockage and helps trigger the cow's milk let-down.

Ideally, the milking machine (or "milker") should be on the cow within two minutes of stripping, and Joan now hooks the first milker over the vacuum pipe, plugs the small "pulsator" box, which governs the air hoses, into the vacuum pipe and the milk hoses into the milk pipe, turns on the vacuum valve, and pulls the four rubber suction cups over the teats. The pulsator interrupts and directs the vacuum suction, so that the milker pulls in alternate pulses at the front and back pairs of teats. Joan and Jeff work opposite sides of the aisle, attaching the other milkers while the first Holstein's distended bag gradually shrinks. After about nine minutes, she is milked out. Joan feels the four quarters of the udder to make sure they are empty, closes the vacuum cutoff valve, removes the milker, disinfects and seals the teat canals with a white plastic solution she carries in a dip pot fastened around her waist, and carries the milker down the line to the next prepared cow.

While Joan and Jeff begin milking the cows, Dick sets up to "grain 'em." He positions a large wheelbarrow under a tin pipe running down the northwest wall of the barn, hits a switch kicking in a small motor, and an "energizer" supplement pours down the pipe from a grain silo outside. The protein content of this grains-and-meals mix is periodically adjusted, depending on the quality of the pasturage and silage the cows are getting. The mix contains everything from vitamins to sodium bicarbonate (yes, for neutralizing stomach acid) to cane molasses, which gives the plug-shaped pellets a wonderfully appealing aroma.

A load of this supplement—which weighs 18,000 pounds, costs about $1,500, and lasts not quite three weeks—could be disposed of in half that time. Cows—and heifers as well—simply think it is the best thing going. At the first sight of the mix falling into the wheelbarrow, the nearest cows' heads plunge in excited anticipation, and Dick fires the rations from a five-pound scoop onto the floor in front of cows ahead of him to prevent them from attacking his wheelbarrow with their massive tongues. A few cows get no "grain" at all, a few as much as fifteen pounds per milking. Ration size is determined by milk production, which varies between cows and in individual cows and is tested periodically. Heaviest producers get the most grain, the operating assumption being that supplement won't increase low production, but is necessary to sustain high production. Dick glances at ear tag numbers, and occasionally refers to cardboard lists of current ration figures tucked in his wheelbarrow, though he quickly memorizes most. He scoops and throws, scoops and throws, the wheelbarrow working its way down the west aisle and back up the east, returning to refill and setting off again around the perimeter of this 204-foot by 32-foot two-story structure which, except for a slightly lowered roofline for increased strength, is very like the barn that had served two generations of Treadways and would have served two more had it not been for that July day in 1977.

"It was a tremendously hot day," Dick recalls. "I remember checking an outdoor thermometer early in the afternoon; it said one hundred degrees." Dick was hauling logs and cutting lumber at the small sawmill on his uncle's farm down the road. "I was in the woodlot loading logs when the storm came out of the west. I got back under the trees for protection; then I looked out across the pasture and these big trees were coming down." He checked his watch. It was four o'clock; Joan would be safe in the barn, starting chores. The fury of the storm passed quickly. Dick hurried up the road wondering about damage and came over the rise to find the barn, broadsided by what they believe was a local tornado, collapsed on itself.

Joan picks up the story. "It was dark and raining. I should have been in the barn, but the baby had a cold, and I thought I'd let him sleep an extra fifteen minutes. Then the storm got worse and the sky turned a sickly yellow and I looked out and the barn was down."

Having found each other, Dick and Joan rushed to a neighbor's to call the fire department ("We were sure the barn was going to burn"), then dug out chain saws and began to cut into the wreckage covering the calf pens. "It was amazing," says Dick. "When the upper story came down the open floor joists of the hay mow set down *around* those pens. Some of the calves were scraped up, but none of them died."

People began to show up in ones and twos—neighbors, friends, strangers—and in the next few days hay was gingerly extracted ("We didn't know when the second story might fall in") from the mow, what could be salvaged in the way of equipment and lumber was ("We almost got the receiver jar out of the milkroom, but we broke off an inlet nipple while removing it"), and the wreckage was dismantled and cleared away. "There'd be twenty-five, thirty people here working on the barn," Dick recalls; "I still don't know who some of those people were."

"We'd drag up to the house at night," Joan says, "and we'd find baskets of food, cases of soda, all kinds of stuff. That still happens. Farmers don't usually socialize much, but when trouble comes, people you haven't seen for six months and won't see again for six months show up to help."

The graining done, Dick joins Joan and Jeff in the central aisle, and, as sunlight begins to find its way into the east windows and the six milking machines slowly leapfrog their way south, the life of the barn carries on. Thorson lies, apparently disconsolate, in the central aisle, occasionally rearing up to attack an itch. Mindy solicits attention after her own fashion, backing her rear end forcefully into the legs of any unoccupied person and looking back imploringly over her shoulder. A black cat lies near Thor, busily cleaning its fur, while the equally inky Blackcap wire-walks the milk pipe at the north end of the barn, jumps nimbly to the vacuum pipe sloping up the wall, and disappears through a missing ceiling board into the hay mow to check her litter of six kittens ("The gray one is mine," says Becky; "I have two cats") luxuriating in an upended plastic wash basket surrounded by a hay-bale wall.

House sparrows cheep and fly about the barn; at least one pair is feeding young in a straw nest perched atop a tin fluorescent-light guard. Several roosters strut and pick down the aisles and perch on the overhead milk pipes. The shyer hens are less in evidence, but two half-sized chicks perch side by side on a ladder leading to the hay mow, moving their heads about in the jerk-by-jerk fashion of chickens. Jeff chortles and points up the aisle, where Kevin's calf, Megan, is sampling the contents of the saw-dust wheelbarrow. Joan laughs: "That crazy calf will eat any-thing. A while back we caught her eating a paper towel."

The cows quickly consume their portion of grain supplement, straining forward and snaking out their tongues to clean up peripheral morsels. When the candy is gone, they munch a bit of leftover hay and chew their cuds. From time to time they take a drink from their water cups, depressing the circular plate in the bottom to activate flow. Eventually—but only after having been milked—most of the cows lie down, something of a trick for a stanchioned animal weighing three quarters of a ton. A cow wishing to rest drops to her front knees, lets her hind quarters begin to sag, then abruptly swings one rear leg over against the other. This move at once traps the udder, holding it out of harm's way, and unbalances the massive hind end, which promptly collapses on the far side.

A cow's udder, especially when distended with milk, is a vul-nerable organ, and from time to time the animals tear them on barbed wire or cut them with a hoof. This presents problems in the barn. A cow with a hurt bag doesn't want it fooled with, but the animal must be milked. Dick seats a "kicker"—a pipe yoke shaped something like a lyre—over the back of an udder-hurt cow just in front of the jutting hip bones. The kicker hampers hind-leg movement, but the cow may plunge and swing laterally as Dick gingerly rubs an udder cream on the cut, a paste de-signed to soothe the injury and keep it soft to promote healing.

If cows care little for this ministration, they like the subsequent milking even less. Last week an outraged Holstein jerked its head out of its closed stanchion, backed into the central aisle, and, finding that the kicker prevented it from running, crow-hopped like a rodeo bronco down the aisle and out of the barn, nearly trampling Brian and Becky in the process. The animal was found on its side in the pasture, kicker still in place, unable to rise. Once the kicker was removed, it rose to its feet and ambled placidly back to the barn.

The interior of a dairy barn is not a comfortable environment for fastidious or nose-finicky persons. Originally white walls are thoroughly stained in a variety of browns. Ribbed tin ceiling, strung power lines, fixtures, and windows are soiled and cobweb-hung. Animal and vegetable detritus collects in windowsills, and underfoot sawdust, hay, and mud mix with abundant feces, in which the cows stomp and recline. For those who believe that cleanliness is next to godliness, a walk down the barn's central aisle is an exercise in terror. A resting cow slaps her tail into the gutter, and the passerby is spattered with a gray-green odoriferous fluid compounded of urine and sloppy-joe-consistency dung.

The milkroom corner of the barn is a wholly different world, and the swinging door between them—brown on the barn side, white on the other—is revelatory. The milkroom is white walls and clean cement and stainless steel piping and sinks and basins and tanks. It smells of antiseptic solutions and raw milk, and looks like a combination hospital kitchen and—thanks especially to the huge hand-blown glass "receiving jar"—Brobdingnagian chemistry lab.

The $350 bubble-shaped receiving jar is at the end of the vacuum power cycle. Two 2-inch stainless steel pipes deliver milk from the two sides of the barn through glass fittings into the oversized jar. When the jar is about half full, a float valve closes the vacuum intake and triggers a pump, which drives the milk through a pipe at the jar's base across the milkroom at head level and into the top of the bulk cooling tank. The bulk tank's job is to hold the milk at 37 degrees until pickup; now, toward the end of the morning's milking, the thermometer reads 46 degrees, the result of the addition of a load of body-temperature milk.

At 6:45 Joan leaves the last cows for Dick and Jeff, and heads for the house to make sure Kevin and Brian are getting ready for the school bus. It is just past 7 A.M. when the milker is pulled from the last cow, and Dick and Jeff open stanchions, set the cows ambling out of the barn, and begin to scrape dung into the gutter.

Meanwhile, Joan has returned to do milkroom duty. She scrubs and rinses the six milkers one by one in a small tub, hanging them in a row over a larger tub adjacent, which is a kind of open-air washing machine. Joan fills two quart jars— one with an acid bath, the other with a bleach-type detergent— and screws them into place under a metal box on the end of the tub. Next she uncouples the milk pipe from the bulk tank, stoppers the hole, removes the paper filter from the pipe (there should be nothing to filter out of the milk, but occasionally one or more teat cups on a milker fall off and suck up sawdust and dirt from the floor) and swings the free pipe around to suspend it over the tub. The milkers are now hooked up to vacuum and milk lines, the tub is run half full of cold water, and the washing cycle is activated.

This ingenious system is essentially identical to the milking cycle, except that the milkers are now sucking water instead of milk, and they deliver it via the receiving jar not to the bulk tank but back to the tub. Joan leaves to look after breakfast, and the cycle continues on automatic. The plug is pulled after this preliminary rinse, then reset, and now the detergent drains into a hot water bath, which circulates as before. After its allotted time, that solution drains, and the cycle is repeated with the acid solution. The woman in the TV ad who finds her mother's dishwasher obtrusive ought to see and hear this system in action. The whole cycle—which lasts just over an hour—operates at top speed, motors roaring and cutoff valves popping like gunshots as the solutions are repeatedly driven into and sucked from the receiving jar while leakage water shoots across the room and the hung hoses twitch spasmodically as if the milkers were live organisms enduring electric shock treatment.

The scraping of the barn completed, Jeff heads for the house, where he must shower and change and breakfast before driving to school. Don appears with a wheelbarrow and proceeds down the central aisle, laying down fresh sawdust in sweeping arcs from a barn shovel. He and Dick pause in the now-quiet barn to exchange an anecdote or two and to talk about today's field work. It is 8 A.M. when Dick leans his scraper against a calf pen and joins his wife for breakfast.

Joan likes morning milking. "Sometimes when we're done I go to town, and the stores aren't even open. They haven't got started, and already we've accomplished something." Dick adds another perspective. "Some people say farmers should help themselves by diversifying. How can a dairy farmer diversify? A milking takes two-and-a-half hours if no problems arise and if four of us are working. That's five hours a day minimum just for the milking. So we put in a thirty-five- or forty-hour week before we start field work and building and machine maintenance. When do we find time to diversify?"

In practice, for three seasons of the year morning milking session (beginning at about 5 A.M.) and evening milking session (ending at about 7 P.M.) bracket the working day, leaving, after breakfast and lunch breaks, between six and seven hours for nonmilking farm work. Weather and other exigencies sometimes dictate a stretch of work after supper as well, so that the usual twelve- or thirteen-hour work day may extend to fifteen or more.

Many farmers have sought to improve their financial situation by diversifying *off* the farm. In fact, just over half of employed farm residents in this country have a primary nonfarm income. Many of these are farm wives and older children, of course, but almost forty percent of adult men are included as well.

*Somebody*, however, has to work the farm. When the farm

family hold town jobs—the wife, say, at the hospital or department store, the kids at Burger King, the farmer himself perhaps a half shift at a factory or farm-implements dealership—much of the farm work must be hired out. The Treadways prefer to stay home and work the farm themselves.

5

JOAN'S PEOPLE WERE FRENCH; DICK'S ENGLISH and French. With the help of town records and a couple of books—particularly William T. Tredway's *History of the Tredway Family* (Pittsburgh, 1930)—they have traced the Tre(a)dway line back eleven generations in this country. The first Treadway is thought to have come over from England about fifteen years after the *Mayflower*. Joan says that the traditional Tredway justification for the tardiness is the claim that the *Mayflower* looked leaky, and their ancestor had waited for a better ship.

Certain it is that a boy, Josiah, was born to Nathaniel Treadway and Sufferance Haynes in Watertown, Massachusetts, in 1652, and that Josiah subsequently supported ten children as a weaver. His second son, James, fathered twelve children, at least two of whom died in Shoreham, Vermont: Josiah in 1790 at age 83 and William in 1806 at age 101. William and Josiah must have been past middle age when they arrived in the frontier township of Shoreham. Its charter, signed by Benning Wentworth, governor of the province of New Hampshire, on behalf of King George the Third (who, as was customary, reserved to his own use "all the white and other pine trees within the said Township, fit for masting our Royal Navy"), was signed on October 8, 1761.

What with the French and Indian Wars, the Revolutionary

War, and the conflicting New Hampshire and New York claims
to Vermont, conditions were anything but conducive to settlement in the early years. According to Reverend Josiah F. Goodhue's *History of the Town of Shoreham, Vermont* (published by
the town in 1861), the first log house erected in the Shoreham
wilderness dates from 1766, and only six families were living
there on May 9, 1775, when Ethan Allen and Benedict Arnold
marched a troop of men north from Castleton to Shoreham's
Hand's Cove, where they holed up into the night in a ravine
awaiting boats to ferry them across Lake Champlain for their
dawn sneak attack on Fort Ticonderoga.

Settlement along the east shore of the Lake quickened with the
end of English and Indian hostilities, and the Treadways became
firmly established in Shoreham. Place records are spotty for the
early generations, but it is recorded that William's grandson,
Joseph, was married and died in Shoreham, and his children—
Hannah, Lora, Betsey, Lewis, Jerusha, Polly, Elvira, Joanne,
Joseph, Lorain, another Hannah, infant male, Jennette, Seraph,
and Andrew—were born in the town as well. (Joseph's wife,
Elizabeth Wright, married at seventeen, had her first child at
nineteen, and continued to give birth, mostly at two-year intervals, until she was forty-four. She outlived her husband, perhaps
in revenge, by fifteen years.)

In a sense, Joseph and Elizabeth's children grew up during
Shoreham's heyday. According to U.S. Census figures, the town
reached its population apogee in 1830 with 2,137 residents, just
over twice the current figure. Men cleared the land (important
by-products of which work were lumber and potash) to grow
wheat. A farm could be bought for twenty-five dollars an acre,
and wheat prices were high. Wool prices were high as well, and
Addison County towns soon became famous for their Merino
sheep. Private enterprise thrived in other directions. The Lemon
Fair River was dammed at what came to be the village of Richville in the southeastern part of Shoreham, providing water
power for mills to saw lumber and grind flour.

Shoreham was then—and remains today—chiefly agricultural.

In 1860—the year Joseph and Elizabeth's first son, Lewis, served his fourth and last term as town selectman—town occupations were listed as follows:

| | |
|---|---:|
| Farmers | 198 |
| Farm Laborers | 148 |
| Domestics | 74 |
| Mechanics | 51 |
| Merchants | 5 |
| Dress Makers & Milliners | 3 |
| Clergymen | 2 |
| Taverners | 2 |
| Physician | 1 |
| Dentist | 1 |

Already in 1860, Shoreham farmers—and Treadways among them—were producing 21,000 bushels of oats, 12,000 bushels of Irish potatoes, 5,000 bushels of Indian corn, 119,000 pounds of butter, 97,000 pounds of cheese, nearly 8,000 tons of hay, 5,500 pounds of maple sugar, and 1,500 pounds of honey.

The problem with evolving New England agriculture has been simple. Whatever it undertook to produce was soon produced cheaper somewhere else. One by one the staples migrated west, grains to the Plains states, sheep to the intermountain West, corn to the Midwest, dairy products to the Lakes states. Like other New Englanders, many Shoreham natives—including some Treadways—followed the wheat to Nebraska, the corn to Illinois, the butter and cheese to Wisconsin. Others stayed to see in the age of mechanized agriculture on larger farms in the home territories.

Among those who stayed were Lewis' son, William Lewis, and William Lewis' son, Guy, whose first child, Donald Lee, was born during the dark days of World War I on the home farm down Cutting Hill Road. Don grew up helping on the farm with two brothers and a sister. Guy and his wife, Ruth Atwood, lost the farm during the Depression, but were subsequently able to reacquire it. They also bought the next farm up the road, and it was here that Don and Irene Quenneville—a spirited girl born in Ontario—set up housekeeping in 1941.

A daughter, Donna Lee, was born to the couple in 1945, and on August 23, 1948—which happened to be her twenty-ninth birthday—Irene gave birth to twins, Diane Rose and Richard Guy. The children grew up on the farm and went through high school in the Shoreham schools. Dick played basketball and baseball, worked on his lessons (and did well in school), and learned farming. He attended Vermont Technical College in Randolph for a year, but, uncertain that college was for him, he returned to Shoreham to farm with his father and, as it happened, to meet a girl named Joan Anne Pelletier from Poultney, a town to the south.

Joan's maternal grandfather, Frank Patenaude, moved from Athol, Massachusetts, to Whitehall, in upstate New York, as a youth. In due course, he married raven-haired Dorothy Lamour, and crossed the New York "thumb" to farm in Castleton, Vermont. Walking to and from the nearby teacher's college, Frank and Dorothy's daughter, Elsie, passed the farm of a French Canadian family named Pelletier. Young Aldore Pelletier would wave to Elsie from the fields. Eventually they married and settled in the nearby small town of Poultney, where Aldore was transferred by the power company for which he worked, and where Joan and two younger brothers ("monsters," she calls them) enjoyed a happy childhood.

A top high school student, Joan headed off to college at the University of Vermont, while her parents—her father having retired from the power company—moved back to Castleton to work the family farm. ("Don't marry a farmer," her mother told her; "you'll have no time and no money.") College went swimmingly for three terms; then, on the night before New Year's Eve, 1967, she met a young farmer from Shoreham at a dance in Poultney.

They dated steadily from that night. On a cold day in January, Dick took Joan tobogganing on a big hill behind the family farm—which Don's brother, Norman, farmed—down Cutting

Hill Road. They flew down the hill and came to rest on the thinly iced-over stream at the bottom. The toboggan sank, leaving Dick and Joan up to their armpits in icewater. "That ought to cool off the romance," Dick's uncle said.

It didn't, and in the spring Dick began to talk about building a house. "What house is that?" Joan wondered. "A house for us," said Dick, who hadn't proposed. That oversight remedied, Dick began to cut timber on the farm and saw it into lumber at the sawmill on his uncle's place. He dug a foundation hole 100 yards upslope from his parents' house. They had the foundation poured, but, Treadways and Pelletiers pitching in, did everything else themselves. They framed, wired, plumbed, finished, roofed. Joan took a job in Middlebury (the county's shire and major shopping town), roomed and boarded with the Treadways, helped with chores. Dick built furniture and cabinets, including a kitchen table, built-in kitchen cupboards, a roll-top desk, a gun cabinet, a breakfront. Dick and Joan were married in December of 1968, and set up housekeeping in their new ranch house, total cost $4,000.

The four of them—Don and Irene, Dick and Joan—farmed the place and kept two households going. In the early years of their marriage, Dick and Joan were avid square dancers. "We'd clean up after chores and drive anywhere in the state to dance," Joan recalls, "then drive home after midnight." Then Jeffrey Lee came along, and then Kevin John. In the midst of these happy times, Irene—having long been a steady smoker at the urging of her doctor, who prescribed it for weight control—was struck down by emphysema. Dick's older sister, Donna, now a fifth grade teacher in the Green Mountain foothill town of Monkton, remembers growing up poor ("but we didn't know it"), and characterizes her mother as the working heart of the farm. Irene had run the household (cooking for hands and in-laws as well as family); had planted and tended and canned the garden; had done chores, often finishing up for Don when, as selectman and fireman, he was called away on town business. She had worked cash jobs as well, taking in a doctor's laundry, picking apples at local orchards—all while raising three children. Emphysema disabled her virtually overnight. Doctors gave her at most two years. (Now, over a decade later, she sits primly on her living room couch, surrounded by oxygen tanks and air hoses, sewing patches on her grandchildren's jeans and continuing to defy medical opinion.)

With Jeff in kindergarten and Kevin a toddler, Dick built a large one-room extension on the south end of the small ranch. Today, with Brian Richard and Rebecca Anne completing the ninth generation of Shoreham Treadways, the cream yellow house is, well, full. All horizontal surfaces—shelves, counters, tables, appliance tops, furniture backs—are likely to be covered with a miscellany of clothes and papers and dishes and toys and fish food and cats and the odd tractor or car part, while scarce floor space is usurped by an ironing board, a sack of empty soda bottles, a box of bolts, a pile of clean laundry. The Treadways do not aim at the living style celebrated by the House Beautiful magazines. Still, they find it a bit much when the dogs, having enjoyed a vigorous roll on the cool dirt-and-sawdust cellar floor, come into the house and climb into somebody's bed or shake all over the living room rug. (Viewing the chaos upon entering a room, Joan will pull up short in mock amazement: "When *is* that maid coming in?")

The Treadway name is not now as common in Shoreham as it once was. Early maps show two Treadway holdings on the next road west and another on the next road, off the north end of the Pinnacle. The mailboxes in front of those farmhouses show other names today, but the north end of Cutting Hill Road remains solid Treadway country. Though Don's brother, Norman, recently died of cancer, his widow, Alma, and their son, Charley, continue to run the farm down the hill. Dick and Joan are buying the farm they work from his parents, and Dick's twin sister lives in the next house up the road. Diane is a teacher and program director of special education for a school district on the other side of Middlebury. But there is obviously a lot of farmer in her too. Chickens roam about her dooryard, and claim the road as well. Sheep pasture across the road along with a goat which from time to time springs over the fence to feast on Dick's crops. ("That goat is lucky to be alive," he grouses.) And then there is the legendary Harry, an aged but robust and impressively hairy donkey. Hairy everywhere, that is, except in the mane, which brought Dick to grief as a youngster. Harry was accustomed to going along when the cows were moved, and once, when the cows had gotten a headstart, he thought he was being left behind. Dick was aboard at the time, and Harry "took off like a train. I didn't have much mane to hang onto, riding bareback, and I fell off and he kicked me—he didn't do it on purpose—right in the forehead." Dick ended up with three steel staples in his head.

Kevin remembers Grandma telling stories about that donkey. "Dad and Aunt Diane would ride around on it together when they were children, and when the donkey had had enough, it bucked them off and bit them!"

# 6

DURING EVERY SPRING, THE NORTHERN LAND-scape is host to a revolving game of floral one-upmanship. Serviceberry—most people call it shad—wins the first round unopposed, but after that the game becomes increasingly complicated. By the end of May, when the apple blossoms and lilacs have faded, pin cherries, hawthorns, and the first winey honeysuckles are coming on in the countryside, while spirea makes a show about farm- and town houses alike. The hands-down winner of the fencerow sweepstakes for the moment is nannyberry, a shrub viburnum no one even notices fifty weeks out of the year. This year its white, multiflowered clusters are so full and abundant that it looks from the roads as if someone benign and slightly touched—perhaps a relative of Johnny Appleseed—had wandered the countryside scattering the seeds of some magical, spring-blooming hydrangea.

Dick Treadway's problem at the moment is not floristic, but it is botanical. Does he plant corn or chop hay? He plans to plant four corn pieces this year, in aggregate about thirty-five acres, and ordinarily that would come first. But May has continued rainy, and the land is too soft to accommodate the heavy manure spreader. There is an option. He can broadcast and harrow in a lighter commercial fertilizer, and spread the manure later on the meadows. But that would mean an extra fertilizer bill.

There's another option. The same rain that has delayed corn planting has brought the meadow grass along ahead of schedule. The Treadways could postpone planting and take a first cutting of hay. But once you start mowing and chopping and filling silos, you're committed to a stretch of time, and risk too long a delay in starting the corn. On the other hand, if you wait and then do corn first, the meadow grasses will have flowered and gotten rank, losing some of their nutritive quality.

Dick sits on the problem through Memorial Day, hoping the land will dry out. It does not, and after morning milking the next day he calls local fertilizer dealers. As he has anticipated, other area farmers have elected the commercial-fertilizer option as well. The dealers are busy, spreaders scarce; but one dealer promises a loaded spreader in an hour or so.

Meanwhile, Dick and Joan set about preparing the corn planter for action. As tractor-pulled farm machinery goes, a corn planter is a light and simple rig. Up front are two large semitransparent, fiberglass-reinforced plastic hoppers, which carry and feed a special starter fertilizer. Behind these are four similar—but much smaller—hoppers, which carry and feed the corn kernels. Joan and Don hunt for grease fittings, passing the grease gun back and forth, while Dick changes "plates," yellow plastic, slotted, Frisbee-sized revolving plates that seat in the bottom of the seed hoppers, where they pick up and drop single corn kernels.

Bag after eighty-pound bag of starter fertilizer is heaved onto the rim of each fertilizer hopper; a quick slice through the bottom of the bag, and the contents spill into the bins. Guarantees are few and far between in the farming business, but the disclaimer printed in capital letters on each of these heavy plastic bags is remarkable: THERE IS NO WARRANTY THAT THE PRODUCT CONTAINED HEREIN SHALL BE FIT FOR ANY PARTICULAR PURPOSE! Certainly the bags themselves are unfit for any purpose, and are hell to get rid of. "Fertilizer used to come in paper bags," Dick says, "which we simply burned. Occasionally the bags got wet, and you'd have ruined fertilizer." So the industry solved one problem while creating another. Dick stuffs rolled empties into one bag, lays it out on the edge of the nearest field, and tries to burn it. The heavy plastic heats up and melts into a puddle, which partially burns, leaving an alarming stain on the ground.

A fifty-five-pound, 80,000-kernel bag of hybrid seed corn just about fills one seed hopper, but it is first dumped in batches into a bucket, where, using a shovel handle, Dick mixes in a small packet of dusty black graphite for plate lubrication and a larger packet of insecticide-fungicide treatment. This shocking-pink powder contains large doses of captan, diazinon, and lindane, which are supposed to protect the seeds and seedlings against damping off, decay, blights, seed corn beetles, seed corn maggots, and wireworms. "We started using this stuff after wireworms got into our corn one year," Don remembers. "The little buggers burrow in and eat the germ. Just a stalk here and there came up that year."

A series of notices on the back of the packet warn that the product is toxic to birds, fish, and other wildlife, and in people may cause "irreversible eye damage" and death "if swallowed or absorbed through skin." "You wouldn't want to sprinkle this stuff on your cereal," Dick jests, but, inured through long exposure to whatever risks agricultural poisons may pose, he does not, as the packet urges, don a long-sleeved shirt and face mask while handling it. His stirring stick turns hot pink, and each bucket of seed dumped into the hopper sends a small cloud of powder drifting downwind.

A bag of hybrid seed corn costs about sixty dollars, and four bags in the four hoppers will plant about five acres. Dick is planting two varieties this spring. He dumps his old standby in three hoppers and a new hybrid another Shoreham farmer had good luck with last year in an end hopper. At row ends he will turn in the direction of that end bin, so that he plants three rows of his traditional favorite followed by two experimental rows. That way he can compare the growth and production of the two hybrids through the coming season.

After lunch, Dick checks in with the fertilizer dealer. They're waiting on a spreader, should be one back any minute. The corn planter is ready to roll except for one hitch. Dick doesn't now remember what the fertilizer-hopper sprockets were set at when the machine was put away last year. Ordinarily, they spread starter fertilizer at 220 pounds per acre, but if it becomes apparent that there will be leftover fertilizer, they "open it up" on the last rounds to use it up. The code for sprocket settings is in the manufacturer's manual, which is missing and which Dick and his father each claim the other has probably lost. They hunt in their respective houses and in the tool shed. No luck. They go back to hunt some more.

Chattering barn swallows, constantly busy about the farmstead, are now tending nests and incubating eggs in various sheds and on the back porches of both houses. ("I don't mind the swallows," says Don, "but I don't care for these damn starlings." Even the popular swallows, the family feel, looking at their thoroughly beshat back porches and picture windows, would profit from some concern for hygiene and aesthetics.) Becky runs down with the news that she has frightened a swallow off its nest and into their house. Joan returns home to catch the bird in an apron and put it back outside.

Brian has spent the Memorial Day weekend home with a

miserable case of chicken pox, featuring lesions even in his gums and tongue. (The doctor will later matter-of-factly attribute the severity of the case to the cortisone he had prescribed for Brian's asthma attack.) Brian feels more energetic now, however, and bikes down to ask if he can cultivate Grandpa's garden. Don tends a tiny garden up by the house and a good-sized one between his house and the barn. A fiercely frowning great horned owl plastic decoy stands guard over each, with backup protection afforded by tin pans rattling on strings. The biggest share of his garden—Irene's lush strawberry bed is no more—is in potatoes, but rows of peas, beans, cabbages, corn, and tomatoes have been planted as well. So far, Don says, he's mostly growing weeds. "It's been too wet. Some of my corn and other stuff didn't come up; must have rotted in the ground." When his watermelon plants failed to appear, he saved a handful of seeds from a store-bought melon and planted them. "I'm not cheap," he declares, "just thrifty." With Becky supervising, Brian begins to work the old-fashioned single-wheel, tined hand cultivator. "Remember," his mother shouts, "*between* the rows."

Dick returns, a bit sheepish, with the planter manual, which had been in his front-room roll-top desk after all. ("I told you," gloats Don; "anything goes in that desk simply disappears.") Jeff arrives home from school, and, since the promised spreader still has not arrived, he and Dick set up the torch to fix a bothersome design flaw on this planter. Changing sprocket settings, which they now have to do, requires driving a pin from a rod with a punch. A metal guard on one side of the rod features a hole through which the punch can be inserted, but there is no hole on the opposite guard through which the pin could emerge, and finagling that pin out has always been a frustrating task. Now they take the time to burn a hole through the second guard with their acetylene torch, a small but satisfying checkoff for Dick's Some Day list.

Afternoon milking time arrives, but Joan comes down from the house with word that the power is out despite a clear blue sky. Dick detaches the meter from the power pole in order to hook up the generator, while Jeff backs a Deere into place to power it. "We just bought this generator on halves with the neighbor last year," Dick says. "It's a good deal for both of us, and since we're on different power lines, we generally don't need it at the same time."

NEXT MORNING DICK HAULS A HAY WAGON loaded with bags of seed and fertilizer—and Becky perched on top—down to the first corn piece, unhitches, and returns to get the planter. The loaded fertilizer spreader had arrived halfway through yesterday's afternoon milking. Don had begun to spread immediately, and Dick and Jeff finished up after supper, harrowing the first piece as well. Now, after barn chores and breakfast, Joan harrows the next piece while Dick plants the first. The tractor chugs along steadily, guided after the first sweep by a "marker" furrow. A marker—a long rod with a round metal plate at the end—extends on either side of the planter. One marker is carried raised, the other—on the side of the direction of the coming end-of-row turn—dragging, making a furrow on which the driver lines up for the next sweep.

The planter is an ingenious mechanism. Four sets of two sharp-edged rotary disks cut narrow furrows, into which a thin stream of starter fertilizer is dropped. Similar sets of disks, offset four inches to one side to prevent fertilizer burn, carve furrows into which corn kernels, passed down a square plastic tube from the rotating slotted plates, are dropped singly, one about every four inches. Four ordinarily tired wheels follow, running over the seed furrows, ideally—it doesn't always work that way in hard clay—closing the furrow and tamping the seedbed.

Planting goes slowly but steadily. Halfway through the morning, Dick pulls the planter over to the edge of the field to dump 720 pounds of fertilizer into his hoppers and to check on Becky, who, on this cool, sunny spring morning, is carefully working with markers ("not," she insists, "crayons") in a Christmas coloring book, patiently turning outlines printed on pulp paper into purple candy canes and green kittens.

Joan stops by, having finished her harrowing, excited about having flushed a fine red fox from the edge of the first corn piece where a small pole barn had collapsed, leaving a nicely roofed rubble that looks like an ideal fox den. A search of the immediate area turns up a fresh meat-cleaned woodchuck leg. "Do you suppose she's feeding pups in there?" Joan wonders; "this close to the house?"

Dick heads back out to plant. "A couple more good days," he says, "and we'll have our corn in."

## 7

"I HATE THIS JOB," JOAN CONFIDES WITH FEEL-ing, and Dick agrees. The corn in, the Treadways turn immediately to the first cutting of hay, which they will chop and feed out of one of two silage silos west of the barn. That silo is now empty, and it is time for the dreaded silo work.

These are not the shiny dark blue metal silos one sees on favored farms—their initial and maintenance costs put them out of reach of most farmers—but weathered white structures made of thin, rectangular cement blocks tied together by supporting-rod hoops. The blue metal "sealed" silo has the advantage over the cement-block "stave" silo that it off-loads from the bottom, so that one can fill and feed from it at the same time. (Off-loading a sealed silo must be managed carefully to avoid creating a vacuum, which can lead to an implosion, leaving a crumpled and useless blue silo on the landscape.) Otherwise, the principle of the two tower silos is the same. (Some farmers store silage in an open cement bunker or simply dump it on the

ground. In either case, the load must be "built" and covered
carefully to prevent spoilage; and to feed it, the farmer must
move it a tractor bucket at a time.) The Treadway stave silos are
fifty feet tall by twenty feet in diameter, and, standing in the
bottom of this one, Dick may as well be at the bottom of a
massive well. Indeed, in the dim light admitted by the small,
semitransparent window in the ceiling, paper nose-and-mouth
mask in place and sweatshirt hood pulled over his head, Dick
looks rather like a diver examining ancient wreckage as he bends
over his unloader.

The silo unloader is hooked via cable to a tripod support in
the silo's domed top. Its three massive arms run circles around
the top of the haylage on cement wheels along with the pickup
chute, whose auger scrapes hay silage—"haylage" for short—to
an open-bottomed, hump-backed off-load chute. The damp and,
as it gets older, increasingly rank mix ("Smell makes you want
to roll it up in paper and smoke it, doesn't it?") is driven via
blower through the chute, which is aimed at one of a row of
doors down one side of the silo and hence down a chute for
feeding. Dick checks and lubricates the unloader mechanism.
Light-colored tin marks a recently installed new section of the
off-load chute. "Haylage acid is even worse than manure acid
for freezing up and rusting and eating through metal." Dick
points to a section of pickup chute eaten through with holes.
"We'll have to replace that soon."

From outside, a silo is a tall, cylindrical, apparently opening-
free structure with a roughly two-foot by two-foot U-shaped tin
chute bracketed down one side. This chute conceals the row of
twenty thick wooden doors—two feet high by eighteen inches
wide—through which, one by one, the silage is off-loaded. As
the haylage level slowly drops, the unloader is dropped, and the
next lower door is opened to accommodate the off-load chute.
Now all the doors are open, and it's Joan's easier-said-than-
done task to shut them.

She works her way up inside the constricting chute on widely
spaced bracketed-rod rungs, tools hung from pant loops and

baler twine. Sweatshirt hood and face mask are most appreci-
ated here, for the chute acts as a wind tunnel, and a pulsing
stream of silo detritus—hay and dirt and chaff and mold—driven
alternately down from above and up from below, penetrates
shirts and pants and shoes and socks and hoods and eyes and
ears. Using a large screwdriver, Joan scrapes dried, caked
haylage—much like what the suburban homeowner scrapes
from the underdeck of his lawn mower—from the door frame.
She then tries to close the door, hammering at it—they open to
the inside of the silo—while leaning in through the door above.
Some doors seat and latch easily; others are obdurate. Joan tries
WD-40 on frozen hinge mechanisms, but in the end it comes
down to hammering, heavy hammering, frustrated hammering.
"Let me know if someone shows up down there," she calls, "and
I'll quit cussing."

Joan climbs down out of the chute, and Dick, having tied the
unloader's arms in an upright position for its coming vertical
journey, inch-worms his way up to close the upper silo doors.
That task completed, Don inserts the bit of a massive ¾-inch
drill into the drive socket of a winch bracketed on the outside
base of the silo, and, squeezing the trigger, begins the chore of
powering the bulky unloader to the top of the silo. He stops
periodically to rest, oil the winch mechanism, cool the drill, and
hear a progress report from Dick, who is watching the operation
through the top silo door. Then the grinding noise begins again
as the unloader is "drilled" into the sky, until Dick hollers down
"Two more inches" and then, "*Hold* it!" and silo number two
is ready for a new 300-ton load of chopped hay.

Silo number one is running down on last year's chopped corn.
Dick feeds his cows a mixture of haylage and corn silage. "Cows
prefer corn to hay," he says; "we mix the two and they eat
both." Once the silo delivery system is set up and working properly, it is a marvel of labor-saving mechanics. A tin trough brings
corn over and drops it into a second trough carrying hay from
the base of silo number two to an overhead horizontal elevator
mechanism which runs back and forth dropping the mixture

into a seventy-five-foot-long cement feed bunk west of the barn.

"We used to feed silage out of a wheelbarrow in the barn," says Dick. "Milking took a lot longer that way, and except in winter the cows had access to it only twice a day. This way, they have free access to corn and hay, and they use it day and night."

Like any other structure, a silo requires maintenance and has a limited useful life. The silo nearest the barn is now twenty years old, and dark rust on sections of supporting hoops shows where silage acid has opened cracks between cement blocks, allowing silage "juice" to run out. A more immediate problem is that the bottom row of one-foot by three-foot blocks is considerably eaten away. "We didn't get a high enough foundation under this silo," Dick says. "And then the dirt and spilled silage and sawdust and stuff pack around the base, and you don't get good drainage."

He plans to have the silo-construction people fix the problem this fall, either by jacking the silo up and replacing the bottom tier of blocks, or by disassembling the whole structure and rebuilding. Dick hopes they can jack it up, which would be a quicker and much cheaper fix. There is worry involved in that fix, however. Jacking silos is a tricky business. Occasionally they come down, and stories of what falling silos do to tractors and cars and barns and living things are legion in farm country.

## 8

IF MAY WAS STUCK ON COOL AND RAINY, EARLY June's weather lottery has come up cool and sunny. The land has completely dried in a week (a week too late, of course) and has now begun to crack. Dick doubts that there's enough moisture in the ground to germinate his corn. "We could use a hot, rainy stretch," he says.

This is, at any rate, lovely weather for mowing and chopping hay, and the Treadways are hard at it. Pockets of light frost showed on the farm this morning, and Don wears a red International Harvester hat and a dark blue jacket against a cool north wind as he heads out on a Deere to mow about nine acres of meadow east from the homestead across two meadows and two corn pieces, where the land rises again toward the ridge beyond their property. This meadow is "cutting a bit thin," Dick says. There is a good alfalfa component, but it is not as luxuriant as it might be, and most of the meadow is knee-high. (By contrast, the richer year-old meadow adjoining this piece to the south is waist-high and taller, and sports a better grass component and rich stands of bee-loud trefoil and red clover.)

Don makes progressively smaller rectangular passes around the meadow, the mower offset to his right. A leading bar bends the grass forward, and a counterclockwise-turning drum spiked with rows of rodlike tines rakes it against a row of serrated triangular knives, which, cutting against a stationary guard composed of similar but plain-edged triangles, scissors it off a couple of inches above ground. The drum then rakes the cut hay up to two furiously spinning counter-rotating slotted drums, which fire it back against the walls of what amounts to an oddly shaped bottomless metal box. These walls slant inward, toward each other, with the result that each pass of the mower constricts a nine-foot-wide swath of cut grass to a three-foot-wide row of piled hay. On the next pass, the tractor operator simply straddles the last windrow with his front tires, and he is lined up for the next cut.

Any windrow shows what the cows will be eating for haylage this summer. Mixed with the alfalfa are brome grass (with delicate, spikelike inflorescences) and orchard grass (short, shaggy inflorescences), red and white clover, and here and there the telltale yellow flowers of mustard and the deep blue flowers of vetch. And dandelions. In some stretches the blown dandelions are so thick that the newly bared land is carpeted with a white, cottony cushion, as if some sort of stuffing material had mysteriously rained down from the sky. Farmers who forget during first cutting to periodically clean their tractors' radiator screens of dandelion "felt" suffer boil-over in the field.

Other foods find their way into the mix. Mowing along formerly damp drainage swales, Don adds waxed-petaled buttercups and the delicately lovely blue-eyed grass. And when he swings around to cut the east end of the meadow, right up against a thriving fencerow of buckthorn, hickory, and tent-caterpillar-bedeviled pin cherry, he contributes one row rich with poison ivy. (Poison ivy apparently doesn't bother Holsteins' innards, but it can do a number on people handling the hay.) Animal matter gets into the hay as well—"a little meat to go with all that salad" is how farmers are likely to put it—not only a variety of insects, but meadow voles (blunt-nosed, short-tailed rodents twice the size of house mice) and the nestlings—and occasionally adults—of ground-nesting birds. Indeed, modern mowing and chopping equipment is so efficient that one wonders how meadow nesters such as meadowlark, bobolink, and Savannah sparrow manage to replenish their numbers.

Don continues to mow, accompanied by what, from a distance, looks like a small cloud of dust, and is in fact an aura of pollen, chaff, and dandelion parachutes which, heading south in streams, is continuously renewed. Above his aura sails a single ring-billed gull, hoping for mower-flushed or -injured voles, while low over the narrowing meadow an ornate tiger swallowtail passes a smaller cream-and-tan satyr jerking along in the opposite direction.

From time to time throughout the afternoon, Don stops, climbs down off the tractor, opens the tool box fastened to its side, and fiddles with the two hydraulic-line couplers. Somehow the lines' slack is proving insufficient, and the couplers are pulling loose. Beyond a certain point, this costs Don his power steering, most of his brakes, and the ability to lift the mower during end-of-row turns. Occasionally a line pulls out altogether, spewing hydraulic fluid for a second or two before the automatic shutoff takes effect. Don works on the couplers with a wrench, attempts to anchor the lines with baler wire to maintain tractor-end slack, hooks up a small spring on the coupler lever. Nothing seems to avail. Don is not the sort to be put off his job by a problem with his equipment; he mows and tinkers, mows and tinkers, wiping at his hands with an oil- and grease-blackened pair of old undershorts. (That evening he reports the tractor "a little low" on hydraulic fluid. Dick and Kevin end up adding the entire contents of a five-gallon drum.)

While mowing the north edge of the meadow, Don runs a rear tractor tire over a massive anthill, actually not a "hill" at all but a thirteen-foot-long by six-foot-wide underground mall ("the damndest pismire I ever saw," Don calls it). Immediately thousands upon thousands of medium-sized black ants boil out of the pulverized ground, gather in the tread prints, and begin work. Some cart eggs, others larvae, others bits of food hither and yon. Still others set about shoving rounded bits of dry soil, apparently starting what will have to be a major reconstruction job.

In late afternoon, a dark cloud bank crawls in from the west and covers the sun, and suddenly the north wind changes from cool to cold. Don mows on. So long as the equipment holds up, mowing, like harrowing, is quick and "clean" work. No stopping to wrestle with seed and fertilizer bags or to juggle catching wagons; no continual pulling and cranking of levers to redirect flying bales or chop. You simply line up, put the tractor in a comfortable gear, and go. As he passes north along the west end of the piece in a shallow dip, only Don's cap and the top of the tractor's exhaust stack are visible from the top of the meadow, and cap follows stack across the landscape with the inexorability and uncannily steady pace of targets at a county fair shooting gallery.

If mowing is relatively fast and satisfying work, there is a lot of mowing to do with more than 100 acres of meadow on the farm. Dick emerges from the barn and gazes across the narrow valley at the meadow Don has just finished, the dark green windrows of hay alternating artistically with light green strips of bare ground. "It looks like we'll have some hay to chop tomorrow," he says.

# 9

SOMEWHERE INSIDE JOAN LURKS A NINETEENTH-century thespian, whose melodramatic tones and stage gestures she occasionally employs to express a particular emotion while at the same time distancing it through comic hyperbole. Today, the role is bereaved mother, and "It's a traumatic day," she wails; "my baby has gone off to school!" It is visiting day at the Shoreham elementary school for next fall's kindergartners. Rebecca, dressed in a frock of her own choosing, has boarded the school bus and sailed off, her mother announces, "in her glory."

The school could not have picked a lovelier day on which to entertain prospective pupils: in the low 60s, with northerly breezes, the sun shining brilliantly out of a sky whose intense blue is highlighted by isolated puffs of white cloud dotting the horizons. Male bobolinks are doing their stiff-winged courtship song flights over the meadows, while barn swallows careen low over planted cornfields and cut meadow in foraging forays.

Heading around the end of the nearest corn piece, Dick's chopping entourage scares up an adult killdeer with four chicks. The adult trots into the bare field, while the chicks (for which Jeff has coined the term "sandpipperlets") scurry along the tractor path. Yesterday one of these stilt-legged, already black-necklaced downy babies had refused to leave the ruts in front of Joan's tractor. She climbed down and caught the chick, triggering the nearby adult's distraction display. One wing extended and hanging limp, the tail splayed to show the orange rump patch, the bird dragged itself forward crying piteously. Joan quickly set the chick down in the field margin and drove away, looking over her shoulder to see the chick run directly back into the road ruts.

Driving Allis—which pulls the chopper, which pulls a catching wagon—down the margin of the mowed meadow, Dick begins to make haylage. The low-slung chopper, offset to the tractor's right like the mower, clanks along over the three-foot-wide hay windrow. Tines on a rotating drum—a smaller version of the mower's rake—sweep the hay back to an auger, both ends corkscrewing toward the center, which concentrates the hay to a twenty-inch-wide mat. This mat is delivered via saw-toothed flanges on a revolving drum to the chopper box, inside which six sharp, heavy knives revolve against a cutting bar to do the actual chopping. The "chop" is then blown up and back through a curving chute aimed at the top front of the following wagon.

Round and round the assemblage goes, neatly engorging hay and converting it to silage. From any distance it looks for all the world as if an endless green shag hall runner were being sucked into some sort of vacuum machine and spit out behind in dusty fragments. Dick grabs and rotates in turn three rods accessible through the open back of the tractor, particularly the one which swings the exit chute laterally, enabling him to fill the wagon evenly and to hit a moving and diminished wagon opening on turns. A second rod manipulates a deflector plate at the end of the chop chute, which controls the vertical angle of the stream, depending on the weight of the hay and changing wind conditions.

Chopping hay is a two-man job, and Don soon appears with the other catching wagon. When the first wagon is full, Dick and his father unhitch and switch wagons, and while Dick goes back to chopping, Don hauls the first wagon back to the barn, where he parks his tractor cheek-by-jowl with another. The Treadways

are now filling the silo nearest the barn, dumping haylage on top
of the diminishing chopped corn so that they'll have silage to
feed while filling the second silo.

Don hooks his tractor's power take-off to the loaded wagon,
and a passive catching vessel becomes a machine in its own
right. Rows of small vertical plates creep forward, dragged by
four chains on the floor of the wagon. As the load inches forward, three "beaters"—axles sprouting double-toothed narrow
plates—stacked one above another in the front of the wagon
spill the chop into an auger lying along the front of the wagon's
floor. The auger shoves the mix out the side of the wagon into
a bouncing, slant-bottomed hamper, whence a short auger carries it to a powerful blower—this latter assemblage powered by
the second tractor—whose whirling paddles drive it fifty feet up
a tube and into the top of the silo. Mowed yesterday and
chopped within the hour, this haylage smells fresh and sweet.

When Don returns to the meadow to switch wagons, he finds
the chopping operation stalled. Having noticed a bad wobble in
his left front tractor wheel, Dick checked to find five of the six
lug bolts pulled out. He heads off for the shop, returning in the
pickup with a jack and some lugs. The rim is warped and must
be replaced, but it will take time to find one. At the moment
Dick is hoping that replacement lugs may enable him to limp
through the day's chopping.

A town-dweller driving down a country road sees a hay-
chopping rig at work and thinks how marvelously efficient it is,
what an enormous amount of labor it saves. The farmer appre-
ciates that point as well. He also sees the rig through a haze of
figures with dollar signs in front of them, figures representing
initial and maintenance costs, costs which are, unlike his take
for the products he sells, continually rising. It would now cost
$15,000 to replace Dick's chopper. A set of six knives, which
can be held in one hand, runs $350, so you take care of them,
sharpening them regularly. The best sharpener available sells for
$1,200. It not only hones the knives' cutting edges, but takes
down the "heels" behind those edges. (Ignored, the heels hump

up with successive edge sharpenings, and will eventually hit the shear bar and shut down the chopping operation.) The Treadways don't feel they can afford this sharpener; they file the heels by hand.

Dick recently shopped around for a new catcher wagon, and, at $6,000, he considers this one a good buy. ("They finally put roofs on these wagons," he remarks. "Chopping with the wind at your back, the old open wagons would leave half the chop on the ground.") And a tractor to pull the $15,000 chopper which pulls the $6,000 wagon? Dick winces and turns away. "You don't even *think* about buying a tractor; you fix up what you've got."

That's no picnic either. Last month the twice-welded gearshift stick on the Allis broke again, and Dick ordered a replacement. In due time it arrived, a two-foot-long, twice-bent hardened steel rod. Accompanying the shift stick was a bill for $158. For a week thereafter, Dick would occasionally take the bill from his shirt pocket, unfold it, and marvel at the figure. "It didn't even come with a knob on it," he says. "We had to use the knob off the old stick."

A $158 shift stick did not break the farm, nor will a new rim for the same tractor. But equipment problems requiring inputs of money—and labor—are continual and cumulative. And the frustrating thing is that the failure of a minor part can shut down not only the machine it belongs to, but a whole operation involving other machines and people.

After a lunch of microwaved grilled cheese sandwiches, Dick is setting up to chop more hay when the Blue Seal feed man arrives to pick up a cellophane-wrapped sample of the new hay, which will be analyzed at the company lab for dry matter as well as energy and protein content. Exuding the confidence of a born salesman, Jim laughs when Dick kids him about the young woman who accompanied him on his last visit. "Nothin' going on," he protests, winking; "fifty-six don't go into twenty-six!" Supremely at home with the male element of the farm commu-

nity, the feed-company rep is expansive and vigorously pro-
farm. He complains about how little townsfolk know about the
origins of their food and fiber. "It's like the lady on the TV talk
show the other day. The guy says, 'What would happen if all the
farmers quit?' and the lady replies: 'That wouldn't be a problem; I'd go to the Stop and Shop.' "

Dick gets back to chopping, stopping from time to time to
check his wobbly front tire, while Don ferries wagons and off-
loads. In midafternoon, Brian, who had felt unwell and stayed
home from school, greets the school bus. Becky, who has, in
retrospect, adopted a no-big-deal attitude toward her day at
school, pronounces the experience "O.K." Dick has come in
from the meadow, and he and Joan climb up the chute and into
the first silo to check the fill. A problem with this system is that
the silos don't fill evenly; the haylage mounds in the center. The
unloader needs to operate on a flat surface; so two pitchforks go
to work tossing the mountain into the surrounding valley.
(Overnight the periphery of the load will settle more than the
center, requiring more pitchforking.) A pigeon sails through the
in-load door and is halfway across the silo when, catching sight
of human beings just below, it wheels about in consternation
and exits in power flight.

It's 4:30, past time to be milking. But everyone seems to
be otherwise occupied. Dick is under the mower, taking off a
bent triangular knife, while Jeff hunts for a replacement in the
tool shed. None is found, and Dick straightens the knife with
gentle hammer taps, starting, as he knew he would, a hairline
crack that will shortly cause the knife to break. "Remind me to
buy a box of knives," he says, replacing the problem knife for
the time being. Kevin's bike has a flat tire, and he is working
near the mower, trying to remove the tire so that he can patch
the tube.

Having been reminded that his Little League minors team has
a game against neighboring Cornwall this evening, Brian has
experienced a rapid improvement in health, and he now emerges
from the house resplendent in maroon shirt (Number 17) and

cap. Don will drop him off at school—whence the team will be driven to the Cornwall schoolyard—on his way to buy a set of extra-long lug bolts, which, secured by nuts, will hold the front wheel on the Allis, Dick hopes, until a new rim arrives. Jeff hitches up to the mower and sets off to start mowing another piece of meadow. But he is involved in a new baseball league, and wants to leave for practice at 6 P.M. "Sometimes," says Dick, "it's hard to keep everybody happy around here."

Brian, at any rate, is happy, even though, as he stands thirty feet behind the third baseman in left field, he will have little chance to demonstrate his defensive prowess. When third and fourth graders play baseball, the result is more theater than sport. In this league, coaches pitch to their own teams, overhand but slow. Some kids, boys as well as girls, don't swing at all, but rather pray for a walk. Others, especially those who have played some with siblings or fathers, do swing (sometimes regardless of pitch location), and occasionally make contact. The result is usually a ground ball, to which the infielders respond in unpredictable ways while outfielders offer advice.

Savvy coaches instruct their players to throw any secured ball to the pitcher-coach, as this stops play. Overcome by excitement, however, defenders often try to get runners out. This is usually a great mistake, and many a soft ground ball in the infield has been played into a double, a triple, even a home run as errant throws and blown catches chase the runner around the diamond.

Cornwall parents (mostly mothers) take their stand along the third base line, Shoreham parents (ditto) on the first base line. They mostly stand in small groups gossiping, from time to time calling out encouragement or consolation to the players. Youngsters too small to play ball chase about in foul (mostly) territory, tackling one another, throwing balls over the fence, trying on batting helmets. A Shoreham mother, keeping as low a profile as possible, positions herself to snap a picture of her on-deck son. A Cornwall mother has caught two tow-headed preschoolers climbing the schoolyard fence. She leans over them in an attitude of mild admonishment, pointing to the electric fence just within. The heifers in the adjacent pasture have seen more than enough of playing kids, and pay the proceedings no attention whatsoever.

By the time Joan and Becky arrive in midgame, Brian's playing stint is over. That doesn't seem to bother him. Nor is it a problem that Cornwall wins the game, by exactly what score no one seems to know or much care. The teams huddle and exchange cheers:

> Two, four, six, eight,
> Who do we appreciate?
> SHOREHAM! (CORNWALL!)

Players pick up their gear and head across the playground with parents or rides, excited about their accomplishments ("I made a run!"), wretched over umpire injustices ("He called me out on a pitch a foot outside!").

Brian has no complaints. He got on base via a walk once, and he chalked up an RBI on a groundout. Not bad for a kid who was sick just this morning.

## 10

MARK TWAIN CLAIMED TO HAVE DISTINGUISHED 136 varieties of weather in a single New England spring day. It was, he said, a situation which compelled one's "admiration—and regret." As it turns out, New Englanders—and others—would give much for a little variety now. The jet stream has shifted north into Canada and a Bermuda High is stuck off the Atlantic coast, with the result that most of the country east of

the Rockies has been sweltering through mid-June. The media
meteorologists have become apologetic as they announce another week of the "three h's" (hot, hazy, and humid) and no
rain. For much of the country, there has been no rain this month.
Drought in the northern prairie states has become severe, res-
urrecting talk of the Dust Bowl years, and the usually well-
watered Midwest and Northeast are hurting as well.

This Thursday is wash day, a twice-weekly event on the
Treadway farm. Joan put a couple of loads through her veteran
washing machine the previous evening to give her something
to hang first thing in the morning. By midmorning the eight
backyard clothes lines are sagging with nine loads of laundry,
mostly jeans, cords, shirts, and bath towels. Line sag comes in
handy for Becky, who can reach to hang her own clothes at
midline.

While her tenth load washes in the combination bathroom/
laundry room ("I'll find a last load picking up the house"), Joan
sets a hose running in a children's plastic pool. Mindy needs a
bath. Water is not, however, Mindy's idea of fun, and when
shampoo and a brush are trotted out, she disappears. Tracked
down and dragged into the pool by the collar, she stands un-
complaining but miserable, splayed legs stiff, while Joan sudses
and Becky rinses from a plastic container. "Fleas are leaving in
droves!" Joan announces, but Mindy is inconsolable. Released
at last, the bedraggled animal slinks off in classic hangdog attitude, her brown eyes throwing an accusatory look back at her
tormenters.

Meanwhile, Don is mowing, and Jeff, who is playing a mild
form of hooky ("It's mostly an exam day, and I didn't have
any"), chops while Dick unloads wagons and checks the silo.
One of the major advantages of storing hay as silage rather than
bales is that silage can be—in fact, ought to be—put up damp,
a welcome fact during the uncertain weather of most springs.
Silage heats up some as it "works," but a by-product of that
fermentation, an acid, limits temperature rise. Then, too, the
haylage, blown loose into the silo, packs well, leaving little room

for air, another check on the danger of silo fires. (Baled hay, on the other hand, must be put up dry. With plenty of oxygen available within and between bales, the heat gain associated with the "working" of damp hay will eventually set bales—and barns and other things—on fire.)

After all this hot, dry weather, however, the meadow grass is mowing dry and quickly gets drier on the ground. Dick doesn't like to see the chop too dry, and he has Jeff's chopper literally chasing his grandfather's mower around a large meadow at the south end of the farm. Longtime members of the town volunteer fire brigade (and Jeff, though technically underage, has just been accepted as well), Don and Dick have seen too many silo fires to want one of their own. Such a fire will likely burn secretly for days or even weeks. A farmer doesn't know he's got one until smoke comes down the off-load chute or the fire reaches and burns through one of his wooden doors; and there isn't much he can do about it once he knows. "We've poured water on top of the load and tried a layer of foam," Dick says, "but you can't get at the fire. It will tunnel this way and that deep in the silage, where the haylage is drier or there's a seam of air." Most often the farmer has no option but to off-load and haul away the entire contents of the silo.

On a clear day, one can see the Green Mountains to the east and the Adirondacks to the northwest from the top of the ladder up the back side of a Treadway silo. In the hot, muggy air of today, one can see but one wooded ridge to the east and three to the west. Down the shallow valley east of the farmstead, the cool, green, waving meadows are gone, and the scalped rectangular fields look oddly deserted under the hot sun, like an abandoned golf course or the vast mown lawns of a housing development that never materialized. The only thriving "meadows" one sees now are in the farmyard itself. Paths and tractor roads, heading between and around buildings and down to the fields, isolate irregularly shaped, never-mown islands, on which are marooned miscellaneous reminders of farm enterprises past—an old hay wagon, part of an obsolete combine, a stark

upright old-fashioned mower bar, an outgrown swing set surrounded by treadless tires, even a collapsed shed.

Dick is not admiring the view. He is standing on top of 290
tons of fresh haylage, trying to get the last ten tons in before
tonight's predicted rain. (It will not rain that night, or the next,
or the next.) Dressed in gray cords, a pink T-shirt, and a red cap
worn backwards, he swings the end of the on-load chute now
left, now right, pitchforking the resulting mound about the silo's
perimeter. Haylage chaff drives relentlessly about the stuffy silo
top, and Dick's T-shirt sports a dark yoke fore and aft. From
time to time a dark spot magically appears and briefly widens on
his shirt front below the dark yoke.

Joan unloads the wagon below, which means that she sits on
the tractor fender with hay blowing in her face watching for
trouble. And trouble comes. The usual roar of the blower is
interrupted by an ominous clattering, and Joan darts around to
turn off the second tractor. The blower has, for no apparent
reason, stalled, packing itself and plugging the chute with haylage. Dick climbs down the silo ladder, removes a spring-loaded
collar attaching chute to blower housing, pulls the bottom out of
the plug, and then rams a twenty-foot length of heavy plastic
hose up the chute, working it to free the packed hay. He then
works with a wooden shovel handle from the top of the blower,
while Joan, on her back in the hamper, legs dangling outside,
pulls haylage from between the blower paddles.

The family takes a quick break for lunch. Dick showers and
changes clothes while Joan makes cold meat sandwiches, slath-
ering on the mayonnaise first. A rumble of thunder occasions an
interested pause, but the succeeding five-minute shower doesn't
even lay the dooryard dust. The real high point of lunch is the
year's first homemade strawberry shortcake. Joan disclaims responsibility for the cake. She was called to silo duty in midbake,
and had to turn it off before its time. She declares the final
product light and fluffy as any brick, but gets no complaints
from the assembled diners.

Don and Jeff head out to mow and chop a small meadow on

the west side of the road, while Joan and Dick return to silo chores. Not half an hour later, Joan looks up to see Jeff pull in past the old farmhouse. "Oh, no," she says, "the mower's down." And then: "This has been a *miserable* week. I told Dick the other day to call the auctioneer." She promptly takes it back ("We're too stubborn to quit"), but clearly this 90-degree anything-that-can-go-wrong-will week has been dispiriting.

Typical of the week's problems has been the front rim for the Allis. Rather than waste a day driving around from dealer to dealer looking for a match that might not be available, Dick had it special-ordered from a dealer's catalogue. The rim arrived with a bill for $199, and it didn't fit. Even the number of lug holes was wrong. "That's what the catalogue calls for," said the dealer.

The next day the same tractor blew a rear tire. Changing these massive tires requires special equipment, and by the time the dealer has pumped liquid chloride into a $72 tube (chloride won't freeze in winter, and a liquid both supports the tube better than air and adds weight for better traction) encased in a standard, nonradial tire ($500), he leaves a bill for $720. ("I think my first Ford tractor cost seven hundred fifty dollars," comments Don.)

Then, last evening, they had found a newly calved cow down with milk fever in the woods west of the barn. Not a fever at all, "parturient hypocalcemia" is a not-uncommon disorder caused by the rapid depletion of blood calcium as a cow starts heavy milk production. Milk fever weakens the animal dramatically, and can be serious, even fatal. Typically, however, cows respond with astonishing alacrity to a vet's ministrations. Arriving in midmorning, the vet ties the cow's head back along her side, exposing her neck, into which he jabs a needle. He then hooks up a bottle of calcium, which he drains into her system, and two minutes later she is up and walking, and will require no further help. It's the sort of cure vets wish they had for every bovine ailment. Still, it's another vet bill for the Treadways.

Small problems are particularly frustrating when they stop a

whole operation. This morning, Don had been unloading a chop
wagon when the beaters and auger mysteriously quit. Dick
found a bit of the end of a rod integral to the safety release
mechanism sheared off. He rigged a replacement with a lug bolt
and two nuts, a fix which enabled the silo filling to continue but
disabled the wagon's emergency power-stoppage system. "It's
not really safe this way," he admits. "I'll have to remember to
order that part."

The Treadways aren't having all the neighborhood's troubles.
A young farmer who rents a spread to the northwest had missed
a heifer three days back and had asked area farmers, including
Dick, to check their heifers for an extra. He now walks into the
barnyard to report that the animal has been found in the bottom
of a well, dead. "There were tree limbs over the well," he says;
"I didn't even know it was on the farm." Dick last lost a heifer—
though not to accident or disease—a few years back, when beef
prices were high. "People just drive a pickup into a pasture in
the middle of the night, load up a heifer, take it home and
butcher it, and bury the hide. There's no way you can find out
who got it."

Dick now climbs down from the silo once again, and, cap and
shoulders mantled with chop and more stuck to wet neck and
hair and eyebrows and shirt, he and Jeff lean over the mower
and ponder a familiar problem. A plate involved in housing a set
of doughnut-shaped counterweights which are instrumental in
steadying the cutting mechanism has twice been welded after
breaking, and it has broken again. Because this particular plate
is not supposed to break, it cannot be easily replaced. A proper
repair would involve taking apart and replacing much of the side
of the mower, and would cost upwards of $1,000, with no
guarantees. Should he try a major repair, or contemplate purchase of a major piece of equipment?

"The only thing keeping me going is the basketball game
tonight," Dick says. Joan and Jeff exchange knowing glances.
They know he looks forward to seeing this NBA playoff game,
as he does many another sports contest on TV. They also know

that he will very likely be asleep in his chair well before halftime.

Farm news is never all bad, of course, and this week has been no exception. The silo will get filled by the weekend one way or another. Corn has sprouted here and there in the four corn pieces, and more will follow when rain comes. The new meadow west of the road is more promising yet. It shows a green blush of two-inch alfalfa, and coverage looks good. And today's mail brings a bit of cheer in the form of a check. A 100-pound bull calf sent to auction last week has netted $106, more than twice the return calves sometimes bring.

Best of all, the calf born to the milk-fevered mother is not only healthy and female, but born of a good bull to one of the farm's best milkers. Already a favorite in the barn, Bunny has every hereditary reason to develop into a top milk producer.

Only time will tell about Bunny, but one needn't refer to the calendar—which notes that the school bus stops for Brian and Kevin for the last time next Monday, the longest day of the year—or to the thermometer to realize that time has marked another season on the Treadway farm. Irene's prize irises—the row of blue and white out front and the beds of yellow with red, solid blue, and magnificent oversized pale violet—have faded along with area spirea, and birdsong has waned as well. In the last of the uncut meadows, rows of tiny yellow lanterns hang from brome grass heads and the first daisies wave over a new generation of thousands of miniature grasshoppers.

Barn swallows are busy feeding nestlings, and from the woods one can hear the nasal begging calls of grackle and crow fledglings. Spot-breasted robin young are independent already, as are the starling young, which zoom about over the farm in squadrons, giving their grating chirring call. Mile after mile of boundary-line vegetation—into which baby rabbits duck at the approach of tractor or car—is awash in white pin cushions thanks to the synchronized blooming of the North Country's foundation fencerow shrub, gray-stemmed dogwood. The very first pastel blue chicory blooms color the roadside from gangly two- and three-foot stalks, and, if another sign were needed, a pioneer monarch butterfly, one of the new generations hopscotching north from Mexico, flits by, no doubt thinking green thoughts of growing milkweed.

Another Cutting Hill spring is over. It lasted, by the most generous of measures, but six weeks.

# SUMMER

As anyone who has ever been in—or even near—a dairy barn knows, milk is not the only generous return cows make on the farmer's investment of grain and grass. Until recently, the Treadways handled manure and urine the traditional way. It was scraped out of the barn, where the urine ran off, evaporated, leached into the ground. They loaded the manure into a spreader, and, snow depth permitting in winter, chucked the stuff onto the fields nearly every day, as often as not when crops didn't need it and the land couldn't absorb it. Much of this manure ended up polluting brooks.

Four years ago, Dick decided to go with the new pit technology. Earth-moving equipment scooped out what might have passed for a huge swimming pool—roughly 100 feet wide by 150 feet long by 11 feet deep—on the east side of the barn. Now, every morning at the end of barn chores, the switch is thrown activating the gutter cleaner, whose chain-dragged vertical plates grind around the central aisle, scraping feces, urine, hay, paper towels, and other refuse out of the barn, where, thinned by water from a hose, the organic sludge works its way down a ninety-foot-long, three-foot-diameter steeply angled cement pipe, then, at a more shallow angle, out into the bottom of the pit. Fed from the bottom, the contents of the pit remain liquid, though a crust forms on top.

Manure pits solve an important problem, but they are not, the family shortly began to discover, without problems of their own. The new pit was filling nicely that first summer when Dick looked out one day to see a large pair of nostrils breaking the surface of the brown lagoon. "I thought it was an alligator," he says. It was, in fact, one of his milk cows. Tracks showed she hadn't fallen into the pit, but had deliberately waded in, and, apparently enjoying herself, had swum out into the middle.

The cow showed no inclination to come ashore, and Dick was afraid she would shortly drown or suffocate. The family quickly fastened together two 20-foot sections of ladder and eased it out on the manure crust. Dick crawled out on the ladders, but his weight was too much; ladders and would-be rescuer sank into the morass. There was no help for it. He waded in up to his armpits and threw a lasso out toward the cow. Eventually she came up inside the loop, and all available manpower hauled on the rope, dragging the aromatic Holstein from the pit. The cow—renamed Esther Williams—seemed to benefit from the experience. "She calmed down a lot after that," Joan remembers.

This is the sort of incident that families laugh about in later years, but Dick and Joan, remembering a sober sidelight, don't laugh about this one. Unbeknownst to them at the time, new images associated with the pit—lurking alligators, suffocating cows—began to work in Brian's subconscious, leading to a difficult psychological period. Night after night he would wake up screaming, the nightmares always about falling. "We couldn't figure it out," Joan says, still blaming herself; "we were so dumb!"

Then Brian's kindergarten teacher called. She was worried about the child. Could Joan come see her? The teacher laid out Brian's recent artwork, all of which had a single subject: a circle, colored black. When they finally made the connection, the solution was remarkably simple: they built a fence around the pit, making sure that Brian participated. The nightmares and black-circle art promptly ceased.

The pit, as it turned out, was not the system's only danger to livestock. Returning from a visit to Joan's parents the following year, the Treadways found the heifers milling around the barn, and one missing. Joan noticed that the cover on top of the manure-pit feeder pipe was stove in, but Dick didn't think a heifer could disappear via that route until a moo issued from it. The Treadways had been warned not to go down that chute for any reason—that methane gas would quickly prove lethal. But the heifer was plugging the pipe; she would have to be removed in any case, and better to get her out alive if possible.

A call to the fire department brought a carload of colleagues and an air pack. Dick donned pack and mask, and, secured by a rope around his middle, was lowered down the cow-pie–lubricated pipe. He found the heifer head-up fifty feet down. The animal panicked at the sight of the flashlight-illuminated Darth Vader–like specter descending upon her and attempted to turn and "run." Luckily, she couldn't do so, and Dick was able to tie a free rope around her head and forelegs. The firemen pulled up Dick, then the heifer. Both, to Joan's relief, were alive. The heifer was "shocky" for a while, but came around. "We're milking Lucky now," says Joan; "she's a good cow."

The chief advantage of the manure pit is that it enables the farmer to store "brown gold" in usable form until it is time to use it, and that time is now. Having missed on the corn planting, the manure will be used to fertilize the meadows. With the haylage silo full and the last of the first cutting now being baled, it is time to get the spreader out. Dick likes to spread before the grass and alfalfa get much regrowth started, since coating the leaves interferes with photosynthesis, and because the plants need time to get the manure through their systems before harvest. "We got a load of hay out of Canada once," Joan recalls; "the cows wouldn't touch it. We found out it had been fertilized with pig manure. It was beautiful stuff; we couldn't smell a thing. Cows are picky eaters."

His name having been drawn for jury duty, Dick is off at court today getting his month's assignments, leaving Jeff to "stir" the pit preparatory to spreading. The purpose of stirring is to break up and mix in the two-foot-thick top crust, which, around the pit's perimeter, supports a luxuriant weed growth. Gigantic overhead eggbeaters would be ideal for the job. Since no such equipment is available, Jeff uses a propeller—like that on an outboard motor, but larger—on the end of a long hitch hooked to his tractor.

Maneuvering carefully—tractors disappear in manure pits from time to time—on the sloping side of the mound enclosing the pit, Jeff drags the prop and its bar guard along the edge of the pit, breaking the crust. He then backs the rig downslope, shoving at the crust to move it and break it up into islands. Then he lowers the prop into the muck, sets it spinning, and begins to stir. The churning soup sets up currents, which circulate the weeded islands of crust. When one sails into reach, Jeff jerks up the hitch and drops it on the island, smashing it or sinking it. Just before breaching, the prop makes an impressive *whump,* like a surfacing hippo, and the liquid manure geysers skyward, like the start of an oil strike, flying clots pattering downwind across the pit's surface.

The smell downwind of a stirred pit is, well, rich and pungent; quite unlike anything most people will ever smell. "It's funny," Joan laughs. "Farmers don't mind their own pit smells too much, but the neighbors' are *horrible.* People will call from miles away: 'Stirring your pit today, are you?' " Today a north wind takes the odor down the valley, away from the Treadway houses.

Wind direction and stirring activity are irrelevant to the grackles, starlings, house sparrows, and single killdeer which stalk the lumpy, sun-dried manure crust feeding on insects while barn swallows tear back and forth low over the surface engulfing escapees. A myriad of small cream-orange butterflies flit and land about the pit's periphery, sipping from the salt- and mineral-rich pee soup. Hundreds of black-and-yellow-banded beelike syrphid flies—whose sluglike larvae will live in the pit manure, breathing through anal tubes—hover and zip about the pit margin as well.

Pit stirring requires patience, patience maintained with the constant roar of a full-throttle tractor engine in your head. Jeff moves gingerly along the pit's east edge, churning liquid, slapping at islands, cutting crust from above and below. Divide and conquer is the plan. But there's a rub here. Patient work will eventually free up wide swaths along the pit's edges, but dealing with the large cake floating in the middle can be frustrating. "It floats toward one side," says Jeff, "and you hustle the tractor over there. By the time you've got your prop in, it turns around and heads the other way." As a last resort, the Treadways adopt artillery tactics, using a pump to bombard the cake with liquid manure, eventually breaking it up.

Jeff quits in late morning, his job perhaps half completed. Yesterday, which the calendar called the first full day of summer, sixty-nine weather reporting stations around the country tied or set record high temperatures, and Jeff can no longer stand the thought of his siblings sporting in the above-ground pool up at the house. (Dick and Joan speak of the pool apologetically, as if expecting to be accused of an indulgent expenditure. "The thing is," Dick says, "it's eight o'clock by the time we get done with barn chores and have something to eat. By then everybody's tired, and we don't feel like cleaning up and driving ten miles to the lake for a swim. This way we can just fall in and enjoy it.") Jeff loses no time changing and falling in. He does handstands on the bottom while life-jacketed Becky paddles about and Kevin and Brian argue over rights to a floating mattress.

Meanwhile, Joan, who has had her hair fixed in town this morning, coffee-klatches on the patio with two farm-wife friends. One has brought a stack of fashion catalogues, which the three leaf through, occasionally urging particular items on one another. "No, thanks," Joan retorts; "I don't really think snakeskin cowboy boots are my style."

"Did Dick try to get off jury duty?" one of her friends asks. "You know John Q. Citizen," Joan replies in mock disparagement, "he does his civic duty." She doesn't add that, some years back, Dick *had* tried to get off jury duty. He explained to the judge that it was a particularly busy time of the year, that once a farmer got behind, he couldn't catch up. "Can your wife drive a tractor?" the judge asked. "Yes." "Can she milk a cow?" "Yes." "Request denied," said the judge. Dick didn't have a chance to point out that his wife had a house and three children to care for, that she had her own farm work—including milking cows and driving tractors—to do, or that she happened to be seven months pregnant. He doesn't know if it would have made any difference.

2

"IT WAS A DARK AND STORMY NIGHT." THAT'S how Snoopy's stories begin, and that is what the Treadways and most other American farmers and gardeners are hoping for on this last Saturday in June. The need for rain is past critical in the Midwest and on the Plains, and is getting critical in the Northeast.

It already looks as if there won't be a second cutting of hay on the farm, and what corn managed to germinate stands ankle-high, baking in the fields. If the second cut of hay is lost and corn production is down, North Country farmers will have to buy both; and because they will be both in demand and scarce, they will be expensive. But the cost of making milk is going to rise even if rain returns to New England. The Rockies-to-Midwest drought has already wreaked havoc with the soybean and grain crops, which means that grain-supplement prices will be up sharply within weeks, anticipating future shortages. And since the individual dairy farmer has no way to stockpile grain, he cannot even buffer or delay the increase. In this state, more dairy farms have already called it quits this year than went out of business in all of last year. With a substantial rise in grain prices, remaining farms which cannot hold on selling milk at or below cost will throw in the towel as well.

Weather forecasters, at any rate, have promised rain tonight, and it looks as if they've got it right. As a mostly clear afternoon faded into evening, a preternatural light glowed orange in the north, and a warming southeast breeze grew steadily stronger. Now, as the light fades, and the first thunder rolls sound, the wind tears north for Canada in earnest. It whips the trees screening dead elms along Cutting Hill Road. The maples and live elms lean north and strain, then whip and plunge chaotically as the gust releases them. The island meadows in the barnyard surge and calm. Don's tin pan garden protectors clatter wildly. Apparently oblivious to the brewing storm, the summer's first fireflies drift and blink in the protected aisle low over the tree-bordered road.

The barn is quiet and smells deserted, which means that it smells more of hay than of animals and animal waste. It is not deserted. Chickens roost on laths over the stanchions. A cat frisks up the central aisle. Calves can be heard munching in their pens, and from time to time one or another of four sore-footed cows clanks a stanchion.

A fat adult raccoon, surprised at its nightly work of pilfering grain pellets and cat food, sidles by the milkroom door into the pump room, clambers up onto the bulk-tank compressor and out an open window. From there it skedaddles around the grain bin and west along the feed trough, out through a hole in whose east end peers the gleaming white black-masked face of a raccoon cub. Its head quizzically cocked, it is a ready-made piece of poster art, whose caption would probably read: "How do I get myself into these fixes?" (The Treadways rather like the several raccoons that regularly raid the barn, but the animals are less popular since an episode earlier in the week, when an adult broke through a screened window to get at the cat food stored in the spic-and-span milkroom, where it pushed breakable items off windowsills and "crapped all over everything.")

Outside, the thunder is less frequent, the wind gusts less strong. From time to time glimmer lightning illuminates a quiet sky, and a few raindrops disappear in the dust. Far to the south, a couple of coyotes yowl argumentatively. A single bat takes two passes by the floodlight on the north end of the barn, and is gone.

The lights go out first in the yellow ranch house, then in the peaked, tin-roofed green farmhouse. Another day ends, like every other this month, without measurable rain.

3

IF LATE JUNE HAS NOT BROUGHT DROUGHT relief, it has at least put a temporary end to the searing heat. This is, indeed, a glorious morning—clear and cool, with isolated cumulus clouds floating in a deep blue sky—for a job that is nobody's favorite: spreading manure. Brian and Becky are playing at the house. Joan works at finding mates for three bushel baskets full of socks from the last wash. Dick is baling hay on the far northeast meadow, hay cut by the farm's brand-new mower. Virtually identical to the old one, but a different brand, the machine was delivered at the pay-later price of $7,700 (plus a trade-in allowance of $2,300), for which Dick has a loan approved in case they can't swing it. "They make a better mower, a rotary disk job," Dick says; "but they're thirteen thousand dollars. We didn't feel we could justify that."

Jeff and Kevin are on manure duty, and if Jeff finds spreading boring, he doesn't offer to trade with his brother. Kevin is the loader. His job is to sit in the Deere and load the Calumet 2250 tank spreader. Between loads he just sits—"this tractor hasn't even got a working radio," he grouses—leafing disconsolately through a toy catalogue. The long six-inch-diameter tin loading pipe—one end submerged in the pit, the other above and in front of the tractor—has a reversible pump, and from time to time

Kevin geysers the manure behind his tractor to relieve the monotony.

Now spreading a meadow beyond the corn pieces east of the barn, Jeff approaches in the rock-music-blaring Allis, pulling an empty tank spreader rolling on four fifteen-inch-thick tires. He drives past the Deere, then backs the spreader into position, its rearward manhole-sized aperture directly under the down-turned pipe spout. He signals Kevin, who throws the pump into forward, and the thick brown soup spews from the pipe into the tank. The 2250 designation in the spreader's name is its capacity in gallons, and Kevin, desperate for something to occupy his mind, times a load. "One hundred seconds," he reports at shut-off, and then, as Jeff backs down the incline, sloshing slops running down the brown back third of the apple-red spreader, takes a calculator from his pocket, punches in the numbers, and announces: "That's twenty-two-and-a-half gallons per second; not bad!"

The Allis sets off doing what it alone of the farm's four tractors can comfortably do—pull a several-ton spreader loaded with nearly ten tons of liquid manure. Jeff pulls the load up to a meadow on the farm's east boundary and spreads, spray-painting a coloring-book-green landscape a dull brown. From a distance it looks as if the meadow is falling under cloud shadow by swaths running now north-south, now south-north. Spreading at a rate of about twelve tons per acre—half the concentration the Treadways use on corn land—the load is exhausted in ten minutes, and Jeff heads back for more, a south-drifting dust cloud accompanying the rig.

Kevin and Jeff load and spread, load and spread as the morning wears wearily on. Two raccoons pad shoulder to shoulder down a tractor path toward the pit; catching sight of Kevin, they duck into high grass and disappear. Now and again a dust devil plays across a tractor road below the pit. Most are tiny, but occasionally one blossoms into a miniature tornado, whirling powdered Shoreham clay seventy-five feet or more into the sky.

When the boys break for lunch, Kevin checks his notebook

and figures the running totals—sixty-seven loads in a day and a half. But that 600-plus tons removed has barely put a dent in the pit's contents, and it looks like the better part of a week of spreading lies ahead. Jeff and Kevin turn off their tractors and head for the house. Up on the east meadow, the newly spread manure quickly dries to a thin scabrous coating on plants and land, in which form it will remain until rain comes.

To Jeff and Kevin's relief, the afternoon is devoted to putting up hay, for which the weather is perfect. Don is baling a large northeast meadow, and Kevin shuttles wagons back and forth between meadow and barn. Jeff and Joan pull the bales from the wagon and position them on the elevator. Dick and Brian, up in the mow, grab them off the elevator and wrestle them into position, row upon row stacked from floor to rafters, hay that will feed calves all year in the barn, where it will also feed the cows and heifers in winter, when pasturage is unavailable.

A load completed, they drag the empty wagon down the lane below Don's garden where Kevin can hitch up after dropping off the loaded wagon. Between loads, the family loafs. Becky plays on a barrel near her grandparents' porch. Brian rides his bike. Jeff dons the welding helmet and works with the torch outside the tool shed. He's putting together a four-wheeled go-cart, for which he has all the parts except a motor.

Dick and Joan sit on upturned buckets outside the barn door and talk. The cows are already gathering expectantly at the gated south end of the barn—milking will be hours late tonight—when a raft of dark cloud materializes overhead. A few large drops fall. Dick stares into the child's wagon parked in front of his bucket: "Look—a raindrop! I'd forgotten what they look like." "The Lord has a sense of humor," Joan comments ruefully.

The cloud passes, and, stepping around the end of the barn a few minutes later to check Kevin's progress with the next load of hay, she catches sight of a blue-purple curtain hanging down the southern horizon. "Oh, look!" she exclaims. "It's raining down in Whiting."

## 4

NORTH COUNTRY NATIVES SAY "IF YOU DON'T like the weather, wait a minute." People had waited most of the month for June to turn from August to anything else, and, on the twenty-ninth, it did. It changed to November. Nighttime lows in the 30s and 40s set records all over New England. But the real news came on the last day of the month, when, without introductory theatrics, it simply rained out of a leaden sky. Up the road in Cornwall, afternoon hail covered bare patches of drought-stricken lawn, converting it to gleaming white beach sporting tufts of emergent dune grass. On top of Mount Washington, in neighboring New Hampshire, it snowed five inches.

On the Treadway farm, it just rained. It rained off and on that day, that night, and the next morning. About an inch total, Dick thinks. That will help, but much more is needed, and nationally the drought continues, and increasingly dominates the news. Barge traffic has all but halted on the shrunken Mississippi River, up whose lower reaches the salt sea ominously creeps. Migrant farm workers are stuck in the Ohio Valley with no money and nothing to pick. Wheat, corn, and soybean futures soar while farm-state politicians deliver dark (and empty) warnings to those who will seek to profit financially from the farmers' plight.

Nothing very dramatic demonstrates the Champlain Valley's lesser drought, but the signs are here. The blooming cycle for area horse chestnuts and black locusts was shortened or aborted. Dick steps gingerly around a half-inch-wide, three-foot-long crack in the ground of his dooryard. "We're thinking of putting a saw-horse over that crack," he quips; "we're afraid somebody will fall in."

The corn, more than anything else, tells the story. "Knee-high

by the Fourth of July" is the rule-of-thumb here as well as in the
Midwest, but on this particular Fourth the corn that's up isn't
half that high. And only half is up. Dick and Jeff dig up part of
an unsprouted row to see if the recent rain has germinated the
seed. Some has, they find; so more corn should be sprouting
soon. With so late a start, however, it will need a great deal of
heat and rain through July and August to put on bulk and decent
ears.

Heat, at least, the corn should get. Last week's brief cold spell
is not only forgotten but already unimaginable, as the 80s and
90s return literally overnight. Not all vegetation is suffering in
the dry heat. In places the road margins look like flower-garden
borders. The small, cut-leafed alien daisy called mayweed
crowds the very road edge under the mower's knife, while the
leggy chicory and white sweet clover nod and wave from the
balcony. In favored ditches and swales, green thickets of day
lilies are showing their first orange blooms.

Jeff, who has finished spreading manure on the meadows,
joins the ongoing business of baling hay. The first hay cutting
has produced an abundant crop, though mediocre in quality.
"It'll fill 'em up, at least," Dick says. Bales are now being put up
in the south end of the barn for the heifers, the elevator track
rigged to run most of the length of the barn. In the remains
of last year's hay, Kevin, who is helping Dick stack bales, finds
a treasure trove in the form of several hens' nests laden with
old eggs. Undeterred by the first rotten egg, which, picked up
too eagerly, erupts in his hand, Kevin gingerly transports the
eggs a few at a time to the open gable end of the mow and
fires them at the cement pad outside the barn door and a rock
outcrop beyond. Dick can't help grinning as Kevin bom-
bards the landscape, bemoaning the duds and celebrating the
explosions.

As so often happens when haying (or some other project) is
under way, afternoon milking is late getting started. The cows
stand outside the south barn gate for over an hour, chewing
their cuds and nosing splattered eggs. Eventually they are ad-

mitted to a barn housing a suddenly burgeoned fly population. Flies are everywhere: in the windows, on the walls and ceiling ("How do flies crap upside down?" Jeff wonders, eyeing the speckled ceiling); on milk pipes and wiring and stanchions; on shelves and equipment and tools; on the wheelbarrow and the light fixtures and the barn phone; on calf pens and heifer pens and gutter scraper. Walking through the hay litter in the side aisles flushes clouds of flies, and Thorson, resting in the central aisle, from time to time lunges and bites at a buzzing fly. ("Sometimes he snaps at a bee by mistake," chuckles Dick.)

Mostly flies attend to the cows, which, stanchioned or not, haven't much defense. They shake their heads, jerk their ears, sweep their tails. They ripple shoulder and flank muscles, and kick their own bellies with the front of a rear hoof. At best this activity momentarily dislodges a few flies; often it doesn't even accomplish that. Clearly, the season for periodic barn fogging is fast approaching.

There are more problems than flies in the barn. At morning milking, Dick noticed some swelling in one quarter of a cow's udder, and it is still swollen. That probably means mastitis—an all-too-common mammary-gland inflammation, usually bacterial in origin—and Joan begins treatment immediately. She fills a syringe with Red Mix—a preformulated antibiotic mix containing penicillin, cortisone, neomycin, and sulfa—inserts the blunt-ended plastic needle up the teat of the infected quarter, and delivers the dose. She then takes a marker and decorates both sides of the cow's rump with the designation RM, a reminder that this cow's milk will have to be dumped during treatment and for eight milkings thereafter.

Red Mix often brings cows back quickly from mastitis, but not always. A cow treated last month failed to respond, and the vet was called. He doused her with more medicines and nutrition supplements. He was convinced the animal would recover, though she might well "lose a quarter." The cow came back only slowly, and, as feared, permanently dry in one quarter. Since she was a marginal milker in the first place, Dick has tentatively decided to sell her for beef after keeping her the required thirty days after treatment. "I hate to do it," he says, "but it's an economic decision."

Meanwhile, Bunny, tied as usual to a stanchion near the south end of the barn, is another object of sympathy. Hand-fed and petted by Becky and the other children through her early weeks, Bunny had been tame as a lamb until her dehorning on Saturday. Holstein milkers are trouble enough without horns, and they are most easily dehorned as calves. It is not, however, a pleasant business. The vet shoves a hollow, gripping pipelike tool down over the budding horn, then twists it violently, hoping to wrench the horn free at its base in the skull. Even when things go right—sometimes a horn breaks instead of twisting off, necessitating a more protracted and more painful removal operation—the calf is left with raw, ugly pits in its head and a new and prolonged fear of people.

It is after eight o'clock when the Treadways emerge from the barn and head up to the house for supper. The family pauses briefly outside the north end of the barn, where Becky and Brian are shoving their Tonka earth-moving equipment about in the nearly exhausted sawdust pile, for a vote. Who wants to rush supper, clean up, and drive to Middlebury for the Independence Day show? Dick and Joan are bushed, and there is little enthusiasm for the idea even among the children. The Treadways decide to pass on the fireworks this year.

# 5

IT IS EARLY AFTERNOON WHEN DICK AND JOAN head out in the van to take care of some chores in Middlebury. Dick drops Joan off in the middle of town. She intends to look for some shorts for Jeff and to get groceries at the Grand Union, where Dick will pick her up.

Dick's first stop is at Brown's Auto Parts. The starter on the International Harvester has been acting up, and it's not always convenient to leave the tractor parked on an incline in case it doesn't work. Brown's is the only place in town that will "go through" a starter, which they promise to do tomorrow. (They do, and find nothing amiss; reassembled and reinstalled, the starter works better anyway.)

Dick's next stop is a brand-new farm-equipment dealership—the result of a merger of two competing outfits—south of town. They have just opened for business. Grass has yet to be planted out front, and half the floor space inside the massive building remains unoccupied. After a ten-minute wait in one of three lines at the counter, Dick orders an oil-drain gasket for a leaking tractor. The parts man grabs the appropriate tractor-parts book and leafs through the pages to find first the tractor model, then the part in question. Having found it, he punches the code number into his computer, which gives him inventory information, including the part's bin number. He returns from the parts room with a small metal washerlike gasket. He punches more figures into the computer, which processes and delivers a multicopy bill for twenty-three cents; with cash-and-carry discount, twenty-two cents. "I think that's the cheapest tractor part I ever bought," Dick remarks on the way out. (The gasket won't come close to fitting; disgusted, Dick will hunt around the shop and find something that will work.)

Meanwhile, back at the Grand Union, Joan heads down the first aisle, pushing one cart and pulling a second. She has brought a piece of paper with an entry or two on it, but most of her shopping list is in her head. Today she is after "some staples and the usual stuff." She drops a bag of onions into a cart, followed by a couple of bunches of grapes and a selection of green, red, and yellow peppers, for which she tears a plastic bag off the nearby roll ("This is how they drive us crazy," she wails, trying to find an end that opens). A gallon jug of vinegar is next, along with ketchup and a bottle of vegetable oil. Back to the produce side of the aisle for two bunches of celery and a head of cauliflower; back to the other side for mayonnaise and a jar of strawberry jam.

Joan stops at the deli counter, where she orders and waits for sliced ham and cheese for today's lunch; then she is off up the second aisle, adding bagels ("Bagels with cream cheese is Jeff's idea of good food"), two packages of cookies, a bottle of cranraspberry drink, and two cans of green beans. At the end of the aisle, she stops to select a bag of nectarines, then moves down aisle three, adding maraschino cherries, six pounds of light brown sugar, cinnamon, cloves, and ten pounds of unbleached flour. Joan is hoping to find the time to do some baking. "I learned to bake apple pies with my grandmother when I could barely see over the counter. She didn't measure anything; it was so many handfuls of flour and a pinch of this and that. I learned laundry with her, too. I remember her warning me to keep my fingers away from the wringer."

Joan's grandmother was a member of the last generation of traditional, "in-house" farm wives. Don and Irene's generation saw a big change. Farmers continued to maintain large gardens and to raise their own beef, but machinery was making both farm work and housework less demanding physically and less time-consuming. At the same time, food and clothing became increasingly available in stores in town, as were cars to get you there and back over reasonably passable roads. Labor, coincidentally, was becoming more and more expensive. And so roles on the farm changed. Wives took to field and barn work, in effect replacing a hired man; which meant that they traded sewing, cooking, baking, and preserving time for saved money with which to shop in town for replacement goods. (As far as women's labor is concerned, the trend now is back in the other direction; few of Joan's farm-wife friends do much actual farming.) Dick and Joan still have a small garden—from which they freeze some beans, corn, and beets, and can some tomato sauce and pickles—and from time to time they have raised a steer for beef. But mainly they eat, like nonfarmers, courtesy of a chain supermarket.

Continuing her serpentine trek with increasingly heavy carts, Joan adds spaghetti sauce, a bag of navy beans, a carton of canning-jar caps, and a package of chocolate candy. At the meat counter she chooses a fresh turkey, a butt-end ham, a large package of ground beef, and a pound each of chicken franks and bacon. Yet another aisle yields three cans of tuna, two packages of fruit snacks ("This stuff's mostly sugar, but Becky loves it"), six economy-size boxes of breakfast cereals, and a dozen cans of cat food ("If it gets any more expensive to feed my cats, Dick's going to tell me to let them catch their own food"). Toilet paper and furniture polish come next, plus shampoo, a gallon of laundry detergent, and a potato peeler ("Mine broke; it was overworked"). The bread section approaches, and into the carts go rice cakes and English muffins and four oversized loaves of white bread.

Like other children, the Treadway kids have their food likes and dislikes. They won't eat broccoli or cauliflower. They hate liver. They abominate succotash. On the other hand, they are fond of pasta, "regular" vegetables, most meats (including chicken and fish), and fruit. And they have their favorite family dishes, among others "toes-in-the-snow" (hot dog pieces in mashed potatoes) and "chopped slop," an old lumberjack recipe for a stew involving bacon or fried salt pork, potatoes, carrots, and onions.

Heading down the home stretch through the dairy and frozen foods section, Joan picks up frozen peas and carrots, two frozen pizzas, two half-gallon ice creams, a mozzarella cheese, a pound of butter, two half-gallons of orange juice and one of grapefruit juice, and three pounds of yogurt. Her last purchases are a bottle of pink chablis and a copy of *Family Circle* at the cash register. Joan says some cashiers are downright short with customers they consider overloaded. The woman she has drawn today does not appear overjoyed, but neither is she unfriendly. She sets doggedly to work, pushing keys with one hand and sweeping with the other, pausing from time to time to help Joan with the bagging.

Sack after sack of groceries goes into the newly emptied carts, and finally the check-out nears completion. Joan takes out her checkbook, fills in date and name, and then the amount: $201.78.

Arriving back home with the groceries, Dick and Joan find Becky and Brian playing in the fold-out camper—in which, on warm summer nights, the kids sometimes sleep—parked in the front yard. "We look at the camper," Dick laughs, "and think about going on a vacation some day. I tell the family they can take it anywhere they want to, on the farm."

Tomorrow the camper is actually going somewhere. The first cutting of hay is nearly in, and Joan will take the three younger children north for a three-day vacation. They will set up camp in a state park on North Hero Island in Lake Champlain, where their only visitors the first night will be raccoons, but where they will have hell-raising teenagers for neighbors the second night ("I just wanted to enjoy the quiet," Joan will lament). They will take a day trip to Parc Safari near Montreal, where they will join a horde of people staring at the animals, which they will enjoy seeing, at the same time feeling sorry for the begging bears and the fat, overheated, miserable-looking wolves.

"I don't much like crowds, or zoos," Joan will conclude. But she will judge the trip a success anyway. The kids will have seen a lot of animals, gone on a lot of rides, and visited with some of their father's cousins. Everyone will have had some good times, and a break from the farm.

# 6

IT IS A WARM, MUGGY EVENING IN LATE JULY, and the village of Shoreham is quiet except for the north end of the large town shed and firehouse building across the baseball diamond outfield from the dome-steepled, Greek-columned Congregational Church. Here in the end stall where the shiny white rescue-squad vehicle is usually parked, six of eight members of the Shoreham First Response Rescue Squad, including Joan and Diane Treadway, stand garbed in yellow firefighter-style coats and hardhats with pull-down face shields and long, heavy gloves in contemplation of a sixties-vintage black Dodge Dart 270 with red interior and automatic transmission. It features what looks like a brand-new leather steering-wheel cover, and a large pair of purple velour dice hang from the rear-view mirror.

The rescue squad has gathered for an "extrication drill" under the informal tutelage of three more-experienced rescue people, two from the Middlebury squad, one from the Cornwall squad. Getting hurt people out of crash-twisted vehicles is serious business, of course, but the spirit here is somewhere between circus and stand-up comedy. "Are we going to wreck this car?" someone objects; "this car's in better shape than mine." "Where is yours parked?" comes the response; "we'll work on it next."

Working crashed cars often involves the quick disposal of windows. Starting up front by ripping off the windshield wipers, the rescuers cut under the windshield gasket with hocked roofer's knives, pull it free, and simply lift out the windshield. ("More recent cars have the windshield glued in," says the head instructor; "you have to break them out.") Large Xs are taped across the other windows to minimize glass scatter, and various squad members stick them one by one with a simple punch, completely shattering them.

Sometimes a door will be jammed, but not crumpled. An instructor grabs a long hand tool, whose heavy curved knife end he drives into the door by pounding on a blunt "stub" protruding from the handle below and away from the knife's curve with a hand sledge, and proceeds to cut three sides of a square above and on both sides of the door handle. He then simply peels the handle section of the door down, reaches into the door interior, and frees the latch.

This trick probably won't work on a badly damaged door, and two instructors with sledgehammers shortly crumple this one on both hinge and latch sides. This sort of door you open with a tool called "jaws," whose double-wedge business end powers either open or closed. The crew starts with its own jaws, a hand-pump-powered four-ton unit. One person crams the jaws into the space between door and frame, triggers "open," and the pumper pumps. This small unit doesn't make much of an impression on the door, however, and, after trying an intermediate unit, the crew hooks up the Middlebury squad's massive jaws, operated by two people and powered by a 3½-horse generator via hydraulic lines.

This tool doesn't fool around. Crammed in between latch and center post, its wedges spread inexorably, crumpling and popping steel and finally wrenching the door from the latch. Now crammed into place above a hinge on the other side, the opening jaws stretch the screaming steel door until it is ripped from the harder hinge. The operation is repeated for the second hinge, and a car door lies on the floor.

What if the driver is pinned by the steering wheel? A huge pair of bolt cutters comes out of the extrication box, and the wheel is simply snipped off in two semicircles. Perhaps the driver is still pinned by the horn rim or steering post. Two heavy chains, one hooked under the front-end frame, the other around the top of the steering post, are attached to the tips of the wide-open jaws, which is then powered closed. Some grill smashing and hood denting ensue, but after three chain resets the steering post is pulled straight up through the windshield hole.

Sometimes the easiest way into a smashed car is through the roof. Joan and a colleague set out with two hacksaws to cut through the front posts. Each breaks a blade, but each completes the task. "Now," says the Middlebury instructor, "here's the quick way." He uncouples the jaws and hooks up an oversized pair of power snippers, with which he simply bites through the heavier center posts in half a minute. Next he takes a single vertical bite at the top back of each rear window, and whacks a dented line between the two bites with a crowbar. Two squad members climb onto the hood and simply bend the top back over the trunk, the purple dice nestling onto the inverted ceiling.

Finally, the instructor demonstrates the "ram," which looks like an outsized car jack. Powered by the same generator and placed between firewall and front seat base, the ram extends, shoving the seat backwards, an alternative way to free a steering-wheel- or dash-pinned victim.

Practice over, the squad sweeps up glass and debris, dumps doors, windows, gaskets, steering wheel and other parts into the wrecked car, and winches it back onto a flatbed truck for its return trip to the salvage yard.

It's eleven o'clock when things are squared away, and squad members begin to leave. Others stay, including Joan and Dick, who has been observing extrication techniques his fire squad may find itself helping with. Route 22A, the chief truck-traffic corridor through the Champlain Valley, runs the length of Shoreham and has produced—and will produce—horrendous accidents, some of them dangerous for those who arrive to help.

Dick remembers a number of big truck accidents, and particularly a gasoline truck sprawled on its side in 8,000 gallons of spilled gas; how they had waded into all that gas, and, holding their breaths, cut the battery cables; how it never occurred to them that this particular truck carried an identical battery hid-

den on the down side of the engine until it suddenly emitted a
shower of sparks; and how they had later been told that they
were spared instantaneous incineration only because the gasoline fumes happened to be in too heavy a concentration to ignite.

Although most emergency-squad "business" involves road accidents, all of these squad members have attended farm accidents as well. Tractors regularly overturn on their drivers, and
tractors aren't the only dangerous vehicles on the farm. Recently, a local farmer was landscaping on a bulldozer. The 'dozer
tipped into a ditch camouflaged by tall grass, throwing the driver
forward onto the hot muffler, which cracked his skull, knocking
him out, and seriously burned him.

All farm machinery, of course, is potentially dangerous. Dick
remembers an ambulance ride north to the Burlington hospital
with a bad-luck farmer. The man had been unloading a silage
wagon, a routine job he had done for years, when the paddle
blew out through the side of his silage blower, fracturing his
skull and nearly taking off the top of his head.

Of all farm mishaps, those involving power take-offs are likely
to be the most hideous. Once a piece of clothing or a limb is
grabbed by a tractor's spinning PTO, the rest of the individual
instantly follows—the human body does not provide enough
resistance to stall a large tractor's engine—and he is quickly
crushed while being pulled through constricted circles. It happened recently to an experienced Shoreham farmhand. A man
standing near him at the time shut the tractor down within
seconds. But the victim had already been through several revolutions, and Dick believes that all of his bones were broken.
"Somehow the machinery removed both his boots," he remembers, "and the laces were still tied."

Children get hurt on farms as well as adults. Joan's memorable first ambulance ride as a novice emergency-squad member
was on behalf of her own daughter. Becky decided to climb
down out of the hay mow, where she and Dick had been working. She stepped through a hay chute—a square hole in the
second-story floor—onto the leaning ladder. Somehow, the lad-

der kicked away, and Becky fell to the floor of the barn, suffering the compression fracture of three vertebrae in her back. The
Treadways know of two other area farm children who have
since fallen from hay chutes. One of them died.

There isn't, Joan says sadly, always a lot you can do for the
victims of serious farm or road accidents. "You get them out
and try to stabilize them. You monitor them and breathe for
them if necessary. You stop the bleeding. Mostly you pray for
the ambulances."

The Shoreham First Response Rescue vehicle is backed into its
accustomed stall, extrication box aboard. A shooting star arcs
majestically behind the church steeple across the ballfield. "Did
you *see* that?" a man asks incredulously. No one responds. The
giant overhead doors are pulled down and locked. The last members of the rescue squad climb into cars and pickups, pull out the
lane past the diminutive Platt Memorial Library, and head down
the road.

## 7

JULY HAS PRODUCED A COUPLE OF WORTH-
while, if small, rains, but what farmers have been looking for
comes finally on the twenty-first. A low-pressure cell moving
slowly across New York state brings the region heavy overcast
and a steady, soaking rain. "This should help the corn," Dick
says, and it should start the meadow grasses as well.

Farmers welcome a rainy day for the change of pace it
brings as well as for the crop benefits. "Rain eliminates field
work," Dick says; "it gives you a chance to do things you've
been putting off." Joan is taking advantage of the break to take

Becky on a shopping trip south to Rutland. Mostly she wants
to get patterns and have Becky choose material for this fall's
kindergarten clothes. ("I learned with Jeff that the only way
to guarantee that the kid will wear the clothes you make is to
have them choose the fabric.") They will look for other things as
well, and Brian and Kevin want to go along for the ride (with
hopes that Mother may be persuaded to buy them a goody
or two).

Dick and Jeff, meanwhile, will stay home and clean the barn.
Recent inspection sheets have complained about a couple of
things, and now there is a special push on. Agri-Mark, the co-
operative which handles the Treadways' milk, has notified its
2,500 dairy farms that the annual federal inspection is coming
up. A number of Agri-Mark farms will be chosen at random for
inspection, and the average score must attain a certain standard.
If it does not, other Agri-Mark farms will be tested; the feds
will hassle Agri-Mark, and Agri-Mark will hassle its farmers.
In short, Agri-Mark has urged its farmers to clean up this
month.

Cobwebs and milk-pipe fittings are the first order of the
day. Dick works his way down a side aisle with broom in
hand, sweeping the wall, windows, and ceiling clear of spider
webs and their accumulated detritus. Meanwhile, Jeff shoves
a stepladder along the stanchion line, climbing up a step or two
to scrub each fitting where milkers plug into the milk line. Dipping his brush in soapy water, he cleans the fitting area, then
slides up the hole cover to insert a round brush into the
pipe itself. State specs call for milk lines to be hung with a
gradual but constant slope, so that milk and wash water will
drain completely, discouraging bacterial growth. But milk pipes,
like other things, move some with time, and from the ladder Jeff
can see dips here and there. Someday the line will have to be
rehung.

"Anybody know a good fly spray?" Dick asks rhetorically.
"As soon as you find something that works, the state or the feds
ban it. I tried some new stuff the other day, and the flies just

laughed at me. I think the only fly I killed was the one I set the can down on." The problem with fly spray—and other insecticides—is that the "good" stuff is also the bad stuff. The Treadways tried a fly powder some time back. Sprinkled on the window sills, it killed a lot of flies. Then the barn sparrows began to drop, and they quit using it. Flies continue to flourish in the barn.

Sweeping cobwebs from the barn's main beams reminds Dick that the milk inspector wants them painted. "You have to either whitewash every year or paint every five years." "Why?" Jeff asks. "I don't know," Dick replies. "I'm not sure they know either."

As in any regulated industry, there is inevitably some friction between dairy inspector and dairy inspectee. Farmers can't always see the sense of rules and regulations emanating from handling organizations and the state and federal governments. Dick quotes as an example a recently instituted regulation requiring every Agri-Mark farmer to buy a rod-shaped fluorescent lamp complete with shock-protection breaker box to hang next to the bulk tank, to be used by the inspector to check the interior of the tank for cleanliness.

"There are maybe ten inspectors checking Agri-Mark farms," Dick points out. "Common sense says they should give the inspectors lights. Why should twenty-five hundred Agri-Mark farmers all have to buy thirty-dollar lights? I suppose they'd say the point is to encourage farmers to check their own tanks, which most aren't going to do anyway. And the inspectors say a lot of the lamps aren't even in the milkhouses anymore; they've disappeared into shops or wherever."

By midmorning the rain has turned the barnyard clay to a sticky mud. Cows lounge in the 'yard and at the feed bunk, ankle-deep in mud and dung. Rivulets of rainwater run down the drive from Don and Irene's place and collect at the north end of the barn, where Jeff wields a hoe to clean out a narrow trench to take the runoff east around the barn. "It's an awful mess when the barn floods," he says.

Barn work is interrupted by the arrival of a load of sawdust. The driver, a local farmer who hauls sawdust from a sawmill in the Adirondacks between times, backs the truck to the rear of the exhausted pile, dumps some, drives forward, and dumps some more. Jeff scoops out the remainder while the driver and Dick stand in the rain and talk about equipment. This load is composed of wood shavings and sawdust. The last load was chewed-up bark, and Dick, suspecting it might somehow have contributed to his increased problem with mastitis, said no more bark.

"That's a tough haul over to Schroon Lake and back," Dick comments as the truck spins in the mud and slowly pulls out. "Two trips a day is all he can manage. I don't see how he makes much at a hundred and ten dollars a load."

Back in the barn, the stepladder and hot-water bucket begin another slow trip around the periphery of the central aisle, as Dick washes the pipeline a foot at a time. The stainless steel pipe, freed from chicken and fly scat and sundry stains and dirt, shines like new, but farmers don't see much point in keeping it bright. Don watches Dick scrubbing away and remembers going round and round with inspectors on the subject.

" 'You gotta wash the pipeline,' they'd say.

" 'Why?' I'd ask; 'that don't make the inside any cleaner.'

" 'Well,' they'd say, 'if you have to open the pipe to work on it, the dirt won't get inside.'

" 'If I ever have to open up the pipe, wouldn't it make sense to clean that section of pipe at the time?'

"Finally they'd just say: 'It's the regulations.' "

Dick and Jeff take a break for lunch. They put a pan of left-over lasagna in the microwave and pour glasses of raw milk from a small aluminum milk can kept in the refrigerator. Fifteen minutes later, food and drink are gone, and Dick drags Jeff away from the TV to get back to barn cleaning.

While Dick works on the pipeline, Jeff, with occasional help from Don, gets started on the stanchions. Stanchions are heir to a number of problems, in large part because they need to move with their captive cows. The bottom is attached to a short length of chain, which is affixed to a bracket, both of which are subject to breaking. More often it is the top of the stanchion that causes the problem. A swivel attachment allows the cow's head and neck to swing from side to side, but that very movement eventually works the swivel through a half-inch of hardened steel, and the stanchion simply falls to the floor. Now a dozen or so stanchions are tied up with baler twine, and Jeff sets to work with screwdrivers and wrenches to replace the swivel units.

Other stanchions have become difficult to close; the sliding side of the triangle requires great force to move. Jeff thinks they simply need oil, but Dick, who has been around stanchions awhile, thinks the problem is at the base of the unit. Using a small monkey wrench, he disassembles the metal sleeve joining the two stanchion pipes at the bottom, removes it, and shows Jeff a chewing-tobacco—like plug of barn litter packed so solidly that repeated hammer blows on a screwdriver barely faze it. Plugs will have to be broken out of all the problem stanchions, and Jeff will oil them for good measure.

"Look at Runt!" Jeff says, spotting a small black kitten watching the action below from a space between barn wall and ceiling. The family has kept three kittens from Blackcap's litter, including Runt, a small black; Gray, a large gray; and Spooky (Spook for short), a black and white kitten that lurks in the shadows. They will be coming down into the barn soon, but for now they continue to play about the mow, their living space now radically restricted by 9,200 stacked bales of hay. Sitting in the hay on the floor of the mow among fly-covered cat-food cans and milk dishes, the rain on the roof skylights sounding like muffled machine-gun fire, one suddenly finds the inquisitive Runt in one's lap, or experiences the surprise of Runt testing his claws on one's back.

Don wanders into the barn to watch the stanchion work. Both he and Dick are currently on jury duty—one in district court, the other in appellate court—and they comment on their judicial experience. Dick has served on one jury, hearing a case concerning a highway-side businessman who felt aggrieved by the price the state paid him when part of his future parking lot was required for a road-widening project. "We gave him some more," says Dick, "but nothing like what he wanted."

Don came close to sitting on a DWI case, but the defense attorney dismissed him when he learned that Don was a town constable as well as a selectman and fireman, apparently on the assumption that town officials were likely to be law-and-order types. Nor was Don that particular attorney's only victim that day. Don chuckles as he re-creates the exchange that cost his colleague a seat. "They always ask if you know either counsel in the case, and this guy says, 'Yes, I know you.' 'You do?' says the surprised lawyer. 'How do you know me?' 'You defended my brother in a trial a couple years back, and you wa'nt no damn good!' "

Stanchion work continues, and Dick is installing a cutoff valve in the water line when a stranger enters the barn. In his thirties, dressed in expensively fashionable outdoorsy clothes, including boots and a wide-brimmed safari hat, he introduces himself as a Pennsylvanian who is interested in buying the next farm west. He has a wife and child in the car, and would like to talk. "What do you do?" Don asks, and the man, caught off guard, makes a vague, embarrassed reference to an "outside" income.

The Treadways know, of course, the property in question. The present owner has been running this farm and his parents' farm up on the Lemon Fair for some time. Now he intends to devote his time and energies to the parental farm, and wants out of the other. Apparently his first thought had been to develop the land for building sites or to sell it to a developer; and, because the land is most easily accessible from the east, he approached the Treadways to negotiate a right-of-way across their land to bring in a road and utilities from Cutting Hill Road. The Treadways, however, don't like the idea of developing farmland—in part for economic reasons, since development drives up the value of land, making it harder to survive farming—and they declined to grant the right-of-way.

The owner's next option was to put the farm up for sale as a farm, which has attracted the present visitor, now joined in the barn by his silent wife and nattily dressed preschool son. He wants the place, apparently as a hobby farm, but he doesn't want the back sixty-nine acres, which border the Treadway farm. How would the Treadways like to buy that sixty-nine acres, which he understands they could have for $60,000? Dick politely points out that little of the land in question is tillable, and that much of it isn't even good pasture. Furthermore, times are tight, and he doesn't plan to expand the farm in the foreseeable future. The family says its good-byes and leaves.

Joan shortly returns with the kids for afternoon milking, and hears of the Pennsylvania couple. The visit had not been at all unpleasant, but it has been symptomatic, and clearly upsetting to Joan. Probably it is not a matter of prejudice against monied flat-landers—though a member of that breed who recently moved into Shoreham and is spreading money around with what area natives call an "I'll-show-the-dumb-locals-how-to-farm" attitude, hasn't helped their reputation—but a fear of change and new problems.

"Everyone wants a piece of Vermont," says Joan with feeling. "The pressure is going to increase on us to do this or do that at others' behest. Sometimes I wish everyone would just leave us alone. I'd like to put on my coonskin cap and live permanently in nineteen eighty-five. That was a good year."

The cows are let into the barn, and soon milk begins to flow through a gleaming pipeline. Jeff remembers that Bunny needs to be treated. She has been eating but not drinking, and hence has become dehydrated. Dick suspects the Red Mix in milk from a mastitis-treated cow may have killed bacteria in her stomachs. Jeff mixes her calf electrolyte formula in water, and Brian gives her her third dose of the day from a bottle.

Just outside the gate at the south end of the barn, two of this summer's crop of barn swallows—their plumage is still mottled,

and the outer feathers of their forked tails aren't fully developed—pass tirelessly back and forth over the watery muck in
the softly falling rain, mostly low, but now and again climbing
steeply a few feet to engulf a higher-flying insect before dipping
back, rising again at the east edge of the barnyard pad to barely
clear the top strand of a barbed-wire fence, then banking and
swinging around for the return pass.

It has never for a moment ceased to rain, and will not until
well into the night. Tomorrow the rain gauges will show a total
of 2¾ inches, and tonight this region's farmers, at least, will
compose themselves for sleep listening to the rain, thinking of
the blessedly sodden land.

## 8

THE "DOG DAYS" OF SUMMER SEEM TO EXTEND
back past memory, and July slips into August under the same
sallow, color-drained skies heavy with heat haze. Along the road
before the yellow ranch house, the buckthorn are berrying up,
and the velvety heads are developing on staghorn sumac. Down
the dusty tractor roads, green- and bluebottle flies buzz about
over the blooming trefoil, chicory, vetch, and Queen Anne's
lace. The flat umbels of Queen Anne's lace are not the only white
highlights in the landscape. Cabbage butterflies—joined by the
occasional yellow clouded sulphur—are everywhere, flickering
low over meadows and waste places. Brome and reed canary
grasses have quietly matured, turning road and field margins a
soft parchment tan, the first substantial crack in summer's green
façade. Early burdock and the first of the goldenrod are blooming, as are the proudly erect pasture thistles, left in manicured
isolation by grazing cows and heifers. And from everywhere

comes the theme music of high summer, the background scratch-
and-trill underbuzz of grasshoppers and field crickets broken
through again and again by the swelling electric-wire drone of
cicadas.

Below the barn, the corn gossips as a southerly breeze lifts and
agitates the long, pointed, crisply crinkled bent leaves, which
tickle their downwind neighbors. The corn pieces are not, however, talking as loudly as the Treadways would like. Many of
the plants simply can't reach one another. Some show leaves
cropped off flat, the result of a recent incident of cow depredation. Mostly the problem is the result of delayed and staggered
germination, some of which followed each of July's three rains.
Some corn is now head high or better, tasseling nicely and starting ears. Other plants in the same row are waist high, knee high,
and ankle high. "If this was sweet corn, we'd be in business,"
laughs Dick; "we'd have a crop all fall." As it is, it will require
a long summer with continued heat and more rain to mature
much of this corn.

In midafternoon the UPS truck drives up to the house with a
package. Thinking it contains books she had ordered, Joan
opens the box and digs down into the protective "popcorn."
What she finds is not books at all, but something in gleaming
white plastic. She knows what *that* is, too. Chagrined at her
mistake, she closes the box back up and stows it under a chair.
When Dick drops by the house before starting chores, she tells
him about the package, and admits to having peeked. "You may
as well go ahead and open it," he says, and Joan takes out a
firefighter-style hardhat complete with her name and insignia,
AFA (Advanced First Aid) and ECA (Emergency Care Atten-
dant). "I'm a bigshot now," she says.

The present—intended for her birthday next week—completes
Joan's rescue-squad apparel, Dick having given her the coat
("Can you believe that coat cost a hundred and seventy-five
dollars?" she asks) last Christmas. One by one the children turn
up in the kitchen to check out the hat, wonder facetiously if their
mother's head is worth the attention, and argue over chin-strap

attachment rights. "Now that I've got the best outfit on the squad," Joan says, "they'll probably sacrifice me. They'll send me into the wreck first."

It is five o'clock when the cows are let into the barn. While Joan rinses milkers, Dick walks his coiled extension cord down the length of the central aisle and plugs in his fogger. Everyone else leaves the barn, and, the north door closed, Dick puts on a nose-and-mouth mask and sets to work. Fogging over two cows at a time on alternate sides of the aisle, he works his way north, the characteristically acrid insecticide odor rapidly filling the barn, biting nasal membranes and lungs. "Watch Them Die!" boasts the fly-spray container, a motto the Treadways have altered to "Watch Them Fly!" This spray at least renders some flies groggy, but most seem to recover. "It just gives them a bad temper," Joan complains; "so they bite more."

A leaking water cup in each side aisle has left a large damp spot on the cement floor. Flies congregate to lay in any kind of moist material, and both darkened patches are now covered with whitish fly larvae. Pausing as they set up to milk, Dick and Joan simply sweep the writhing maggots into heaps and shovel them into the gutter.

After chores, the kids hit the pool while Joan works on dinner. Friends—an agricultural extension agent, his wife, and their two daughters—are coming over, and Joan is making two salads and bread to go with ziti, a pasta dish popular with the children. Sue and her daughters arrive; John is working on a problem in the barn, and will be along. The Treadway children climb out of the pool to allow Sue and the girls a peaceful dip.

Jeff is excited by a phone call. Someone is coming over to look at the 1977 Chrysler Cordoba he has advertised for sale. A relative had given him the car, but he spent a fair amount of money in repairs before giving up on it. He has advertised it at $400, and now has a hot prospect. (Dick and Joan share his enthusiasm for the sale. They will be grateful for some room in the front yard they call "our used car lot," a yard housing, in addition to the Cordoba, a gray 1980 Chevy Luv pickup, the '79

Jeep Renegade, a white and gold '85 Dodge Caravan—the family's "town" car—and Jeff's replacement car, a wine-red '82 Plymouth Horizon TC3.)

John arrives, and he and Dick have their dip in the pool. The house is much too hot to supper in, Joan decides, and she begins to cart food dishes, plates, and utensils out to the front-yard picnic table. The light is fading when supper gets underway, and then two teenagers drive up to look at the Cordoba, down the yard a few paces. They start it up, listening attentively to the engine. Apparently seasoned mechanics, they poke about under the hood, check out the back end, and ask Jeff questions. Then all three pile into the car and head off down Cutting Hill Road.

While the kids put away ziti, the adults talk about common interests. They talk about last winter's sugaring ("We were sold out three days after we quit boiling," Dick says); about raccoons and skunks in their barns ("It's a riot when the big 'coons try to go out what we call the cat hole in the middle of the barn," Joan says; "the front end goes through easily, but then they get stuck, and they churn away with their hind legs, and you hear this sort of 'pop' when their fat butts sail out"); about what farms are for sale, and which others will probably soon be on the auction block.

"How's jury duty going?" John wants to know, and Dick, who won't discuss pending cases, describes a recently completed one. It seems a bartender at an area town's American Legion post set off after work with a receipts bag containing something over $1,000, which bag he claimed to have dropped off in the bank's night deposit box. No such bag was subsequently found by bank employees. The bartender's explanation was that the deposit box must not have worked properly, and that somebody came along later and walked off with the money. The bank claimed the deposit box was foolproof, and the bartender's employer had him arrested on embezzlement charges.

"They took us out to the bank so we could look over the situation," Dick says. "They showed us how the deposit box

worked, and darned if a minor glitch didn't show up first
time. We went back to the courthouse and talked it over. We
agreed that the guy probably had taken the money, but we
didn't think the state had proved it beyond a reasonable
doubt. He walked." Editorializing, Dick adds: "Of course, it
isn't fair. Either the bartender or the bank (or the manufacturer of the deposit box) was responsible, and somebody
should have made restitution. But the system doesn't provide
for that, and the American Legion post ends up taking the
loss."

The Cordoba, which left with two headlights burning, returns
one-eyed. Jeff rustles up a flashlight in the house, and the prospective buyers get busy once again, under the hood, in the
trunk, under the car. The three youths huddle in the dark, ne-
gotiating. Title and payment are exchanged, and the new owner
climbs behind the wheel and turns the key in the ignition. The
starter labors valiantly, but the engine won't catch. "Come
onnn!" Dick urges under his breath, and finally the big
eight roars to life, and two cars set off for parts unknown. Jeff
comes over to the picnic table a bit concerned over the circum-
stances of the sale—the buyer declined to give his name, and
paid $340 in cash ("Is it real money?" queries his mother)—but
he's relieved to have gotten most of his investment out of
the car.

The other children have left the table when Jeff sits down for
a late supper. His brothers are watching TV in the house. Becky
and her friend Sadie, with whom she starts kindergarten next
month, alternately spy on Kevin and Brian (lifting one another
up to peek through a window) and carry out sneak attacks on
the adults, working their way toward the picnic table belly-
down in the grass, infantry style.

There is little traffic at any time on this road, and none now.
Conversation stalls, and one becomes aware of familiar heat-
of-the-night music, the music of male orthopterans anxious, like
other living things, for space and love. There are the continuous
high, thin trills of field crickets, and beneath those the unending

pulsing buzz of the tree crickets (the very heartbeat of a summer night, and, like other heartbeats, usually assimilated then ignored). More importunate are the sudden and sporadic rasping zaps of the katydids, which sound for all the world like linen being torn before hidden microphones, or like minor electric appliances shorting out at random.

It's eleven o'clock. John and Sue's younger daughter lies in her mother's lap, thumb in mouth. John rises from the table. "Gotta get up in the morning," he says; "thanks for the supper." Their friends off, Dick and Joan stack and carry in the supper things. "Just set them down," says Joan; "I'll think about them tomorrow."

# 9

NATIVES OF THE SOUTHERN CHAMPLAIN VALley will tell you that the only certain thing about summer weather is that it will rain often and hard during the second week of August. This is the traditional week for Addison County Farm and Home Field Days—a combination agricultural fair and carnival popularly known as Field Days—an event held for the past forty years, the last twenty-odd years at permanent grounds in New Haven, north of Middlebury. It doesn't always rain this week, of course, but the gods do seem to enjoy the sight of some thousands of people scurrying for cover, and, at going-home time, a couple of thousand cars—headlights pointed every which way in the farm-field parking areas—spinning and churning in the mud.

Probably nothing could induce rain this summer, but when forecasters predict periodic showers for Wednesday, Dick and Joan decide to take in the fair. Jeff, Kevin, and Brian decline to go. They are currently in thrall to a new TV video game, which involves steering little guys named Mario and Luigi over and under hazards and barriers and chasms while shooting down or jumping over attacking turtles and gnomish animaloids. The game presents eight worlds of increasing difficulty, and, as nobody has yet got through world four, it clearly represents a challenge before which the fun of a country fair pales to insignificance.

Becky and her parents arrive in time for a run through the livestock tents before the noon clown show. In the sheep tent pens are fine specimens of Suffolks, Perendales, Hampshires, Dorsets, Romney-Merinos, Blinking Finns, Corriedales, and Southdowns. In the cow tents, as in the sheep tent, animals stand under lineage cards, to which are thumbtacked ribbons won in prior shows. The Treadways wander down the wood-shaving–covered aisles past teenaged handlers trimming hooves, pitch-forking dung into wheelbarrows, and loafing on equipment trunks. Dick and Joan check the posted names of owners—some of whom they know—and examine their Black Angus, Simmentals, Ayrshires, Holsteins, Jerseys, and Guernseys.

Like everyone else, the Treadways stop to marvel at the Scottish Highlanders. These strange animals—a girl working on them says she has heard adults call them everything from horses to water buffalo—are a smallish but stocky breed of cow. All brown, Highlanders are noted for hirsuteness (ears, head, and body are particularly hairy; even the tail is hairy from stem to tip) and for the longhorn-steer–style horns. A small calf lies before its mother, looking for all the world like a baby bison with its truncated snout, curly forehead hair, and dainty hooves. Children quickly learn that the mother, despite the frightening rack of horns, is the very soul of placidity, and they crowd in to pet the calf and offer it hay.

The Highlanders' owner, a grizzled old farmer from Vermont's Northeast Kingdom, seems to enjoy the attention. The breed is a beef animal, he says, and thrives anywhere. He claims it fattens on pasture, needing neither grain nor corn. What doesn't seem to suit Highlanders is this lowland heat. Tied in a row, their eyes half-closed, the cows doze fitfully, their shaggy heads rocking up and down in time with their labored breathing.

The tent housing small livestock has a particularly rich and varied population this year. There are dogs and cats, gerbils and piglets, ponies and goats. Rabbits large and small and every conceivable variety of show pigeon are on display, as well as two ferrets ("Keep Your Hands Away," the sign warns; "We Bite") and a llama named Rico Tubbs. One whole end of the tent is devoted to fowl, exotic and domestic—chickens, ducks, geese, turkeys, golden pheasants, a peacock. Something about the crowded conditions or the heat or the people seems to have gotten on these birds' nerves. One or another, vocalizing at the drop of a hat, sets off others, and in seconds a full-alert cater-wauling is under way, cocks crowing themselves red in the face, neck-up geese threatening and braying hysterically, and, when further upmanship seems impossible, the high-pitched, long-drawn grating siren wail of the guineafowl caps the fowl cacophony.

Time to head cross-lots for the show tent, where the music has begun for the Rosie and Herbert clown act. Herbert appears from behind a red curtain at stage back, replete in multicolored pants and double-long patent leather shoes, his white-painted face sporting a bulbous nose and topped by a derby hat. Herbert talks to the kids and starts to juggle balls. Rosie appears, decked out in a frilly cape over pantaloons and pink stockings. She has a great mop of black frizzy hair, and painted on her face are red cheeks and black diamonds across the eyes.

Herbert just wants to juggle, but Rosie makes a shambles of things, snatching balls out of the air and miming depreca-tion of his talent behind his back. They juggle separately and together and do some slapstick, poor Herbert being repeat-edly victimized. Herbert introduces 5½-year-old Herbert, Jr. Arrayed in face paint, red-and-yellow suspendered pants, and purple-and-white striped socks, Herbert, Jr., is said to be "working his way through clown college." His specialty is magic tricks, and he proceeds to make a flower change colors under a magic cloth and to cause a rabbit to appear in a previously empty box. His segment complete, Herbert, Jr., perches on a folding chair near the end of the red curtain to watch the rest of the show.

Rosie scans the audience for a fearless volunteer, and chooses a reluctant, chunky preteen. Placed squarely in the middle of the stage, bubble gum under both feet to prevent a dash for freedom, balloon in mouth, the embarrassed lad is to have bowling pins juggled past him front and back, "risking his life," as Herbert puts it, "for your entertainment." While the mothers (and a few dads) in the audience seem to be enjoying the act, their children are of two minds. Some faces are fixed in rapt delight, while others are glum and abstracted, their owners appearing to be suffering through a long day in school.

The volunteer is eventually dismissed unscathed, and Herbert introduces with solemn warning a dangerous hippopotamus. Out comes a massive hippo head covering Rosie's upper half. Tiring of terrifying Herbert, the hippo climbs down from the stage and menaces the front row of the audience, taking entire heads into its gaping jaws, dragging a child across the floor by a leg. Charging offstage behind the red curtain, the hippo does some real damage, accidentally collapsing Herbert, Jr.'s, chair and flattening its occupant, who commences to scream. Rosie does some impromptu juggling while Herbert hustles Herbert, Jr., offstage and delivers him to an associate for comforting and safekeeping.

The show must go on and does, and concludes. Rosie and Herbert's considerable pains are rewarded by a scattering of polite applause, leading one to wonder if television exposure to top-notch international circus acts hasn't cast a pall over acts of this kind, and if so whether Herbert, Jr., mightn't be wise to transfer from clown college to barber college or business school.

Dick, Joan, and Becky work their way east down the north

flank of the fairgrounds, where the major exhibit buildings are located. These buildings house a goods-and-services catalogue come to life. One passes—after a while in a daze—by booths selling jewelry, wraparound madras skirts, vacuum cleaners, diesel equipment, TV satellite dishes, Christmas decorations, pots and pans, quilts and potholders, seed and fertilizer, T-shirts, wooden toys, stuffed animals, work boots, honey, fudge, custom caps, tools, kitchen items.

The National Guard booth features glamour photos of airborne jets; the Ducks Unlimited booth, ammunition. Home Health Care is here and a fundamentalist church and a Right-to-Life display and a basement-waterproofing outfit whose statuary mascot is a man holding aloft a dripping boot. Republican and Democrat booths are passing out campaign buttons and bumper stickers. Dick and Joan, in particular, are enjoying themselves. "Field Days is like a farm auction," Dick says. "It's a chance to take a break from the farm and see everybody you know." He and Joan stop to talk with their seed dealer, who lounges in front of his company's booth.

The Treadways move on to the 4-H Exhibit Hall, where prize-winning entries in categories from paper jewelry to apple trees sprouted from seed to bluebird houses are displayed proudly hung with their ribbons. Less proud as the days pass are the vegetable entries, the peas and beans, squash and melons, lettuce and tomatoes. Baked goods are aging more gracefully, the jams and jellies not at all. People pause before the University of Vermont Extension's entomology case, wondering at this bug or beetle or that butterfly. "Here's a luna moth," Joan says to Becky; "remember that luna moth we found down at the barn one year?"

But Becky wants to see the horses pacing about the warm-up and show rings with their elegantly habited riders, and beyond the rings the ox-pulling contest has attracted a small but appreciative crowd. The cement weights on the sled now approach four tons, but five teams are still in the competition. A teamster walks his pair of oxen around in front of the sled and backs them up by flicking his whip at their knees. As soon as their hitch is secured to the sled, he shouts the pull command, and the beasts strain ahead. A light rain, which no one seems to notice, drifts in from the north. After a time, the shower turns serious, however, and people begin to move under the sparse cover of a nearby fencerow. Others head back toward the midway, among them the Treadways, who wait out a heavy fifteen-minute shower in a covered maple-sugar–equipment exhibit. Dick is unfamiliar with the manufacturer's name. "It's a Canadian company," the dealer explains; "they're not well known now, but they're gonna be."

The passing shower over, the family sets a southwesterly course for the 4-H food tent. It's difficult not to suffer constant hunger at Field Days, assaulted as one is on every side by the sight and smells of hot dogs and hamburgers and barbecued beef, of subs and hot sausage, of baked potato "with six toppings" and French fries and deep-fried onion rings and fried dough, of ice cream and candy apples and cotton candy and chocolate-covered bananas. Thirst builds in this weather even without advertising encouragement, and the food stands must be breaking records for soda dissemination.

After a quick lunch, the Treadways wander about the outdoor-exhibits area. The farm-equipment dealers are here, representing John Deere, Deutz-Allis, White, Ingersoll, Massey-Ferguson, AgriMetal, Ford, Kubota, Houle, Hesston, Gehl, Sarrazin, Badger, Dion, New Holland, Farmhand. Kids climb about on the tractors, but Becky is already thinking about rides. Dick asks a dealer whom he knows what he's getting for his 120-horse Deere tractor. "It lists for fifty-seven thousand," the dealer replies; "but I can let you have it for fifty-one."

Other entrepreneurs are doing—or hoping to do—business here. There are mobile-home dealers and water-well drillers, plumbing-and-heating outfits and log-home builders, cattle-breeding services and computer portrait takers. There are fence systems set up for examination. There are livestock trailers for sale, and cars, trucks, boats, and petroleum products. A motor home dealer has driven a number of models to the fair, including the mammoth Eurocoach with a price tag of $85,852; and across the way is a booth selling socks, hundreds and hundreds of pairs of socks.

Scattered about the midway are raffles (for everything from a boat, a fire extinguisher, and a lawn tractor to a hand-spun and hand-woven afghan) to benefit youth groups and volunteer fire associations and the wool-spinners' guild. And, of course, there are the games of skill and chance played for prizes of doubtful value. Stopping before a darts-and-balloons game, Dick remembers how as a kid he and a couple of friends had gotten a dart board and practiced all winter. "That summer we went down to the Rutland Fair and threw darts at balloons. I think we had three or four teddy bears apiece before the guy running the booth told us to get lost."

Dick and Joan remember when Field Days was mostly an agricultural fair. Then the carnival element hitched on, adding— to the delight of children and teens—games and rides. Becky isn't much interested in games. She wants to ride rides. Dick and Joan have in the past been reluctant to allow the children to do fair rides, which are continually breaking down and whose general appearance fails to inspire confidence. Nor do they find reassurance in the image of the typical carnival roustabouts who set up the rides and run them, mostly tough, dropped-out youths in sleeveless T-shirts who lean passively on ride railings, lifting cigarettes with tattooed arms. "One year they busted some of the ride attendants for drugs," Dick says. "They were leading them out in handcuffs, and their rides were still going."

This year, however, Becky gets lucky. Perhaps because her brothers aren't here to call foul, she is allowed three rides. She passes up the Cobra, Scrambler, and Tilt-A-Whirl in favor of a ride called Flying Bobs, which for some reason is decorated in a winter motif featuring snow-covered Alp-like mountains, Swiss chalets, snowmen, and seminude female skiers and ice skaters. Achingly loud heavy-beat rock music starts up, and Becky and her mother are off. Flying Bobs is a sort of shallow roller coaster

whirled around a center, so that the two-person cars are bottoms out as they fly the hills and dales. Joan, her arm protectively about Becky's shoulders, is flushed but holding her own
when the ride slows and stops, only to start up again in reverse.
As the cars gain speed in this mode, Joan's face turns ashen, the
forced smile fades. But she survives, and Becky declares the
experience "fun."

She proceeds to ride the Ferris wheel and the merry-go-round,
and then, as the afternoon is getting along, Dick announces that
it's time to leave. On the way out, Joan buys a candy apple to
share with Becky on the ride home. Becky has never tasted a
candy apple, and, to her parents' surprise, cannot be persuaded
even to try it.

## 10

AUGUST CARRIES ON HOT, HUMID, AND LARGELY
rainless in much of the country. Young joggers die of heat ex-
haustion in New York's Central Park. Cities are filled with the
collective hum of air conditioners, with metropolitan brownouts
resulting. It is hot in the Shoreham countryside as well, but the
constant humming here is generated by crickets. Patches of hol-
lyhocks brighten the east end of the older Treadway house. Don's
potatoes are beginning to bloom, and at the far end of the garden
a luxuriant stand of ragweed is holding candelabra spikes three
feet off the ground.

The near-record-volume first hay cutting, which has filled the
haylage silo and put nearly 12,000 bales in the barn, was completed before Field Days, and the Treadways turn immediately
to the drought-stunted second cutting.

Baling hay makes chopping it look easy. More steps are involved, and so more time is involved. The trick is to get the hay dried. Damp hay might well seem the least of a farmer's worries in the middle of a drought; but the meadow is cut green, of course, and, what with high daytime humidity and the occasional nighttime dew, the hay tends to retain its moisture.

The answer to damp hay is tedding, and on this hot but breezy afternoon, Jeff pulls the tedder up to the high meadow under the east ridge to do just that. He starts work only to find that half his tedding apparatus isn't working. A crucial pin is missing. Jeff pulls the rig back downslope, around a corn piece, past the barn, and up to the shop, where he will craft a replacement pin.

Mission accomplished, he returns and begins again to work the hay. The tedder's long axlelike rod, running on four wheels, supports four "racks," round platters with six bars jutting out and down toward the ground, each bar ending in a two-tined (or, thanks to breakage, a one-tined) fork. The row of racks, perpendicular to the tractor's axis, just covers two rows of mown hay, and, as Jeff aims the tractor between rows, the four racks work as two pairs, one tedding each row. The outer rack of each pair spins clockwise, the inner counterclockwise; so that each pair works through a row of hay like a pair of eggbeaters, chucking half the row outward and half the row inward.

A dust cloud drifts downwind as the whirring forks unmake the neat rows of green hay, and soon the barn swallows and tree swallows are swooping about that cloud, engulfing fleeing insects. Jeff proceeds in narrowing rectangles, working half the meadow at a time, leaving the hay strewn in knobby bunches, fluffed for good air penetration. Indeed, a tedded meadow looks precisely as if somebody with a grudge has walked the mown rows kicking. That method, in fact, would work perfectly well on a farm with tiny meadows or numerous obtuse enemies.

Becky has come along to the high meadow, but finds tedding boring. She busies herself trying to catch grasshoppers, of which every field on the farm must support hundreds of thousands. They are alert, however, and good flyers as well as quick jumpers. She stalks hundreds, and nearly catches two or three. But at the first touch of jumping grasshopper on hand, she sings out in alarm while jumping backwards and throwing out her opened hands. Chagrined by this uncontrollable sissy impulse, she slips under the fence into the heifer pasture to look for frogs in a stream now reduced to a few small pools surrounded by heifer prints.

Brian drives up on the red Honda three-wheeler. He is searching for a stand of red clover, a favorite food of his white guinea pig, Willy, and would appreciate tips. A great raft of altocumulus cloud, rippled like a washboarded country road, works its way down the sky from the north. Brian chugs off on his search, and Jeff is tedding the far end of the meadow. Momentarily it's quiet, and from the pasture beyond the fencerow comes the soft, exquisite warble of a bluebird.

Once tedded hay is sufficiently dry, it is raked back into rows preparatory to baling. While Jeff teds above, Don rakes the meadow below him with the small International Harvester pulling a French-made Kuhn rake. Supported by two small wheels, the rake is essentially an eight-foot-diameter horizontal wagon wheel with nine spokes, each of which ends in a six-tine comb, which looks like the business end of a pitchfork. Put in motion, the rake spins quietly counterclockwise, the combs sweeping the scattered hay to the operator's left side, where each spoke in turn pivots, lifting its comb, depositing the hay in a neat row against a stationary comb guard.

Don drives rectangles around half the meadow. An eight-foot sweep collects little hay; he incorporates that row in his next sweep and the result of that in his next, leaving only one row for three sweeps. He then turns around, lines up the comb guard on the outside of that row, and sweeps a fourth and final strip back to the now-substantial row, which is left for the baler. "This is just about a waste of fuel," Don says from under a straw hat. If this meadow were any thinner, the Treadways would have left the mown hay for green manure.

A meadow is often retedded; sometimes twice. The hay in this meadow, spread to dry, got caught by a nighttime shower, and had to be tedded again. (This doesn't amount to a great deal of extra labor and expenditure, but the farmer pays another price. Tedder and rake are marvelously efficient, but they beat up the hay. Each handling knocks off more of the alfalfa's triplet leaves, which are the best part of the forage.) Dick certainly doesn't want to ted and rake this hay again, and, with an eye on the darkening clouds, he follows the rake in a Deere 4000, pulling the New Holland baler and hay wagon.

Twenty-one feet long from hitch to end, the baler is the space shuttle of the farm's field equipment. It has a whole series of independent jobs to do, all of which must be integrated in a crucial timing sequence; and everything must perform flawlessly while the three-wheeled rig clanks along over uneven ground. As Dick drives along the left side of a windrow, a revolving rake—a smaller version of the chopper's rake—pulls the hay into a bin, where moving pairs of elephant-tusk-shaped pointed rods drag it into the baler's central chamber, an elongated chute. Here the hay encounters the "plunger"—a battering ram with a heavy knife blade for one edge—which drives rhythmically into the hay, at once compacting it, driving it forward, and slicing the side clean. The bale-to-be inches down the chute with each slam of the plunger, two lines of baler twine—fed from rolls housed in a bin behind the rake—laid along its long axis.

When the preset bale length has been reached, the critical tying cycle is triggered. Two 28-inch-long, curved, pointed heavy steel bars with twine lines threaded through holes in the pointed ends (hence the name "needles") slam up from below between the rear end of the completed bale and the fore end of the forming bale. The needles having completed the twine loops, the "knotter"—a complex double unit of plates, disks, wheels, and ratcheting cogs on an axle—sets about tying. Two pairs of jaws called "bill-hooks" grab and twist the strands into knots, knives whack through the twine lines below the knots, bars shove the knotted twine lines off the bill-hooks, and the needles retract. This whole sequence—from needle entry through tying cycle through needle retraction—must be completed during the interval between plunger thrusts, an interval lasting just under one second. ("You hate to have to play with anything on a baler," says Dick, "because then you have to retime every-thing.")

The tied bale continues its slow journey back along the chute, shoved now by the next bale, which is shoved by the plunger. Finally, it works its way back to the up-slanted ejector, or "kicker," where a series of pulleys drives a pair of foot-wide reinforced rubber belts, which spin furiously, like assembly-line belts gone mad. Its lead end fed between the whirling belts, the hitherto slow-motion bale is accelerated through the kicker and is catapulted up and back into the trailing hay wagon.

Round and round go tractor, baler, and wagon, the baler eating up loose hay and spitting out bales. It soon becomes apparent that the second cutting on this meadow will amount to only about two 120-bale wagon loads. When the first load is complete, Dick leaves Don to bale the remainder, and pulls the first load back to the barn. He eases the wagon up alongside the base of the elevator, unhitches it, and moves the tractor down to the end of Don's garden.

Jeff pulls out the pipe blocking the wagon's side "door," and Joan climbs aboard to wrestle the bales down to Jeff, who, having started the elevator, positions them on the climb-ing chain, whose equidistant teeth anchor them. Meanwhile, Dick, Kevin, and Brian have climbed to the mow, through whose open gable end the climbing bales come to be trans-ferred to a second, horizontal "elevator" running high up down the middle of the mow. (This track must run high, since the bales it carries will be stacked up on either side nearly to the roof peak.)

The barn mow is now three quarters full, and Dick and the boys start on the north end. A curved deflector plate, fastened above the moving chain, turns the bales aside and drops them where they are wanted. Or *some*times drops them. Often a bale will "stick," bumping gently against the plate until the next bale comes along and gives it an extra boost. As the Treadways take turns wading in under the elevator to grab a spilled bale, they keep a wary eye on the overhead situation. Will the next bale fall or stick? Occasionally, a bale starts out bumping like a sticker, then falls, and once in a while one of these catches someone below on the back of the head. Dick bales small so that all the family but Becky can pick them up and lug them. But when, as now, the stackers are working on the floor of the mow, the bales are dropping a long way, and even a thirty-five-pound bale packs a wallop if it catches you right. ("Kind of rocks your back teeth, doesn't it?" grins Dick after a mishap.)

The stackers grab a bale by the nearer twine loop, haul it to the side wall, and swing it into place (fine-tuning with a foot) end out. Rows are just beginning to build along both walls when the outside elevator is shut down. The stackers gather at the open gable. "What broke?" "Nothing broke," replies Joan; "I think this hay is too green." "Stick your hand into a bale," Dick says; "see if it's hot." "It doesn't feel hot," she says, "but it's unloading heavy." Heavy hay means too much moisture content, and Dick doesn't argue with her judgment. "O.K.," he concludes; "send up what's on the elevator, and we'll put the rest in the shed."

Dick recently built a covered machine shed, hoping to extend the life of his more valuable machinery by getting it out of the winter weather. In the summer, they fill it with overflow hay, feeding it first so that they can get the machinery in before snowfall. A third of the shed is already full. Having spread black plastic on the earthen floor of the shed's middle section, the family goes to work off-loading and stacking the rest of the load.

(The increasingly popular round-bale technology eliminates much of the time-consuming transportation and handling required by conventional bales. On the order of thirty times larger than oblong bales, these mammoth rolled bales are mostly fed where formed, in the meadows, since to move them requires forklift equipment. Over the course of the fall and winter, however, the outside layers of these bales mold in the weather, and cows are sometimes reluctant to strip away rotten hay to get to palatable feed.)

"Speaking of barn fires," says Joan, knowing that no one had, though they had all been thinking on the subject, "I wish you'd get lightning rods on that barn; I have enough to worry about without having to lie awake stormy nights and think about that." Dick isn't sure how much lightning rods help, or how much anybody knows about lightning. "We had a lightning-rod salesman come here some years back," he recalls. "He gave the farm buildings the once-over and says: 'This big barn is up here on ledge; you oughta put rods on it. The little barn down the hill is perfectly safe; I wouldn't waste a dollar on it.' I said I'd think about it. A week later a storm comes along and that little barn down the hill took a direct hit. It exploded; blew the ends right out of it. This barn up here has never been touched."


THE TREADWAYS ARE IN THE MIDDLE OF AFTER-noon milking on the following Sunday when they hear, from Don and Irene's house, the continuous ring of a fire call. Don hustles down from the house. It's a barn fire down in Orwell, at a farm owned by a couple who are among Dick and Joan's best friends. Dick and Don grab their apparel and head out, leaving Joan and the children to finish up chores.

Less than two hours after the call came in, Joan loads her rescue gear in the pickup and drives west and south. She stops briefly at the Shoreham corner store to pick up two cases of soda for the firefighters. "Either the fire department will pay for this or I will," Joan says to the woman. "It's O.K.," she replies; "it's a donation." The smell of smoke is heavy in the air miles north of the farm, but one by one the Shoreham fire trucks pass Joan heading for home.

Joan drives up to the farmstead to find no sign of a fire. A teenaged son emerges from the barn and points down the road. Driving on, she finds cars and pickups lining both sides of the road, as well as a few remaining Orwell and Whiting fire trucks. Below the road, neatly piled rows of mammoth round-loaf hay bales smoke and smoulder. Not until one notices a bit of standing northeast corner does one realize that these bales had been housed in a barn. The timbers are thinned and charred black, the color of the mud they lie in; the metal roofing and sides of the Quonset-style barn have simply melted away.

Their work done—there wasn't much they could do—the firefighters, mostly defrocked for the heat, stand about the road in knots, some of serious mien, some jocular. A supply of beer has come from somewhere, and Joan's soda mostly goes begging. The farm wife walks up and down the road, alternately talking with friends and looking at the ruined hay. She had learned of the fire from her youngest son, who had said: "Mommy, the hay barn's on fire; is Daddy going to cry?" She laughs. The laughter dies, and tears well up. Joan embraces her friend.

Back in the truck, Joan turns around in a driveway, threads her way back through the parked vehicles, and starts for home, driving past the now-deserted farmhouse, where she and Dick were supposed to have suppered last night. "They called in the morning and invited us, and I said, 'Sure.' As it turned out, Dick had a lot of hay he wanted to rake and bale, and we hadn't even started chores when suppertime came. We called at the last minute and canceled out. I feel bad about that.

"It could have been a lot worse. It could have been the milking barn. When ours blew down, we were lucky. We drove our cows down to Uncle Norman's, and he let us use his barn. Still, we had to get up in the middle of the night to get our cows in and milked and out so he could get his in and milked. Then we milked again at night, after he was done milking. I'll never forget those weeks. What with early and late chores, and carpentering all day on the new barn, we were dead."

Joan's thoughts return to her friends' misfortune. "The two hundred bales in that barn were the equivalent of six thousand regular bales. They lost half their winter's feed supply today. I hope they have contents insured as well as buildings." She drives in silence for a time. "At least," she says, "nobody got hurt."


## 11

THE HEAT WAVE CONTINUED THROUGH AUGUST in most of the country—fifty widely scattered weather stations reported record high temperatures on the sixteenth—but just past midmonth the Great Lakes and Northeastern states turned delightfully cool, and remained cool for most of the rest of the month. Acquaintances meeting in town would stop to comment: "It's only right. We had August in June; now we've got June in August."

It is the last Saturday of the month, and on the Treadway farm one of those days when no farming other than the obligatory milking is going to get done. Brian has fallen in the house, twisting a knee. He lies in the rocking chair in the living room, complaining of the pain, his leg in a soft temporary cast supplied out of Joan's emergency gear. Becky hovers around him, curious about his injury, while Jeff and Kevin, sitting on the floor pursuing a video game, offer no sympathy.

Joan calls the Middlebury hospital to see if emergency business has the facility tied up. Cleared for a visit, Dick and Joan move Brian into the van for a trip to town and X-rays. "Grandpa should be back any time," Dick reminds Jeff; "see what you can do with the baler."

The baler has been a recurrent headache this summer. First, one knotter wasn't tying consistently; and a bale of hay without two secure ties isn't a bale at all, but a spineless U-shaped hump that won't ride the elevator, won't carry, won't stack. Beyond that problem, the baler has been showing signs of metal rot ("That's partly our fault," Dick says; "we left it to overwinter with some bales in it"), and Dick wasn't sure it was worth fixing. He followed up a promising line on a good used baler, but the machine didn't materialize. He checked out new balers at area dealers, who tempted him with no-payments-till-after-the-first-of-the-year deals. Still, the $9,000 (plus trade-in) price would have to be paid, and Dick decided to have the knotter worked on. The dealer sent out a couple of men, who labored through an afternoon, replacing most of the knotter's parts. Their opinion was that the baler wasn't in bad shape, that it ought to carry on for a few more years.

Earlier this week, the second knotter began to act up. The trouble seemed to involve a lax spring, and, remembering the $360 bill for the other knotter work, Dick and Jeff rebuilt it themselves. Both knotters then worked famously, which is when the tongue hitching baler to catcher wagon broke its metal-fatigued attachment point at the base of the baler's central chamber wall.

Don returns from a local shop with a three-foot piece of heavy angle-iron, which he and Jeff hope to incorporate into the weakened section where the wall corners into bottom to provide sound attachment material for the tongue. Jeff opens up this section of the baler chamber by removing parts. Those bolts the air wrench won't budge are cut off with the torch. Kevin has been pressed into service as fireman, dousing torch-started hot spots with a squirt bottle. Becky, perched on the baler above the action, wants Kevin's job. Kevin, who had been less than enthusiastic about it in the beginning, is now determined to keep it. She pesters Kevin until he orders her home, a command she disdainfully ignores.

Don and Jeff lay the length of angle-iron in place, only to find something in that corner out of square. They rig up two jacks, one from below and the other from the side, and force the remains of the original frame and chamber metal to snug up to the angle-iron. This maneuver widens to a gap what had been a crack around a bracket attaching a supporting plate to the baler's rake housing. But the plate doesn't seem to be load-bearing, and the mechanics on duty declare the new problem noncritical.

The baler rests where all equipment under repair rests—at the moment the upslope manure spreader awaits a tube for a flat tire, the downslope tedder nearly a complete set of double-tined teeth—below Don and Irene's house and outside the door to the shop, into which Jeff sends Kevin from time to time after a tool and into which Don disappears to hunt up new bolts. People whose idea of a shop is the huge, brilliantly lighted, sterile edifice inhabited by white-coated men which they glimpse through swinging doors from the potted-plant-decorated and canned-music-soothed service department waiting room of a large auto dealership can have no notion of what an old-time farm shop is like. The Treadways' is housed in a long-unmaintained outbuilding featuring a sway-backed, permanently open hanging door, warped siding boards, and windows with slumped frames.

The low-ceilinged, dimly lit interior smells and feels of grease and iron filings and is cock-a-jam with a bewildering jumble of ancient, old, and newer stuff: tool boxes and loose tools, boxes of bolts, drill bits, welding equipment, a grinder, batteries, extension cords, clamps, tires, motors and parts of motors, saw blades, a rake head, and, piled in odd corners, barrel and pail after barrel and pail, emptied of oils and lubricants. It is virtually impossible to walk directly on the shop floor. One proceeds on and over cables and chains, mower teeth and six-inch-long nails, shock absorbers and a sledgehammer head, grease guns and wrenches, soda can tops, a pulley wheel, a pair of purple pants.

Dick would like to tear down this building along with the old horse barn behind the sawdust pile, and build a large heated shop where they could work on machinery during the winter. "As it is," he says, "the equipment sits through the winter when we've got some time, and by spring, when we're getting busy again, I've forgot what's broke." Another item on the Some Day list.

Jeff drops his welder's face mask into place and sets to work cutting bolt holes through the angle-iron. There is no problem with hole positions here. He simply directs his flame through the original bolt holes. The torch pops; sparks fly. Slowly the flame eats through the iron, emerging as a red point, and then a hole opens, sending a blob of sun-orange molten iron rolling down the angle-iron like an egg yolk across a skillet. Kevin dumps water around the newly cut hole. The water beads up on the angle-iron's horizontal surface, sizzles, and boils away.

Having located replacement bolts, Don leans on the baler and watches as Jeff begins work on a second hole. Remembering a story out of his past, he chuckles, and launches into it. "There was this group of guys, all good friends, who used to spend time together in a bar in Brandon. This one guy—he was French—was always telling Polish jokes. Now the butt of these jokes—I never could pronounce his name; it had a lot of z's and y's in it—never said much, but apparently the jokes got to him. One day, when the other guy had finished one of those jokes, he says, blunt-like: 'You know, do you, why these Polish jokes are always so short?' 'Don't know as I do,' says the other fella. 'Well,' he answers, 'they had to keep 'em short and simple so Frenchmen could understand 'em.' That shut that guy right up," Don concludes, in full rippling chuckle now: "He didn't have nuthin' to say to that!"

Jeff lifts his mask and casually mentions his intention to proceed with welding, a comment which reopens a standing disagreement between him and his grandfather. Jeff is proud of his skill at welding. He is convinced that a couple of anchoring bolts are sufficient here; that he can finish the job by welding the top of the angle-iron to the chamber wall. Don, on the other hand, is not a great believer in welds. "They bolt 'em together when they make 'em," he says. "Put a couple more bolts in and then you can weld to your heart's content."

The afternoon wanes; the baler job will not, in any case, be completed today. Dick and Joan return with Brian, fixed up with a soft Velcro-fastened leg cast and crutches. The hospital news is mostly good. No bone has been broken, at least, but Brian must see the doctor in a week to check on the possibility of torn ligaments. Meantime, he will enjoy chair rest and added attention, the privileges of the newly injured. His main worry at the moment is nighttime temperature. "I hope it gets cold tonight," he says; "this cast is *hot*."

Dick changes clothes and stops by the baler to see how Jeff and Don are getting on and to recruit help for barn chores. He wants to get on with baling the second cut, and to proceed with a new round of spreading manure on the cut meadows.

As it happens, the weather will scotch both plans, the first temporarily, the second for good. It will rain steadily tonight, and again tomorrow, with booming morning thunder showers thrown in for good measure. The two-inch rain will delay haymaking and will cancel manure-spreading, since, by the time the land dries out sufficiently to make spreading practicable, the meadow grasses will be showing regrowth, making it inadvisable.

Dick will not, however, grouse about this rain. The land is still dry, and a good soaking rain will mean a growth spurt for his multistage corn. And Jeff, who would have had to spread the manure, and Kevin, who would have had to load his spreader, won't complain about the rain at all.

## 12

"WE SHOULD SHOOT THE LITTLE BUGGERS IN the barn," says Dick, trying to summon conviction. The margin of his far southerly corn piece looks as if livestock have run amok. Random gaps penetrate six and eight rows into the field, the broken corn stalks lying every which way on the ground. In fact, until one notices the neatly pulled-back shucks and the kernel-stripped cobs, one doesn't realize he is looking at raccoon, not cow, depredation.

A 'coon simply climbs a corn stalk until its weight snaps the plant off at a low node, then strips and feasts on its one or two ears. Dick doesn't begrudge the 'coons the ears, but these whole plants are lost to him. The corn chopper will pass over downed plants, leaving leaves and stalks to rot on the ground. To add insult to injury, the stalks won't rot fast enough; they will impede the plowing of this field next spring.

In the meantime, raccoons must be figured into the equation determining the harvesting schedule for the farm's corn. Dick wants to leave it as late as possible, to enable late-germinating plants to mature. But the later he waits, the better the chance that fall rains may prevent timely chopping; and at what point does 'coon damage overtake and negate corn growth? A hunter friend has told Dick that the price of 'coon hides is down, that they probably won't be much hunted this year, leaving the dark prospect of more inroads on the cat food and corn in future.

It is a warm early September day, breezy out of the south, and Dick is hiking the farm, checking corn pieces and meadows. Heading east now, he climbs up onto 'Coon Ledge, a north-south–running ridge rising abruptly to a small vertical cliff face on the western flank. Its flat crest only fifteen or twenty yards wide, 'Coon Ledge is timbered in maple, hickory, basswood, white birch, and red oak. The thin soil under the canopy supports an abundance of fuzzy-headed white snakeroots, their dark green leaves decorated with the light involutions of leaf-miner work. A delicately elongated brown walking stick perches—its long axis aligned with that of the tree—eight feet up on a massive oak.

The farm's raccoons are believed to headquarter up here, and a small pile of round-ended woody porcupine pellets in a rock hollow and a fresh coyote scat near the western dropoff show that other animals are here as well. Dick laughs over a remembered encounter from earlier this summer. "We were coming along in the meadow below here. Joan was driving the tractor; I was riding in the wagon. A big coyote stalks out from the trees at the base of this ledge, and walks right toward us. Joan stops the tractor. The coyote gets pretty close, and Joan is scrambling up on the tractor seat; I wondered which way she was going to jump! He took a good look at us, then calmly turned and loped away."

The Treadways think a pair of coyotes may den somewhere in 'Coon Ledge's craggy caves. There must be a lot of open space under this ridge. Upslope drainage simply disappears into gaping holes, some of which plunge straight down out of sight through the ledge.

Dick emerges from the wooded ledge into his southernmost meadow. Grasshoppers in the hundreds jump and scatter out of the dry grass. Most are medium-sized, and their blurred transparent wings carry them off in a straight-line rush of five or ten yards. Now and again the walker scares up one of the large brown 'hoppers, which shake out yellow-margined, black leathery wings and lurch off cross-lots in every direction like small diurnal bats.

The patchy distribution of alfalfa indicates that this high meadow is nearing the end of its cycle. "If I were a more aggressive farmer," says Dick, "I'd have replanted this meadow last year. But I hate to plow under good alfalfa, even when the grass is crowding it out." The grass is not, this dry summer, crowding anything with much vigor. The meadow looks like short-grass prairie, not what a Northeastern farmer expects or wants to see.

Dick climbs a fence into the farm's easternmost pasture, and, at a jog in the fence, locates the remains of an old barn effectively concealed by hedges of nettles, thistles (mostly going to seed), and newly blooming goldenrod. Nothing stands now. The barn is a jumble of foundation rocks and timbers. A mammoth eight-inch by ten-inch beam lifts like balsa wood after decades on the ground.

Dick remembers this barn well. "I came up here as a kid and worked with my father. We used to store hay in this barn. I remember the stalls. They had twelve or fifteen cows, which was about all most farmers could handle in those days. We'd come up here with a lunch packed to work all day. We'd sit up under those trees to eat lunch. That stub down there by the fence was a pear tree. It had the best pears on the place."

Lost in boyhood memories, Dick pokes about down the gentle pasture slope. Clouded sulphurs cruise aimlessly back and forth; a large black swallowtail is busy at thistle flowers. Just below the barn's west foundation line, a circular jumble of stones and boards shows where a small silo had stood, the boards and poles now "furred" with British soldiers lichen. Below the silo site, slab stone still defines the well, two pole timbers crossed over the top for heifer protection. One can see water eight feet down, and even in this dry summer the wall stones are well mossed. Down-slope and north a short way, Dick locates the remains of the old hen house.

A short walk south of the barn site, backed, like so many abandoned New England cellar holes, by a grove of black locust, is the foundation of the farmhouse, which Don remembers standing a half-century ago. It is difficult to imagine what this house looked like, or even how it stood on the land, whose earlier contours have been lost in the swells and gullies of time. Brambles and buckthorn heavy with dark blue fruit grow within the remains of foundation walls, while thriving hedges of reddening-berried barberry crowd the perimeter.

The big elms which had shaded the house in summer are long dead and coming down in stages. North of the house site a pair of mockingbirds flip their tails and dart for insects among a tumbled heap of barkless, polished elm boughs looking from a distance for all the world like an elephant graveyard. A long-thrown-up road, now a heifer path, runs south from the farm-stead past the wreck of an old butternut and a huge mulberry. Except for a fluted, pumpkin-shaped kerosene lantern glass found hidden in a barberry thicket, no sign of human habitation remains.

"Who were these people?" Dick wonders. "Where did they come from, and where did they go?" He falls silent, perhaps thinking about the several other cellar holes and barn foundations on the place, reminders that his farm is after all an incorporation, an assemblage of horse-powered family farms whose stories are lost forever. Or perhaps he falls silent in response to the mood of a warm summer afternoon, the quiet broken only by crickets and cicadas, by the small but persistent *dee-dee*ing of a foraging chickadee, and, once, by the sudden distant cackling of an alarmed kestrel.

What eventually registers on Dick's consciousness is the dull throb of Jeff's tractor pulling the repaired baler up and down the meadow below 'Coon Ledge. He rises abruptly and heads off to join the hay-making operation.

## 13

PUTTING UP THE LAST OF THE 15,000 HAY bales in the machine shed has been an experience quite unlike that of stacking bales in the barn a month ago. The boys took a thermometer up into the mow then, and on a typically hot, dry day it registered 111 degrees. But the dramatic break in the drought in mid-August has fortunately continued, with delightfully cool weather (and seasonable rainfall) ever since. Now, a week into September, the second hay cutting is complete, the baler retired—with a sigh of relief—for another year, and summer chores are complete.

Like most seasons on the farm, this summer has been a mixed bag financially. On the down side, there has been a typical array of machine-related expenses, from repairing the baler and tedder to fixing flat tires to replacing the Allis-Chalmers' muffler, which Dick, working along the edge of a field, caught in overhead tree limbs and snapped off. These expenses are expected. The feared drought-related increase in grain prices has come and has hurt. A few dairy farmers in the area have cut back on grain rations, substituting cheaper whey or brewer's yeast. Dick, like most, is paying more, and hoping the price will shortly retreat. The Treadways have been able to switch back from 18-percent-protein to 16-percent-protein grain, but the same mix that cost $153 a ton two months ago is now in the $190s, a rise which, should it hold, would amount to an annual increase in the cost of milk production of about $6,000 on this farm.

Not only is milk more expensive to make, but there is, just now, much less of it to sell. At peak production, the Treadways make roughly 3,600 pounds a day; now they are milking just under half that. The weather hasn't helped, since cows give less milk in hot weather. But production would be down now in any case, since the Treadway herd has peak numbers of "dry" cows.

Probably most Americans think of cows as—what agricultural science has attempted to make them—milk-secreting machines, animals that line up dutifully 365 days a year to deliver milk. They are not; and do not. Cows are mammals, and, like other mammals, produce milk to nourish their young, and hence must be kept on a regular breeding cycle. Toward the end of a cow's pregnancy, her bag begins to swell (called "springing") with colostrum. She is checked to make sure that she is eating well and feeling good. She gives birth ("freshens") either outdoors or in the barn, and for much of the first week her colostrum- and antibody-rich milk goes to her calf. She then goes on line as a milker, working up to peak production in a matter of weeks.

Between forty-five and sixty days after freshening, the "open" cow comes into heat, in anticipation of which a vet gives her a thorough examination, with particular attention paid to uterus and birth tract. If she is in good health, she is watched carefully lest her brief heat period slip by unnoticed, and she is bred. The cow's next heat period is watched for as well. The cow may not "settle"—that is, the insemination may fail, or the fetus may be aborted—in which case she will come back into heat, and must be bred again.

About eight months through her nine-and-a-half-month gestation, the cow's declining milk production comes to an end. She may dry off quickly or more slowly. If the latter, she may be milked once a day for a short time, will have her water cut back, and will be kept out of the barn, where the sights and sounds of milking encourage the conditioned reflex of milk let-down. A dry cow—treated with antibiotics to prevent mastitis—enjoys a two-month resting period. Freed from the burden of milk production, she regenerates her strength and energy and tones up for her coming freshening.

A dry cow is, of course, a consumer but not a producer, and hence a financial burden on the farm; and now, at milking time, the empty stanchions testify to a milking herd reduced from sixty-odd animals to near forty. Noticing the fact, Brian is ebullient: "That's great! Chores won't take long now." "No," Joan responds, "and it won't take long to spend the milk check either."

There has been positive financial news as well. Dick's sporadic bouts of jury duty have paid $30 a day, "the first steady money I've made in years." (Those bouts weren't always convenient, of course. Last month, Dick was directed to appear on his birthday for an attempted-murder case, whose jury would be sequestered for some time. As it turned out, the case was successfully plea-bargained the day before it was to start, and Dick was able to celebrate his fortieth at home.)

Serendipity has added modestly to the farm's coffers as well. One day a man with a landscape business drove into the farmstead looking for squared-off foundation stones to turn into walks and patio walls. He examined the stones in two of the farm's cellar holes and bought them on the spot, to truck them away as needed. This amounts to "found" money, and is welcome here as it would be anywhere else.

Better news yet came from the state legislature. Federal dairy policy supports milk prices, of course, but it ties the level of support to production. When the federal government is forced to buy more than a predetermined amount of milk, it cuts the support price by fifty cents per hundredweight, theoretically discouraging overproduction by forcing marginal dairy farmers— opponents read "small" for "marginal"—out of business. (Something has certainly been shutting down dairy farms. In the twenty years prior to 1980, three-quarters of this country's 700,000 dairy farms were lost.)

When a fifty-cent price cut was triggered this year, the Vermont legislature promptly undid it, initiating what the Associated Press described as the "nation's only state-funded dairy subsidy." Paying fifty cents per hundredweight up to a million pounds—and restricted to people who make at least half their income from farming and whose net income does not exceed $32,000—the program will pay the Treadways $5,000, half of which they have already received. Though this money represents less a gain than a cancellation of a loss, it is welcome on this, and many another, Vermont farm. The state subsidy idea has attracted the attention of other dairy states desirous of retaining their farms; should it catch on in the big milk-producing states (in descending order of production, Wisconsin, California, New York, Minnesota, and Pennsylvania together are responsible for more than half this country's milk supply), the federal government will have to think up a new way to discourage overproduction.

Dick and Joan have spent time this summer mulling over another new state initiative, a tax-abatement program that would save them, at current rates, $1,700 a year. Although a tax break would be more than welcome, the Treadways finally decided against joining the program. They had doubts about the clause which grants the state an option to buy the property at the price of any accepted offer, should owners in the program decide to sell. The advertised purpose of the plan is to preserve open space; so presumably the state would step in to buy a farm threatened by development only to see that it stayed farmland.

The state is not, however, expressly restricted in that regard.

"Say we decided to retire to a little house on five acres up on that hill," the Treadways say, "and sell the rest, which we could do under the program. We get an offer for the farm, and the state steps in and matches it. Now, there's no guarantee they're going to farm it. They could decide to build a prison here, and we'd be left looking down at that." One suspects that Dick and Joan are not so much distrustful of the state's intentions as they are reluctant to trade away their control over the disposition of their farm.

The most satisfying good news of the summer, however, lies not in one-time subsidies or sold stones, but in the results of the farming itself. A bumper hay crop is baled and out of the weather (though that in the middle bay of the machine shed pot-bellies precariously: "The boys stacked that," Dick laughs; "we put some ropes across and hope it stays put"), and it now looks as though the weather and the 'coons will leave more corn for winter silage than once looked likely. And tied next to Bunny— who is quite mature now, and, apparently having forgotten her dehorning, happy to be petted again—in the south end of the barn are two new calves and more soon to come, which means progressively fuller bulk tanks ahead.

Farming is a curious business. Most people work to save, then spend it while loafing. A farmer rests to save money he will lose while working. That is, winter is at once the farmer's easiest and most profitable season. He has milk to sell but no field work to do. During the other three seasons, he has, on average, less milk to sell and milking-to-milking field work, together with the expenses in seeds, fertilizers, pesticides, herbicides, machine parts and maintenance, gas, diesel, and oil, and on and on, involved therein.

Now it's September, and Dick can see easier money times ahead. "If we can pay our bills this month and next," he says, "we'll be O.K."

*FALL*

"How early in the year it begins to be late!" Thoreau wrote in his journal, an observation as apt in Shoreham now as it was in Concord then. The first adult shorebirds abandon the tundra nesting ground and overfly New England in July. Tree swallows and barn swallows are already massing—lining up on power wires and sunning on barn roofs—in early August, when flocks of fall-plumaged bobolinks begin to work the cornfields.

It is nearly two weeks before the autumn equinox when the Treadways turn from hay to wood, but the signs of fall are unmistakable. Kettles of broad-winged hawks are drifting down out of Canada, and the odd sharp-shinned hawk, kestrel, harrier, and osprey as well. Mile after mile of gray-stemmed dogwood fencerow is maturing its clusters of white berries, staple food for resident birds and particularly for migrating robins, bluebirds, and other thrushes, for mimics and tanagers, even for flycatchers. Big, hairy, rusty-buff acrea moth caterpillars are rippling their way across roads, undertaking their annual mini-migration prior to taking shelter for the winter.

Not everyone scans the Champlain Valley skies for migrating hawks or drives its roads on the watch for caterpillars. Not everyone notices that the summer-quiet blue jays are suddenly raucous again and restless, or that the birds massed on the utility wires are no longer swallows but starlings. Everyone does notice the crews of Jamaicans picking the Cornwall and Shoreham apple orchards, and surely no one is oblivious to the great yellowing swaths of goldenrod along road and field margin, or to Act One of the fall foliage spectacular, as the ashes turn a dark plum-purple (an elegant shade somehow at once warm and cool), the first egg-shaped woodbine leaves come in on the burgundy side of red, and the narrow sumac leaflets begin—lower leaves first, working gradually up to the fuzz-covered seed spikes—to turn that strong red that fires the landscape in late-afternoon sun.

It will be a couple of weeks before the legions of down-country leaf-peepers arrive to witness the triumphant maple act of the play, but already the odd red maple and stressed sugar maple limb are showing color as Dick hitches his Bush Hog splitter to the International Harvester and drives the tractor road south toward 'Coon Ledge, below which he has, this morning, felled and sectioned three disease-killed elms. He backs the splitter into position among the bark slabs and sawdust piles alongside the first elm, a tree fully two feet in diameter at neck height where Dick has cut it, leaving the butt to continue its fence-post duty.

The little fifty-five-horsepower International Harvester is ideal for splitting wood, both because it is maneuverable in the woods and because it has a good hydraulic system, which, rather than the power take-off, powers the splitter. An efficient and relatively simple tool, the splitter is essentially a horizontal I-beam frame along which a lever-controlled piston with a plate on the leading end drives toward an upright steel wedge fixed at its far end.

Dick starts with the easily manageable limb logs, placing one end against the wedge and pulling the lever forward to activate the piston. This super-dry limb wood is gray straight through, and most of it splits nicely, popping crisply like watermelon rind, often after only a few inches of wedge penetration. Trunk wood is another matter. Less dry, with pale cream heartwood, it splits harder and requires more splits. Dick starts a trunk log by splitting concave slabs off the perimeter. "These logs remind me of a carrot," he says; "the outside peels off, leaving a solid center." Then he splits chunks off the heartwood core, processing the larger trunk pieces into a dozen or even fifteen firewood logs.

The butt pieces of this tree must weigh 100 pounds each, and they are a real chore to handle. Dick rolls one down to the splitter, and, sweating freely in the cool, crisp air, wrestles it up over bent knees onto his thighs before heaving it onto the splitter. He pauses to catch his breath. "When we built the house, gas was seventeen cents a gallon, and we heated with it. Now it's around a dollar, and we cut wood, which saves us about a thousand dollars. Still, the boys say they don't see any of that saved money, and there's something to that. I suppose we should take five hundred out of the farm account and put it in a vacation account." Dick feels that the ten cords of wood they put through two stoves is too much for their small house. "I'd like to take the siding off, put in better insulation, and put up nice clapboards." Another major item on the Some Day list.

At the moment, Dick is alone on the farm. Kevin and Becky are in school, and Joan has taken Jeff and Brian to a specialist in Burlington to check on their asthma. Dick interrupts his work in midafternoon to drive to the house for Becky, home on the bus after her afternoon kindergarten session. She changes into play clothes, and they return to work wood together, he lugging, positioning, and balancing the logs, she operating the lever. The scatter of woodstove logs grows on the meadow's edge, and, after Dick splits the last butt log (which had served as a prop to stabilize the splitter), the processing of the first elm is complete.

The second and third felled trees lie above the tractor road just to the north, where white pine, sugar maple, elm, red cedar (female trees already heavy with chalk-covered berrylike cones), and barberry are cheek-by-jowl over a bank of poison ivy. Dick sets up shop once again, and splitting continues. As with most dead elms, the bark-stripped limbs of these trees are liberally decorated with bark beetle engravings, which look like over-sized, skinny-bodied centipedes. The two-inch-long central tunnel is an egg gallery, dug by the tiny adult. The wavy centipede-leg side tunnels are the work of the larvae, and they broaden toward the "feet" as the larvae grow. Eventually the larvae pupate and leave as adults through holes in the bark, flying off in search of new trees to attack.

The second elm has not been dead as long as the first. It is not as dry, and its pink-tinged, wavy-grained heartwood resists splitting. Occasionally, indeed, the splitter succeeds only in embedding the wedge. Dick then swings his sledgehammer against the log end, trying to drive the log free of the wedge. Usually this works. If not, he drives in a free wedge and splits by hand until the log comes free. In either case, the log is then repositioned for another try. Even when the splitter is successful, these logs don't really *split*. Rather, the tough, fibrous wood is wrenched apart, accompanied by the agonizing straining and tearing sounds one associates with houses succumbing to bulldozers.

Dick stops and picks up a chunk of newly split wood, as something dark backs out of a tunnel. He watches as a heavy-headed, yellow-banded insect looking rather like an overlong, stout-bodied hornet emerges and works its wings. Soon other pigeon horntails appear on the woodpile, insects whose larvae eat wood softened by a fungus with which the adult female anoints her eggs. These insects, despite the ominous tail-end spear, are harmless, but Becky wants no introduction. Nor is she enthusiastic about the inch-long white grubs—probably borer beetle larvae—also found inhabiting the tree. Long since bored with levering the splitter, she sits on an upended log seat with a handkerchief neatly spread over another, apparently hoping that some unexpected occasion will require the laying of a formal table.

These two elms are smaller trees, and the splitting is finished by chore time. Dick and Becky head for the barn, and quiet returns to the fencerow. A flicker laughs from a dead elm down the way, this one protected by a thicket of pine, cedar, and citrus-scented prickly ash. A single monarch butterfly flutters by low, trying to make headway against a south breeze. The Treadway children have often brought monarch eggs home in summer or caterpillars in the fall, keeping them to watch them develop and metamorphose. This year they will be unlikely to find any milkweed-munching black-, yellow-, and white-banded caterpil-lars. For some reason, the midsummer monarch flight from the south simply didn't arrive, and the September return migration has been reduced to a trickle.

Back at the barn, Dick asks Jeff and Kevin if they'd like to take the open-bed manure spreader down and pick up a load of split wood. Not particularly. He then asks which they would rather do, pick up wood or milk, and, as Dick puts it, the boys are "out of the barn like a shot."

A COUPLE OF DAYS LATER, MORNING CHORES and breakfast completed, Dick decides the weather is right for working up more wood. He carries his chain saw down to the shop, where he secures it in the table vise. After installing a new part, he touches up the saw's curved teeth with a rat-tail file, counting strokes as he goes. He loads the chain saw into the back of the pickup, and he and Becky head south and then west to the pasture-bordering woods above Cutting Hill Road, fol-lowing Joan, whose Deere pulls the open-bed manure spreader. "We have put up wood with a foot of snow on the ground," Dick says, "but this is a lot easier."

It is another cool, crisp day, still in the upper 40s as Dick gasses and oils his saw and prepares to fell three manageable elms. He stands at the base of the first tree and chooses an avenue in which to drop it, one that will damage few other trees and will make the felled tree accessible to the splitter and wagon. He primes and chokes the saw and, bracing it with one arm, yanks on the starting cord with the other. It roars to life, and Dick cuts a wedge—straight cut first, then angle cut—out of the base of the tree facing the fall lane. He then slices halfway through the back of the tree toward the missing wedge, and the tree leans and falls. While he cuts the tree into eighteen-to-twenty-four-inch lengths (starting with two-inch-diameter branches for kindling), Joan maneuvers the wagon into position, unhitches, and is off to pick up the splitter, left down along the pasture edge, and to bring it up alongside the spreader.

The tree down, Becky is allowed out of the pickup, and she and her mother take turns operating the splitter and chucking logs into the wagon while Dick finishes the sawing. Finally, the shrill, throbbing, head-bruising scream of the chain saw ceases— Dick and Joan speak approvingly of ear protectors, but don't in fact use them—and quiet returns. "These woods are so beautiful in spring," Joan says; "violets everywhere. They're beautiful now, too. I was down in the far woods the other day looking for a couple of missing heifers, and it was so nice with the sun filtering through the leaves, and so quiet."

The second tree leans away from the direction of the desired fall. Dick stops his back cut short and drives two wedges into it, and the straightened tree drops where planned. The splitter and wagon can't be gotten close to the third tree, so he hooks a chain around the butt end to pull it out of the woods. He cannot pull it out in a straight line, however, and at one point he stops to rehitch the chain on the other side of a tree barring the way. It still doesn't clear, and when Dick gets the tractor stopped, the butt end is only inches from a direct collision with the standing tree, and the cut elm is much too heavy to roll over. "Sometimes you can fool a tree," he says. He backs the tractor up, loops the chain slack around the far side of the butt, eases the chain tense, and pulls. Sure enough, the tree promptly rolls over, and can then be dragged past the standing tree and out into the pasture for processing.

At eleven o'clock, Joan and Becky leave in the pickup. Becky will change into school clothes, and her mother, having driven the eleven-mile round trip to school in Shoreham village, will prepare lunch. Meanwhile, Dick finishes splitting and loading the three trees. The spreader is not quite full, and he cuts up a downed beech top and a downed hardhack to complete the load. He pulls the wagon back home, leaving it just past the front door, and he and Joan take a break for a lunch of grilled ham and cheese, fresh apple and raisin salad, and raw milk.

The Treadways seldom dawdle over meals, and this lunch is no exception. Fifteen minutes after sitting down, they are out front unloading wood. Joan stands in the spreader passing logs to Dick, who throws them through a paneless window into the cellar, where, in odd half-hours, the family will work at stacking.

The Treadways head back for the woods, Dick, in the pickup, shaking his head over Joan's latest emergency-squad experience. A call for help had come from Sudbury to Middlebury at 1:30 A.M. a couple of nights ago. "Joan figured she could get there quicker than Middlebury could, so I drove her down." They found a car parked on the side of a back road and a man lying face down in the ditch screaming bloody murder. On closer approach, they saw that it was not the face-down man who was screaming, but the young man—his son—upon whom he was lying in an attempt to restrain him.

"I tried to help his father hold him, but he fought like crazy. He was hollering that Satan was his father and loved him, and that he would be avenged on us. He said Satan would rip off our arms and kill us and we would roast in everlasting Hell." Joan tried, during a calm interval, to monitor his vital signs, but he screamed and swore and spat at them, and Dick pulled her back. After a time, state troopers arrived and handcuffed the young man, and the Middlebury ambulance took him away, leaving the Treadways not only saddened by yet more evidence of drug use in the area, but worried about the cult implications of this case.

Back in the woods, Dick brightens up, despite a clouded sky that now begins to spit rain from time to time. Late in the morning, he had spotted a larger Dutch elm disease victim, "a whole load in one tree," and he enjoys the challenge (and can't resist teasing Joan, who is always nervous about felling larger timber). There is no easy place to drop this tree. He studies various options, and finally decides. "If we can get it past that beech, she'll come down O.K." "We've got a twentieth anniversary coming up in December," Joan says with an edge in her voice; "put on your hardhat."

Dick gasses and oils his chain saw, and sets to work. The sixteen-inch bar is barely adequate for this tree. The front wedge-cut is no longer a simple double slice, but multiple around-the-tree cuts, and the wedge must be knocked out with the sledge. He checks his escape route, and works his back cut around the base of the tree. "It's coming!" Joan shouts, and Dick backs out in a hurry to avoid the danger of kickback. (The Treadways well remember the young professional logger from Shoreham who was killed in the woods nearly a decade ago— Joan had his son in catechism class at the time—when the butt of the tree he had cut kicked up and back, crushing him against a nearby tree trunk.) This tree does not jump off the stump, however. It twists off, and then comes down with a rushing, wrenching, tearing, smashing roar, like the soundtrack of a shipwreck in stormy seas. Halfway down, the elm top encounters a large beech, which it attempts to drive into the ground. The beech buckles but wins, ripping a major limb off the elm which the beech, in whipping upright, hurls back toward the elm's stump. It isn't enough to worry about kickback. "You've got to look up to see what's coming back," Dick says. "My father was cutting wood once by himself, and a limb came back and knocked him out. He eventually came to and got himself home, but there was blood all over."

Splitter and wagon are maneuvered into place, and Joan splits and loads while Dick cuts logs, starting at the top of the tree. This is not, at the moment, an ideal work site. Recent rain has left low spots, wheel ruts, and the six-inch-deep "anklesprainer" cow prints standing full of water, and fresh cow pies— on which orangish, hairy, long-legged, long-winged dung flies are mating, and on which their larvae will feed—are as perilous underfoot as banana peels, and less pleasant.

Two hours later the easy work is over, and Joan drives the pickup home to meet the school bus, leaving Dick contemplating the massive trunk sections and hoping Jeff will show up soon feeling muscular. He does, and he and his father take turns hoisting elm-trunk pieces up onto the splitter beam, knocking off the outsides and splitting up the heartwood. A colony of big, black carpenter ants boils out of one section of trunk, and Dick thumps the pieces on the ground to encourage evacuation. "Otherwise, they'll warm up sometime this winter and roam around the house."

Finally, only the butt pieces remain, logs which nobody wants to think about lifting, and which would be too large for the splitter in any case. Dick heaves the first up on end, spits in his hands after the manner of Paul Bunyan, and, wedge end of his sledge forward, swings over and down into the log, aiming for the outer margin of the heartwood. Too big a bite, and the wedge buries fast. Two small a bite, and the tool head glances off, endangering the wielder's legs and feet. Just right, and a concave slab peels neatly off the log. Dick moves in two circles around the butt piece, first knocking off the outer wood, then splitting off perimeter sections of heartwood, after which the log can be hoisted onto the splitter and finished up.

Jeff wants a try at hand splitting. With more height but less heft and experience than his father, he winds up for a terrific blow with the sledge, the downswing lifting both feet off the ground and the cap off his head. At first, he misses with his aim, but soon Jeff is knocking off elm exteriors, too, and he and Dick take turns hand splitting and power splitting the last of the mammoth butt logs, a task they finish wet with sweat.

The old elm presents one last problem, a limb hung up overhead. Dick unhitches the splitter, backs the tractor into position, throws the log chain around the reachable end of the limb, and pulls the "widow-maker" down. Jeff cuts the limb into lengths and splits the larger logs. It is chore time, and the two hitch up the wagon and start for the house, where they will recruit the three younger children to chuck this full load down cellar while they and Joan let in the cows and rinse milkers.

Better yet, another half-load of split elm lies ready for pickup down in the woods, something Dick and Joan, at least, will think of with satisfaction and comfort tonight when, for the first time since early spring, the temperature will fall into the 30s.

## 2

THE TREADWAYS WORK PUTTING UP WOOD FOR
ten days, off and on, and when the stacked rows in the cellar
look like ten or eleven cords, Dick puts the chain saw away and
turns his attention to the corn. For nearly a week he watches the
corn, watches the weather, and, as Joan puts it, "tinkers with the
machinery." The better part of an inch of rain falls, and then
dry, cool weather returns, with no immediate sign of Indian
summer. The corn isn't gaining much, and the 'coons are; Dick
decides on a Sunday to start chopping.

Jeff brings in two wagon loads, and then, he says, the chopper
"blew up." A universal joint in the power take-off shaft—whose
sole purpose is to enable the chopper to swing back behind the
tractor so that the rig can pass through gates—has, for no apparent reason, shattered, breaking one of two yokes holding it as
well. The chopper has not exactly "blown up," but it has been
completely disabled. The next morning, Dick calls around for
parts. The U-joint is available locally, but not the yoke. He
orders one next-day air through a Deutz-Allis dealer, and hopes
for a phone call.

The call comes late Tuesday morning, and, after lunch, Dick
loads both broken yoke and good yoke into the back of the
pickup and drives northeast into Middlebury and then north
on Highway 7 for Hawkins Bros. in Ferrisburg. Dick likes
Hawkins Bros. "I guess you'd say they're old-fashioned. They
don't have a big, fancy building like some of these other dealers, but I figure somebody has to pay for those buildings, and
it's probably the customer. Hawkins has been around for a
long time. They don't just sell equipment; they work on it,

too. And you can go right into the shop and watch and talk to them."

The sales room up front is shaped like a railroad car, and is no bigger. Not much room for displays here beyond some small tractor parts, some stacked lubricants, and a new-tractor-brochure rack. A Royal Crown soda machine stands beside the door, while prominent on the long counter is an open—and "weathered"—file of customer accounts. A man appears, says hi to Dick, and reaches him two packages from behind the counter. "You suppose I can get this put together?" asks Dick. "Sure," the counter man replies; "take it out back, and one of the boys will do it for you."

Dick pushes open a limp-knobbed door and walks down a ramp into a new equipment-storage room, where several men are loafing. A mostly eaten plate of ribs rests on the hood of a small tractor. Dick and the men pass small talk for some minutes, until someone feels like tackling the U-joint. After a time, someone does, and heads through another door with Dick into the shop. One side of the shop is dominated by two tractors under repair, including a mammoth Allis-Chalmers "broken" clean in two at the forward end of the cab. Boxes and a variety of parts and a crane stand on the shop floor. Medleys of hydraulic hoses hang from the ends of support beams jutting out under ceiling storage bays. A basketball hoop—long since isolated from use by changed storage patterns—hangs from a massive trolley door.

The man stops at the kerosene bath and cleans the original part—the good yoke attached to an override clutch which mediates between power take-off and chopper knives—then clamps it yoke up in the table vise. An examination shows that this yoke has been affected by the accident as well; its two holes are out of alignment. A second man joins the job, and, while Dick leans on a twelve-cylinder tractor engine and watches, one man anchors the vise while the other attempts to beat the twisted yoke back into true with a sizable hammer. A hammer blow goes awry, and the vise man, peering intently at his hand, says dispassionately: "That was my thumb, Henry; you spoiled my thumb."

Pounding doesn't help; so Henry drags a torch and tanks over to the bench, heats the twisted end of the yoke, and uses a pipe and hammer to straighten it up. A New Hampshire farmer drops by. He has glitches in several pieces of equipment, and, while they work on the U-joint assembly, the Hawkins men talk with him about them, asking questions and suggesting fixes. When the yoke seems to be in good alignment, the men seat the needle-bearing-lined caps through the yoke holes on two ends of the cross-shaped U-joint. When it doesn't turn easily, they fine-tune the yoke's alignment with hammer blows until it does.

They now install the new yoke over the other arm of the U-joint, and cap the ends. They secure the assembly once again in the vise, and once more take the hammer to the yokes, until at last they turn freely around the U-joint in both planes. Finally, they install a grease fitting in the U-joint and replace a second, which they have broken, in the override clutch. "Aren't you sorry you didn't tackle this job at home?" one of the men asks. Dick picks up his bill at the front counter: yoke, $55.50; universal joint, $22.50; next-day air freight, $17.50; labor, $25. "Not as bad as I thought it might be," he says, hoisting the assemblage into the bed of the pickup; "I'd like to get it installed before chores."

Dick settles back for the drive home, and ponders his new role as ambulance-driver-trainee for the Middlebury rescue squad, for which he is now taking Saturday classes. Don has groused some about his absences from the barn, but Dick has decided he wants to get into rescue with Joan. "The thing is, we think about the farm twenty-four hours a day. Rescue work gives us a break, something to look forward to. And we're helping people at the same time." He remembers a call that came through this summer. Joan and a colleague were first on the scene of a two-car accident on Highway 30 in Cornwall. "There were two broken necks in those cars; from what the medical people said later, it seems pretty certain they saved their lives."

There are no broken necks at the moment in the Treadway family, but more than enough other injuries. "I've always said they should name a wing of the hospital after us for all the business we give them," Joan says, "but this has been the worst year ever." This month has been especially taxing for Irene, who likes to send over cookies or pudding when a grandchild is sick or hurt. No sooner was Brian off his crutches than Kevin suffered a broken finger while wrestling with Jeff in the backyard. If Jeff was at fault, retribution was swift. Last week, while racing for the barn—first man in for chores gets to choose the radio station—he tripped and fell on cement, tearing up a knee.

"I mean, it was ugly," Joan declares. "The emergency-room doctor cut away a lot of tissue, and when he was done you could see through the hole in his knee right up into muscle tissue." At least nothing was broken. The doctor installed a drain in the knee, wrapped him up, sent him home with an antibiotic introduced just last year and without which, the doctor said, Jeff would have had to spend two weeks in the hospital for fear of infection.

Just home from school, Jeff hobbles down to the shop to help his father finish installing the U-joint assembly in the chopper. Dick has had to unbolt the gear box and remove the belt from the blower drive in order to widen the power take-off-shaft aperture and get the unit into place. Soon all parts are back in place and tightened down. Dick, Joan, and Kevin start barn chores while Jeff uses the grease gun on the two new fittings, and then—having been ordered by the doctor to stay clear of the bacteria-rich barn—he fires up the Allis and sets off to try the chopper.

When the milkers are on the first cows, Dick emerges from the barn and looks down the tractor road, up which a tractor pulls a wagon load of corn. "Looks like the chopper's working," he says.

3

THE DAYS ARE NOTICEABLY SHORTER NOW, and the Treadways are milking later in the morning. It is 9 A.M. by the time the cows are out of the barn, and, the boys already off to school, Don, Dick, and Joan finish chores. Dick is chucking bales of hay into the calf pens while Joan feeds fresh corn silage from a wheelbarrow, dumping a pile in front of each stanchion. With the unloader raised while the corn silo is being filled, the cows are getting only haylage in the feed bunk; so corn is being fed in the barn by hand. Joan goes back for load after load, powering the chop via auger directly from wagon to wheelbarrow.

The gutter cleaner scrapes its way around the central aisle, down which Don pushes the other wheelbarrow, throwing arcs of clean sawdust. "We don't need any more excitement today," he says, musing on yesterday's misadventures. First, a wheel came off a loaded corn wagon, and picking up a corner of a loaded wagon is a real chore, requiring a three-point hitch and tractor and two jacks. In the afternoon, a fire call came through. A barn in Orwell. Jeff was coming home on the bus and saw the smoke. "They say he was jumping up and down," Don says; "the bus wasn't going fast enough for him." The fire brigades weren't fast enough, either. "We saved the milking barn, but the one beside it burned down, and they lost some heifers in there."

Jim, the Blue Seal man, drives up just as chores are completed. He has come to bag a couple of samples of corn chop for analysis. "It's awful green," says Dick, and the two walk over to check the corn silo. Exactly a century ago a University of Minnesota bulletin recommending the virtues of chopped-corn silage defined a silo as "only a preserving can on a large scale." If so, this particular "can" is leaking pretty freely. A quarter of the way up, at the present level of fill, the juice in this green corn froths out interstave cracks like bubble bath and runs in constant streams down furrows and, leaking around off-load doors, down the chute.

Already the narrow area between silo and barn stands inches deep in liquid, and a ditch between the two silos takes the spillage south toward the feed bunk. "The cows are crazy about corn juice," says Joan. "When it gets down toward the bunk, they line up to drink it." "If we get some warm weather," Dick adds, "this silo will smell like a brewery." He had planned to have the silo repaired this fall, but the short corn crop has changed his mind. There are still a couple of doors of last year's corn in the silo, and Dick plans to add this year's crop. The silo, he figures, will run dry about midsummer next, which will give the silo men time to work on it and have it ready for more corn in September. In short, the drought will have provided a handy interim for silo fixing. At the same time, the Treadways will now have another winter through which to worry about the silo's stability. (Joan wasn't at all anxious about the integrity of structures until their barn, which was solid as a rock, came down; after that, she says, she found herself looking up all the time.)

Joan announces that she will shortly expire if a cup of coffee is not forthcoming, and invites the men up to the house for homemade apple pie. They walk through the living room—where Fred, the yellow tiger cat, lies, eyes closed in blissful peace, on the back of the couch between Becky's stuffed Alf and Kevin's current reading matter (2000 *Insults for All Occasions*)—into the kitchen, where Joan cuts pie and pours coffee. Jim is ebullient as ever, jesting and jousting, roaring with laughter. Like the ex-football player in the beer commercial, he tries to make trouble between Dick and Joan. They play along, enabling him to conclude with delight: "She's gonna *kill* you, Treadway!"

"He's more of a friend to us than a salesman," Dick says,

when Jim has hit the road, and he tells a favorite story. Dick had
stopped by the Blue Seal headquarters in Brandon to pick up
several rolls of barbed wire, and he asked for six Blue Seal
one-size-fits-all caps. "When you've got four kids, you don't ask
for two caps; and Joan and I each wanted one for the barn." The
counter man asked in the office, and returned to say that he
could have only two caps. Dick was ticked. "It seemed like when
you do something like thirty thousand dollars' worth of business
with an outfit, they could give you twelve dollars' worth of
caps." He walked out, leaving the barbed wire behind. "Next
morning, we're sitting here at the kitchen table. The front door
opens, a cat food bag shoots across the room, and the door
closes. We looked in the bag; it was six Blue Seal caps, six Blue
Seal pens, and six Blue Seal key chains. Then the door opens a
crack, and Jim says, 'Is it safe to come in yet?' " (Jim might well
have wondered whether it was safe to show up today. The latest
load of grain from Blue Seal was billed at $201 a ton. Dick asks
if grain has "topped out," but Jim is noncommittal.)

Joan will stay at the house this morning. In an hour, she will
take Becky to school, then drive into Middlebury, where she will
be on emergency-squad duty for the afternoon. Dick hitches a
catcher wagon to the chopper and drives the Allis down to the
far south piece of corn. An early frost has touched the corn in
the low corner of the field, but Dick would love to have seen a
hard frost hit the whole piece, draining the corn of excess water.
He knows this corn will chop "green," but it is particularly risky
to wait on this field. It is hilly in places, and a drainage swale
runs across the north boundary, both of which mean trouble
after autumn rains. If he does have to work on wet ground, the
smaller, flatter fields closer to the barn will be easier.

A sharp-shinned hawk takes a turn over the woods margin at
tree-top level, looking for a songbird lunch while drifting into a
southerly breeze. The sharpy moves on, luckily for the cuckoo
that flies up out of the corn and slips into the woods as Dick
begins to chop. He heads straight down the field from the gate,
where a starter alley has been left. It isn't quite adequate, how-

ever, and the tractor knocks a row down as the chopper works to the tractor driver's right.

The actual chopping and blowing of corn is identical to that of hay, and is accomplished by the same machine. The chopper "heads"—the delivery systems—however, are as different as the corn and alfalfa they are designed to handle. Dick has replaced the rotary-rake-and-auger hay head with a corn head, whose three flat-bottomed, torpedolike projections skim the ground out front, funneling two rows of corn back to pairs of dessert-plate-sized rotary knives, which whack off the stalks. The freed stalks are immediately captured by chain-driven pairs of soft belts, which "walk" them back to the chopper. A flat-bottomed U-shaped bar above prevents the plants from falling to the sides, and, as they approach the chopper, bends the tops forward, so that the stalks are fed to the knives butt-end first. As with hay, the chopped corn is blown up and out a curved chute into the following wagon.

Dick chops straight down the piece's interior, leaving two rows of mostly ten-to-twelve-inch stalk stumps, then swings around the western perimeter along a fencerow of cherry, aspen, elm, gray birch, white pine, sugar maple, ash, and sumac, among which stands a single red maple colored a glorious rose. West across a meadow on Norman's farm, a sugar maple in the woods margin shows spectacular orange-side-of-red foliage. These two trees are all the more conspicuous for their lack of competition, and now, on the last day of September, doubts begin to surface about this season's color. Basswood, hickory, and box-elder leaves are yellowing and coming down, but few maples in the Champlain Valley are turning the anticipated dramatic oranges and reds. Perhaps the drought has short-circuited the color show.

Don pulls up on a Deere with an empty wagon to exchange for a full one. "I'd sure as hell hate to be a squirrel this winter," he says, looking up into three nut-bare shagbark hickories. But the beech mast looks good this year, and, what with the corn being left on the ground on end-of-row turns and thanks to 'coon and cow work (thirty cows got into this field earlier in the week), there ought to be plenty of food for deer and raccoons, turkeys and squirrels this winter. When Dick has a load, Don drives the empty wagon into the piece, where he leaves it for Dick to back out of the way to unhitch and rehitch to the full wagon. "I could back anything with a team of horses," Don confides, "but these wide-front-end tractors are something else."

Two passes around the perimeter of the west third of the cornfield complete another load, which Dick drives to the barn. He gasses up the tractor, climbs up the corn-silo chute—trying to avoid the cascading rivulets—to tighten the off-loader belt, and walks up to the house for lunch. The kitchen is even more crowded than usual. A bucket of small potatoes stands by the refrigerator, and covering the floor at the far end of the table are three clothes baskets full of cucumbers and one of tomatoes, the raw materials for Joan's pickles. (Don has made pickles for the first time this year. "I never expected so many cucumbers could make so few pickles," he complains. "Irene told me they'd shrink, but I never expected they'd disappear.")

Dick puts cheese slices on two pieces of bread, adds sliced tomatoes and green peppers, puts the concoction in the microwave, and pours a glass of tea from a pitcher. He is thinking about yesterday's barn fire, and about the loss of livestock. "The thing is, it's hard to get cows out of a burning barn. They think they're safe in their barn, and even if you can drive them out, chances are they'll run right back in. Then it gets too hot to go in there. You can hear them bellowing, and there's nothing you can do. We used to want to shoot them, but the fire people say no. In the smoke and confusion, and with firemen around, somebody could be hurt or killed."

Dick's thoughts turn to his uncle. "Norman lost a barn to fire. Somebody was driving by about midnight and saw it. When we got there, the flames were burning up through one end of the roof. He lost ninety-some cows; just about his whole herd." Dick remembers his uncle with fondness. "He was an animal man, just as Dad is a machinery man. His cows and heifers would follow him around like dogs. He knew how to work. He'd work all day, and a lot of nights, too. He was right down the road all the years when I was growing up. Whenever we had a problem, he'd be right there."

Lunch over, Dick hitches up the empty wagon and returns to the south piece, which makes up perhaps a third of this year's thirty-five or so acres allotted to corn. This is the best corn on the farm. It has matured more evenly than that in the other fields, most of it at least seven feet tall and much of it eight to nine feet, with a full ear on nearly every stalk (and sometimes a second, smaller ear as well). The Allis pulls chopper and wagon steadily along, and soon Dick heads back for the barn, hoping Don has unloaded the other wagon after lunch.

Autumn marches forward, despite increasingly warm afternoon winds. If color is stalled in woodland and fencerow, it proceeds nicely in grown-up pastures and what wildflower guides call "waste places." The neatly aligned vertical rows of milkweed leaves are turning yellow, unchewed by monarch caterpillars. More dramatically, the waving fields of goldenrod are now counterpointed by two- and three- (even four-) foot clusters— living bouquets—of violet-purple New England asters, while smaller, pale-pink-lavender-blossomed arrow-leaved asters light up the woods and shady side of fencerows.

Far more numerous than either, but getting much less attention, is the tiny-flowered small white aster of roadsides and field margins. A particularly rich stand lines the fence on the east boundary of this corn piece, just above a sedge-filled low place edged with a hedge of pink-blooming smartweed. This three-foot-high shag carpet—its thousands of white blossoms attended now by flies and scores of honey bees—is impenetrably thick, except here and there a mysterious dark oval shows where a black and yellow argiope spider has drawn the flower stems aside, creating a hole in which to hang its web.

A bluebird calls from somewhere up the fenceline. Pregnant female praying mantises are thick in the meadows now, and in the pastures the crickets and grasshoppers, though still numerous, are less noisy and less active, the latter flying less vigorously when disturbed. Female field crickets are busy with egg laying. They search out cow pies of a certain age, pies soft in the center but dry, tan-crusted on top. Then, fifteen or even twenty-five crickets per prime pie, they crawl slowly forward, dragging their spearlike ovipositors. When the sensitive tip encounters a hole or crevice, they simply back the ovipositor down it and pump out their eggs, which will overwinter in place.

Jeff drives up in the Renegade to see how the corn chopping is going. Not many loads will go into the silo today, but it will be a different story over the upcoming weekend. With three hands working—one chopping, one off-loading, and one ferrying wagons—corn makes a load in a hurry. "If it doesn't rain, we ought to be able to finish this piece this weekend," says Jeff; "and that ought to fill the silo about half full."

## 4

A WEEK LATER, THE TREADWAY CORN IS IN. The corn silo is full, and Dick raises the unloader in the second silo and dumps the last couple of loads on top of the dwindling haylage. The volume of the corn crop is down about 15 percent, which is not as bad as Dick had feared (and not nearly bad enough to qualify for federal drought aid, which requires a 35 percent drop). If the third hay cutting is good, the farm will have an adequate supply of silage to feed through the winter.

Family fortunes, for the moment, have been less lucky. Infection has been discovered in Jeff's knee. Two strains of bacteria had been cultured and fought with antibiotics; a third strain had been missed, and flourished. Jeff went back to the hospital for surgery, and the bad luck continued. Spinal anesthesia proved

inadequate, and he had to be knocked out with sodium pen-
tothal. Surgeons cut straight across the knee, cut away the "hamburger" tissue, cleaned out the wound, and sewed up the knee,
leaving him to spend the better part of a week in the hospital
hooked up to IV antibiotic jars and enduring a constant spinal-
hangover headache.

As if Jeff's late-afternoon surgery appointment weren't
enough ("Dick says it's a mother's duty to worry," Joan says,
"and I was doing it"), Brian chose that particular day to get into
trouble at school. In the morning, a group of kids including
Brian were convicted of picking on a girl, and in the afternoon
he was hauled into the principal's office for talking in line (which
he denied). The principal informed the coach that Brian was not
to play in that afternoon's school soccer game. Brian came home
on the bus upset, and Joan called the principal to inform him
that she was shortly headed for the hospital where her oldest son
was having surgery, that she had spent an hour on the phone
arranging for rides to and from the soccer game for Brian, who
lived only for soccer, and that he, the principal, ought to be able
to think of an alternative punishment.

Recounting the story of the altercation, Dick shakes his head
in a mixture of chagrin over the whole incident and admiration
for Joan's spirit. She was trying to be nice about it, Dick says,
until the principal made a mistake. He was a busy man, he said,
and had been working on school problems from nine until four.
It is never wise for nine-to-fivers—much less nine-to-fourers—to
complain to farmers about their working hours, and particularly
not to one who two nights before had been down on the Richville Dam Road at 2 A.M. cutting the top out of an overturned
car to get at four beery teenagers, including one with a thrice-
broken neck. The parent-principal conversation, in any case,
came to an abrupt and unmellow conclusion. Joan sums it up
this way: "I couldn't afford to, but I gave him a piece of my
mind."

It is midmorning now, and Joan leaves for town to visit Jeff
before lunching and serving her shift at emergency-squad head-

quarters. (Jeff, who had looked forward to a soft hospital life—food in bed, attention from pretty nurses, twenty-eight TV channels—she will find, on his second day, already bored and planning escape.) Dick and Don, meanwhile, have their hands more than full with uncooperative cows. With the haylage unloader raised, only corn silage can now be fed in the feed bunk, and Dick doesn't want to feed straight corn. There is good food available in the big corn piece south down the valley and in an adjacent meadow too short to mow but with good alfalfa grazing. The trick is to get the cows to this feed. Earlier in the morning, a tractor had pulled a wagon ahead of the herd, dumping small piles of corn from time to time. About half the cows, successfully pied-pipered, now graze and pick corn contentedly, and Dick and Don are trying to drive the rest south. "If we can just get them to where they can see the others," Dick says, "I think they'll go right along."

But these cows have no intention of heading off into the southerly unknown. They are accustomed to feeding at the bunk and being milked in the barn, a routine they find entirely satisfactory. The thirty or so Holsteins are 150 yards from the barn and getting nowhere. They slip up into the woods, clamber down over ledge, stand stock-still. Their drivers holler, swear, and swing sticks, darting up hill and down to turn those that swing back toward the barn. It's frustrating work, and soon several animals break through the line of defense, leading a stampede north. Don gives up in disgust and follows them back to the barnyard. Dick sticks with a knot of forward beasts, and eventually succeeds in adding four animals to the south herd.

Dick stops at the mailbox on his way to the house for lunch, and comes away waving over his head in triumph a bill stamped PAID. "The mower's paid for," he says with satisfaction; "now we've got to come up with nearly four thousand bucks for town taxes." He enters the house to find Becky—undoubtedly pleased to find herself without sibling competition—jumping the TV video-game hero Mario (or is it Luigi?) over chasms and killer turtles. Her midday kindergarten group had met in the morning today, so that the whole class could visit a local orchard. Dick fries up a lunch of loose hamburger and sliced potatoes, after which Becky passes out small red apples, part of her morning's take at the orchard.

Back in the barnyard above the shop, Dick and Don set about the task of once more changing heads on the chopper. The corn head is through for the year; it will sit on the tractor path between the Treadway houses through the winter or until a place is found for it in the machine shed as hay bales move to the barn. Removing the corn head is no picnic. Don strains to lift the torpedo-studded front end with a massive bar to free connecting pins Dick is trying to drive out. When the head is finally off, Dick maneuvers the chopper carefully into position to attach the hay head. But the ground under head and chopper is unlevel, and the two U-shaped flanges don't quite line up in any plane with the large, axlelike rod they are supposed to grab. More straining fore and aft on the pry bar, and finally the flanges are forced over the chopper's attachment rod, and the two support bars angling to the bottom of the chopper are worked into place as well.

Yesterday morning marked the first substantial goose flight down the Champlain Valley, and now, as Dick adjusts the drive chain on the hay head, the tell-tale bugling from the northwestern sky resolves itself into a flock of ninety-odd Canadas. The birds advance, not in the classic V formation, but in a stretched-out, shallow U. A half-dozen geese, either latecomers or displaced birds, sidle back and forth in the pocket behind the lead birds, looking for an entrée into the tight line of flight. "A flock or two always stop on their way south and work our corn pieces." Dick is not, himself, a hunter. (His sympathy for the animal kingdom may have been inherited from his mother. His sister, Donna, vividly recalls an episode of forty years ago. She and her mother were cleaning out the chicken house, when, in the process of forking out soiled hay, they exposed and jumbled a number of baby-filled rats' nests. Irene surreptitiously re-formed the nests around the blind young.) The Treadways enjoy seeing geese on their land, and, says Dick, "we don't say much about it while they're here."


It is mid-October, a week since the first goose music was heard, and high autumn has arrived in central New England. Except for shaded sections, the mile after mile of gray shrub dogwood fencerow has turned from green to dull plum, the better to advertise the clusters of white berries to their seed-dispersing bird consumers, and robins are beginning to flock up and work those fencerows. White-throated sparrows and yellow-rumped warblers have flooded in from up-mountain and out of the north. On South Bingham, Cutting Hill's feeder road to the northeast, the annual September and early October slaughter of road-sunning snakes—mostly garters and northern browns, but the occasional red-bellied as well—mercifully nears an end, and the acrea moth caterpillars have passed from the scene, turning over the job of tirelessly crossing roads to their better-known relatives, the black-and-brown-banded wooly bear caterpillars.

It is still in the 90s in wide areas of the West, where smoke still rises from several terrible summer fires, but the drought already seems a distant memory here. It is a typical fall day, blustery and unsettled after a cold, showery night. Blue sky shows here and there, but high, dark clouds dominate the sky, and well below them bank after bank of white clouds hurries east from the Adirondacks, a few of whose outlines are darkly visible from the top of the northernmost rise on Cutting Hill Road. From this vantage point, the land drops away to the west and south, and in the distance the sun arbitrarily illuminates patches of the dark landscape, yellowing part of a hill here, whole mountains there. This will not go down as a great foliage-color season—the leaves of too many trees are simply rusting and dropping—but there is good color to be found, and in the middle distance the solar beacons highlight a clump of yellow aspen or orange and red sugar maples on the Pinnacle and in the nearer woods. Lining a rough drainage through a roadside meadow, the umbrella-shaped cloned colonies of staghorn sumac continue to flame even in the dull light.

Starling wolf whistles, robin peeps, and song sparrow alarm notes sound from a nearby fencerow. From the woods beyond come the nasal *erk* of a white-breasted nuthatch and the reso-nant, rolling trumpet of a pileated woodpecker. Crows and blue jays keep up an intermittent dialogue, and a single bluebird note floats up the hill on the west wind. To the south, the land drops abruptly to a stream, and on the upslope beyond, Diane Tread-way's sheep are discernible, head-down at pasture, and on the hill beyond them stand two familiar silos, a hay-filled machine shed, and parts of yellow and mint green houses.

On the farm, the vegetable world is wrapping up a season of growth. The new alfalfa meadow west of Diane's house is thrifty as can be. The eighteen-to-twenty-inch-high triplet-leaved plants are so thick and even that the meadow looks from a distance like a rich green lawn. In the tiny marsh isolated in the alfalfa, ten-foot-high narrow-leaved cattails undulate in the wind, and in the field corners maple sprouts are making a valiant attempt to color. Black-capped chickadees have flocked up into indepen-dent troops for fall and winter foraging, and one such flock, a solitary golden-crowned kinglet in tow, now sweeps into field-border white pines to search for insect tidbits.

Just beyond the south fence, in the heifers' wooded pasture, a massive red oak—measuring nearly seventeen feet in circum-ference—stands in splendid isolation. (Three major trunks sug-gest that it may originally have been three trees; if so, the seams in the bark tissue have long since become invisible.) The tree's leaves are turning straight from green to dead brown this year. What a glory it must be in other Octobers, with a spreading crown of brick red. In an open stretch of pasture beyond the oak, some goldenrod and a few late Queen Anne's lace are dominated by thousands of New England aster blossoms, holding their color though beginning to curl up after several hard frosts.

On higher ground to the north, buckthorn and barberry are showing good fruit, and red cedar and the prickly ground juniper are hanging heavy, promising a good waxwing winter and more than the usual few overwintering robins. Several clouded sulphurs are active in the pine- and cedar-studded pasture. The high, thin *tseet* note of a brown creeper issues from a stand of pines, and the dry chip notes of yellow-rumped warblers come from all directions.

Yellow-rumps are at work on the farmstead, too. One is stationed in a dead tree at the west end of the old horse barn. It flits from branch to branch, intently watching for insects. Now it sallies forth, grabs a flying insect, whirls—showing the yellow rump patch—and returns to the tree. It works up and down the tree on the barn side, examining the siding boards for lurking prey, and periodically flies up into the open mow door, taking flies at the hover. Two more yellow-rumps work the row of trees lining Don's garden, whence one flies over to try the pickings on the north end of the milking barn. It hops down the slanted power wire, darts up to the barn wall, detours to the mow door, deftly snapping up flies. Yellow-rumps will work the farm buildings and silos for flies (a feast awaits on the corn-juice-sweet first silo) for a couple of weeks before moving south.

Dick, Don, and Joan are in the barn cleaning up after morning milking, scraping out the two pens holding older calves and feeding hay. More cows have freshened, and nine new calves lie in hay along the stanchion lines. They moo mightily (one's voice in particular is surprisingly basso), sounding burry, like adult moos delivered through trumpet mutes. Two calves, their tails stained yellow from loose bowels, aren't vocalizing. Joan ministers to their "scours," a bacterial ailment common among calves, working giant pink caplets down their gullets. One of these calves—the circular black eye patches on its white face look like slipped earmuffs—hasn't been on its feet this morning.

Its nose, which ought to be pink, is a deathly white. Its ears droop and are cold to the touch; its eyes are slightly sunken.

"I don't like the look of that calf," Joan says. Then the animal coughs twice, deep down, and she suspects it has pneumonia. "I'll take its temperature when I get a chance," she says to Dick, "and we can give her penicillin if she's got it." "Don't bother with the thermometer; go ahead and give her a shot." But it is Dick who draws the penicillin into the syringe and administers the shot. (Joan hasn't given penicillin since the day she administered a dose to a cow named Stubby. Stubby's legs promptly splayed out, and she dropped like a stone. "Oh, my God," Joan wailed, "I've killed her!" "Seems like it," Dick responded, calm as ever. The penicillin-allergic cow was, in fact, nearly dead by the time they pumped adrenaline into her and reversed the reaction.)

"Let's do this heifer's foot now, too," Dick says, and Joan heads for the north end of the barn and hauls back the "foot box." A beam hook—it looks like a pair of ice tongs minus the handles—is the first tool needed for foot work. Dick hammers the pointed ends of the curved bars into the beam over the gimpy heifer, hangs a pulley from the secured hook, ties and hoists the right rear leg up to the level of the heifer's back. The animal strenuously objects to this treatment, throwing her weight from side to side on her free hind leg. Dick selects a foot knife—a knife with a long, thin blade which at the tip curves back on itself to form a U-shaped cutting edge—and takes advantage of the heifer's calmer intervals to attack a bad case of foot-rot.

Cows are forever injuring their feet, mostly stepping on nails, wire, tin, whatever, and the farmer doesn't know it until the infection has advanced to the point where it causes limping. Dick carefully slices away the bad tissue from the inside surfaces of the "claws" and from the footpad lying deep between them. The heifer doesn't think much of this operation, either. When he thinks he's gotten the worst of it, Dick rubs on a paper towel a thick smear of a black, tarlike substance advertised to draw rot and binds it up, towel and all, with a roll of gauze wrapped around the foot. Finally, he administers two shots of penicillin through the tough heifer rump hide, stabbing the inch-long needle up to the hilt.

Dick and Don find time to mow, chop, and unload a couple of wagons of hay after breakfast, and then it's lunch time. Joan puts a tuna-noodle casserole dish on the table with beans and milk, and finally convinces Brian to try some. He has stayed home from school, complaining of head and stomach pains. "Brian's already got enough problems for one kid to carry," Joan says, and now she fears he may have her family's digestive-tract troubles—everything from bleeding ulcers to colitis—as well.

After lunch, Dick and Joan climb into the pickup and drive south to the far meadow, where all the cows have finally learned good grazing is to be had, and where the problem now is to drive them back to the barn with the help of the headlighted three-wheeler in the mornings. Two cows freshened in the meadow sometime last night, and the Treadways want to transport the calves to the barn. Hundreds of generations removed from the pressures of natural selection, dairy cattle differ widely in terms of maternal behavior. Some ignore their calves from birth; others are fiercely protective.

The first calf is nowhere to be seen on the east edge of the meadow, where it had been spotted early this morning. The mother has hidden her calf, and is now feeding across the meadow with the herd. Dick and Joan begin to search in opposite directions along a rough stream drainage bordering the meadow. The calf may be well hidden, and in any case it will lie still and be silent. Joan pokes about through the heavy herb and shrub vegetation, and comes upon the calf secreted in a patch of goldenrod and brambles.

Like other heifers in her age class, the first-time mother of this calf was bred to a Jersey bull to ensure a small—and, it is hoped, easily delivered—calf. The resulting Jersey-Holstein cross is a soft brown color and calendar cute, with astonishingly long and thick eyelashes fringing large, limpid eyes in a doelike face.

"Thank God," says Dick, finding it a bull calf; "we've already got more heifer calves than we can keep." He ties a baler-twine lead around its neck, helps it to its feet, and urges it up the slope. Maternal orders, however, were to stay put, and it declines to follow, leaving Dick to hoist it into his arms and carry it back to the truck.

The second calf lies in the open on the far side of the meadow. It is a full Holstein calf, and a big one. Dick pushes and pulls it toward the truck, and is just heaving the struggling animal into the bed when a cow charges in response to the calf's distressed cries. "Uh oh," he says. "It's O.K., Spuds!" Joan hollers; "it's not your calf!" Spuds settles down, and other cows join her, until the pickup bed is ringed with staring bovine faces. Joan says cows are "nosy ladies," and they are curious about more than calves. Dick once checked a circle of staring cows in a pasture and found them puzzling over a flock of half-grown wild turkeys; and recently, when a stanchioned cow failed to eat her grain, they examined her and found fifty-three porcupine quills embedded in her nose.

The brown calf is perfectly placid during the ride back to the barn, but the bigger calf has other ideas. Suddenly it is on its feet and straining at the held baler-twine leash. Surprisingly strong and well coordinated for a newborn, it nearly succeeds in backing off the lowered tailgate before Dick manages to tackle it and throw a leg over it to discourage further forays.

Joan drives up to the barn to find a red pickup parked outside the milkroom. She and Dick exchange significant glances, and set about unloading the calves. A young man emerges to announce an unscheduled barn inspection by the Massachusetts Department of Agriculture. (Much Vermont milk goes to Massachusetts and Connecticut, and both states inspect here, as well as Vermont and Agri-Mark). Not all inspectors have a talent for getting along with farmers, but there is no trace of officiousness about this visitor, and the tension is soon broken. When he gets around to problems, they are the usual ones, and nothing of serious concern. ("You've got chickens in here." "Not as many

as we did yesterday; 'coons or something got two last night."
Fowl, which contribute their share of dung and dirt, are expressly forbidden in milking barns. Don has always liked to have
a flock of chickens around, however, and he continues to defy
authority by keeping a few. Barn inspections are like driver's
tests—you can miss a few and still pass—and so every new and
repeat inspector at the Treadway farm writes "Get chickens out
of barn" to no avail.) He points out that a particular part of the
bulk tank has not been properly cleaned, and he will return in a
week or two to check it again.

This was supposed to have been a haylage-making day, and
now milking time looms again. Don, at least, has been mowing
much of the day, so there is haylage to make. Dick hitches up the
chopper and sets off for a mowed meadow east of the farmstead.
Joan returns to the house to see after Brian and to study for a
recreditation emergency-squad test. That test will be given this
evening, as well as Dick's ambulance driver's exam. Joan is
looking forward to working shifts with Dick. "I'll be giving him
orders," she says with a crooked grin: "I hope he won't take it
too hard."

5

AFTER WEEKS OF UNSEASONABLY COOL WEATH-
er, a weekend's worth of Indian summer arrives on southerly
breezes, and on Saturday Joan proposes a picnic hike up Money
Hole Hill after church on Sunday. Evening milking nearly
puts the kibosh on the plan. When a cow began to back out
of a stanchion Joan was closing, she grabbed at the animal
in an attempt to stop it, and the Holstein swung her massive
head to the side, smashing Joan's hand against a wooden par-

tition. X-rays were inconclusive, but the doctor thought her index finger might be fractured. He put a cast on it and sent her home.

By Sunday morning, the cast was off ("It was a bother"), and Joan played the organ for the church service as usual ("I sneaked in a Protestant hymn," she says, feeling slightly wicked). The picnic may as well proceed, she decides ("It's my hand that hurts, not my feet"), and store-bought grinders, potato chips, and a large bottle of soda are divided among three school back-packs. Joan packs her camera case as well, and she, Kevin, Brian, and Becky pile into the van and head down Cutting Hill Road, leaving Dick and Don to make haylage while Jeff hobbles about the house in his soft leg cast.

Joan pulls off the road on Norman's land and parks beyond a farm dump sporting rolls and rolls of baler twine, fencing wire, paint cans, innertubes, tin roofing, a set of bedsprings, two re-frigerators, and a rusted cash register. The family pass a couple of dozen bee hives backed up to the base of the hill, their east-facing entrance slots busy with activity on this 60-degree day, and start up an old logging and sugaring road already filling up with maple leaves. The road climbs inside the hill's west-facing cliff face, and here and there one can see across the narrow but deep valley to a heavily wooded ridge beyond.

The road turns away from the cliff and then ends, and soon the party emerges from woods into an open, parklike plateau which the Treadways call the butternut orchard. As a nut pro-ducer, the grove has seen better decades. The trees are what foresters call "post-mature," their hollow trunks holding aloft nearly as many dead limbs as live. "I can remember cracking butternuts to make fudge with my grandmother," Joan says; "your hands would be sore for three days afterward." Kevin, who has scouted the trip with his father and grandfather, leads the way cross-lots, coming at last to an old stone wall, rising and falling in an east-west line across the land.

The wall is in surprisingly good shape, four feet high for long stretches and supporting great fallen trees without complaint.

The hikers turn west along the moss- and lichen-encrusted wall, stepping over maple and beech leaves and the tiny lilac blossoms and hairy leaves of scattered small-flowered cranesbills. There may be autumn colors in the canopy, but summer lingers on the floor of this shady woods. While pasture mulleins have long since been reduced to bare stalks, a five-foot specimen here still holds its velvety leaves, and yellow blossoms adorn the head of its flower spike. Along the wall, three Canada violets hold up yellow-throated white blossoms showing just a blush of light purple.

A second stone wall ties into the first. It heads purposefully north, suggesting intentions long since abandoned to the homogeneity of these second-growth woods. The wall descends a hill to the north, and from the top one can see it deviate—for no apparent topographical reason—in graceful arcs to left and right. Presumably the builders were skirting obstacles of which no trace remains, working at a time when stones were plentiful (they still are) and labor was cheap. (The astute English observer William Cobbett found that the typical American farm laborer earned $1 a day, or a third that with room and board, in 1817–18; a half-century later, a USDA report still lists average wages for Vermont farmhands as $1.08 a day, or 69 cents with board. A general hand today, should the Treadways need to hire one, would expect $200 per sixty-hour week plus housing and milk for his family and a side of beef a year.) Continuing west, the first wall abruptly disappears, giving way to fifty feet of zig-zag rail fence. Then more stone wall, and then Kevin gestures beyond and announces: "Here're the money holes!"

Just below the wall, indeed, are several minor declivities, like incipient Florida sink-holes, which a passerby would be unlikely even to notice. Beyond these, however, is a kind of slope-sided trench, perhaps five feet deep and eight feet wide at the wall end, becoming shallower and narrower through its twenty-foot length. Two dead trees rise from the trench, now grown up to maple saplings and clumps of leathery-leaved marginal woodferns. If this really is one of the original money holes that nearly cost a Treadway ancestor his life, it must have been quite a digging before two centuries of time and weather worked to fill it and soften its outlines.

The Reverend Josiah Goodhue, Shoreham's last-century chronicler, reports the story this way: "About the year 1794 many people in this and the neighboring towns were excited, by one of those singular instances which in former times was regarded as an omen of some hidden treasure, revealed by a mysterious supernatural agency. The cause of this excitement, which lasted several years, and induced many to dig for money, is thus given by one living near the scene of operations. 'A man of the name of John M'Ginnis dreamed one night that a man came to him and said if he would, in the morning, take his butcher knife and go to Mr. Treadway's and grind it, and not tell any one why he did so, a large dog would come to him while grinding the knife, and if then he would go alone to a certain place and commence digging by the side of a log, a small sized man would come to him just as he should get near the money, and that if he would not speak to him, but kill him, he would succeed in getting it. The next morning M'Ginnis began to follow out the suggestions of his dream. While grinding his knife, Treadway's dog came to the grind-stone. He then went to the place designated and commenced digging. After digging for a while, he took his crow bar, and striking it into the ground he thought he heard a noise, like the jingling of dollars, when he involuntarily exclaimed, "There, I've found it!" and looking behind him, he saw Mr. Treadway close by him, answering in appearance to the vision of his dream. Instead of killing the man, as directed, he kept on digging, but heard no more jingling of dollars, and found no money. But others, excited to dig for the precious treasure, saw strange sights, and heard strange sounds, which for a long time kept up the mania for money digging.' "

The kids pick out a picnic spot north of the money holes and divide up the grinders ("I love ham!" says Becky; "I want salami!" says Brian). "The Treadways owned all the land along here," Joan says. "There were something like five Treadway farms on the next road west. Unfortunately, your great-great-grandfather Will took to the bottle after he was blinded by a falling barn beam, and he lost most of it." If the family's genealogical records are accurate, the Treadway who figured prominently in the money-hole incident must have been either William, along with his brother Josiah the first Treadway in Shoreham, who would have been about ninety, or one of his middle-aged sons. From the story we know only that he was apparently small of stature; and whether that might have described William or a son no one now knows.

"According to the tale," Joan continues, "people dug here and there all over this hill during the following years looking for treasure. Two old women—they called them the two witches of Shoreham—lived down at the end of our road. They sold food and things to the fortune hunters, and they seem to have worked at keeping the legend alive." Brian suggests that earth-moving equipment be brought up here to settle the treasure question once and for all.

It is a soft, lazy day, quiet here except for the talk of crows and jays, and, from time to time, the mechanically punctuated squeals of a chipmunk back in the woods. The younger picnickers soon tire of food and of the view over a low woodland opening thick with goldenrod and snakeroot, both now fuzzing out to seed. Kevin sets out to explore along the stone wall with Becky. ("Yes, Mom," says Becky, unprompted, "we'll be careful." "Thank you, Becky," Joan responds, smiling.)

Brian, meanwhile, has found a natural climbing tree, and, despite his mother's objections, proceeds to climb. The tree is a granddaddy hop-hornbeam, nearly four feet in circumference. At head level, its trunk gives way to major limbs, which swing out and then up, like candelabra arms. "It looks like the tree is flexing its muscles," comments Brian, at ease in the tree's interior. Kevin and Becky return, and Becky starts to inch her way up toward Brian's yellow T-shirt. Brian discourages her advance by bombing her with leaves stripped from a neighboring maple and with handfuls of the hop-hornbeam's shreddy bark. Becky cries foul, prompting maternal intervention.

The children get back to work on grinders and chips and soda, and soon the lunch is finished. Antsy to get on with something else, they don backpacks and start back over the wall. "I just want to take a nice nap," Joan groans, getting up to go. On the way back she stops two or three times to take a picture. She points the camera into a downslope glade of young sugar maples, hoping the film will somehow catch October peace and quiet and warmth as well as vertical trunks in soft light, but fearing she will get only another picture of trees. She laughs apologetically as she puts her camera away. "Dick will say, 'What did you take that picture for?' "

## 6

AUTUMN COLOR NEVER LASTS VERY LONG, AND this year a week of off-and-on wind and rain write a quick finish to a less-than-spectacular foliage display. Late-turning maples hold their lower leaves for a time, but they, too, succumb to alternating rains and frosts. "I'd rather see snow than this cold rain," Dick says, collar up in the muck of a drenched barnyard, and Joan agrees that, when the skies are as gray as the woods, the month before Thanksgiving can be a dispiriting season.

Late October is not at all gloomy for Brian, not as long as soccer lasts, and he is back in the good graces of school officials in time for the big game with Cornwall, long a soccer power in these parts, and undefeated again this year. The teams square off—Shoreham in maroon, Cornwall in red—on a playground field sloping gently to the west. It is hustling, competitive soccer, with good rushes on both sides. Brian is a defensive wing, working the middle of the field trying to frustrate Cornwall attacks. Both schools have enough players for two teams, and the eager sideliners hang about the coaches, pleading to be inserted. ("I'd like to get in there and play, too," responds the young man in jeans coaching the Shoreham team.)

Like soccer games at all levels, this one is a defensive struggle, both teams having trouble finishing off rushes. The score is 1–1 going into the final minutes when, urged on by home-field fans, Cornwall turns up the heat, carrying play into Shoreham's end. Two final attacks end in near-misses, and the parent acting as timekeeper hollers time. That the tie is a moral victory for the visitors is clear in the teams' demeanors. The Cornwall kids walk off the field in mild dejection, while Brian and his teammates leap about and scream for joy.

Back at the ranch, the Treadways have been working between rains to get the last of the haylage put up before Halloween. If the second cut of hay was abundant but of relatively low quality, the third proves to be the reverse. Mostly alfalfa, it is rich stuff—testing 22 percent protein—but there isn't much of it; the cutting fills but half the second silo. Dick will simply divide the amount of haylage in storage by the number of days until first-cut hay will be available next spring, and the resulting figure is what the cows will get, a short ration supplemented by baled hay fed in the barn.

Halloween follows a cold night, the first of the season to reach the teens, and the hard frost leaves car windows glazed opaque and roof shingles whitened. Afternoon finds Dick stirring the manure pit and hoping for dry weather ahead, so he can spread the harvested cornfields and plow them. Joan, meanwhile, is folding laundry. Piece after piece of load after load is added to one of six piles growing ceilingward on the kitchen table. She isn't always sure to which pile a particular shirt or pair of jeans should be consigned, and Becky, home from school, adds a second opinion. "Those are Kevin's," she says of a pair of pants her mother has added to Jeff's pile.

Socks are much the biggest challenge. Joan first sorts them into subsets: all white here, red stripes there, blue stripes, gray stripes, brown stripes, mixed stripes. Then she takes them a pile at a time, trying for size and pattern matches. "Here's a pair," she announces triumphantly, and turns one sock inside out around its mate. She is not discouraged to end up with the better part of a bushel of unmated socks. Perhaps some of their fellows are merely lost, and will turn up in the fullness of time.

Jeff arrives home from school driving one of the Shoreham fire department's tankers, whose engine has been worked on by his high school mechanics class. He shortly leaves in the tanker with Don. They will pick up a load of water and deliver it gratis to a new house in town, whose septic tank needs to be filled and covered before the ground freezes. Jeff is supposed to return early to help with chores, as Joan has promised to take Becky and Brian trick-or-treating. Once the cows are in place and milking begun, Joan leaves for the house to check on costumes and hit the candy trail. Jeff has not returned, and Kevin and an upset Dick are left to milk alone.

Becky is a bunny this year. Zipped into a pink sleeper pajama, she sports pink bunny ears and a round cotton-ball tail. Joan paints black whiskers on her cheeks and reddens her nose, and she is ready to venture forth. Brian, who is less enthusiastic about the costume aspect of the holiday, wears an old pair of overalls, a bowler hat, and a truly hideous mask representing some sort of subhumanoid creature, gat-toothed and with little, round, misaligned porcine-cruel eyes.

The kids pile into the van with their plastic treat bags, and Joan heads out into Whiting, plotting the order of stops, wondering who will be home and serving at this early hour. A couple of houses are not yet receiving ("Uh oh! No porch light here"), but probably Laney will be home baby-sitting her sister's new baby. Laney is home, as well as her boyfriend, John. LeRoy, an old beagle mix, is also home. LeRoy doesn't like the looks of the pink bunny or the subhumanoid. He barks and barks. Laney passes a basket full of boxed caramel corn. Joan would like to see the new baby, but it is sleeping.

On the way out, the Treadways bump into Laney's sister, just coming up from the barn. "You may as well go on up to our place," she says to Joan; "we're headed home now." She and her husband have just completed a new log home, and Joan and the kids are happy to stop for a house tour, commenting on the good smell of wood and the open spaces. ("Wow!" says Brian, staring up from the living room all the way to the roof over the second story.) They leave the house just in time to meet LeRoy huffing it up the drive. He glares at the bunny and the subhumanoid. He barks and barks.

Joan drives back into Shoreham for more stops. The van pulls up at the house of Brian's gym teacher, who rotates among area elementary schools, and at the home of Jeff's girlfriend. ("Well, she's not exactly his girlfriend," Joan says. "She's fifteen, and her parents won't let her date until next year. With all the problems teens are susceptible to, I think that's great.") They stop at Bob and Terry's, and at the house of Donna and Yves, the Treadways' neighbors and close friends, with whom they eat out from time to time or attend a dance. When it's time to go, Becky has long since disappeared with confederates, and she is nearly left behind. Donna laughs: "When I've got Becky here and call up about bringing her home, and I get one of her brothers, they say, 'Don't bother; you can keep her.' "

Back in the van, Joan says: "We'll make one more stop and then go home. O.K.?" Apparently satisfied with visits to eight or nine friends' homes, Becky and Brian agree, and at 6:15 the three arrive home to find the lights out in the barn; perhaps Jeff had returned in time to help after all. Joan elicits Jeff's help now with getting the dogs indoors, fearing one might bite a trick-or-treater. "I don't need a lawsuit," she says; "it's only Monday."

Dick has cleaned up after chores, and emerges from the bathroom end of the house in town clothes. He did his weekly 6 P.M. to 6 A.M. emergency-squad shift in Middlebury last night, but has agreed to take today's evening shift for a colleague who wants to attend a dance. Kevin has a dance tonight as well, at the junior high school. He is going as an Aussie, dressed in bush shirt, safari hat, and riding boots. (To the disappointment of his brothers, he has no boomerang or Crocodile Dundee–style knife.) The dance hours are, like Dick's shift, 7 to 10, which will provide him handy rides both ways. On the way out the door, Dick says to Joan: "Number thirty-six has started to freshen. Will you check up on her tonight?"

Jeff stokes the cellar wood stove, eats a bowl of cold cereal, then flops down on the living room floor to put Mario and Luigi through their video paces. Becky wants the pillow he's lying on, and, when he ignores her request, enforces it by walking up his back. Joan turns the responsibility of handing out candy over to Jeff, pulls on her barn boots, grabs a flashlight, and hikes down to the barn to see what progress the mother-to-be is making.

She switches on the interior lights, revealing a barn full of stanchioned cows—they continue to spend days outdoors, but remain overnight now in the barn—mostly chewing hay. She upends a petroleum bucket several cows down from number thirty-six, and sits down to keep watch. The freshening cow is lying down, a narrow wooden platform placed behind her to cover the gutter. She is breathing hard, but shows no sign of discomfort. Protruding from the birth canal is the leading bulge of the amniotic sac, turgid like a water-filled balloon. Vaguely discernible through the white membrane are two feet, Joan hopes *front* feet (rear feet or one of each or all four first means trouble). The amniotic sac, she knows, is tough. "You hope it breaks when the nose is born, so the water is gone when the calf takes its first breath."

Thirty-six stands up, and the sac retreats out of sight. She lies back down, and shortly the sac reappears. Her body heaves with a series of contractions, and the bagged feet ease rhythmically out an inch and back, out an inch and back, out and back. Runt climbs into Joan's lap and snuggles, a miniature black panther with a soft spot for people. Thirty-six gets her feet under her and heaves herself erect, Joan groaning even before the extruded calf parts slowly disappear. Some births are quick and easy; others take hours. "It's best to let them do it at their own rate. My father throws twine around the feet as soon as they appear and drags the calf out. He says he hates to see the cow suffer. But we think they do it best at their own speed."

The cows begin to lie down now, many relieving themselves of dung and urine first, making Joan's seating situation precarious. (The platform is placed behind the freshening cow not so much to prevent the calf's injury through a fall into the gutter as to prevent its drowning therein.) Runt apparently finds all the plopping infectious. He climbs down from Joan's lap, paces sedately to the nearest pile of clean sawdust awaiting morning spreading, and, with an air of great dignity, digs a pit, defecates, covers, and returns.

Thirty-six is down again and up again, the calf feet emerging and retracting, the lubricating birth fluids drooled out in viscous ropes. When after an hour the birth has made no progress, Joan walks up to the end of the barn for a pair of plastic gloves and surprises a raccoon drinking at the cats' milk pan. It skedaddles—after the rump-high fashion of its kind—down a side aisle, and Joan returns to check the cow, working a gloved hand in over the extruded sac. "The head's right there," she says to the would-be mother; "let's get on with it." She breaks the sac, which sometimes precipitates the birth. But thirty-six is in no hurry.

Runt climbs about Joan, luxuriating in the stroking. His littermate, Spook, sneaks into the north end of the barn for a quick drink of milk. Oddly enough, this cat, born to the same mother and afforded the same treatment in the same environment, cannot yet be closely approached by any human being, leading Joan to wonder if perhaps Spook had a different father. Their mother approaches Joan, and Runt—now the larger of the two—is down in a flash and confronting her, spitting and showing the claws of a raised paw. "Is someone jealous of attention here?" Joan asks.

After what seems ages, the borning calf begins to make real progress. Its front feet separate, and a new series of contractions produces the end of a nose, from which hangs a purple tongue. (Runt chooses this moment to launch an attack on the tuft of hair at the end of the laboring cow's tail, batting it with his paws. "Come on," Joan objects; "she's got enough problems.") Thirty-six is pushing seriously now, and slowly the calf's head emerges. Joan cleans out the nose and strips the amniotic membrane from the eyes. The black head hangs limp over jutting white legs. To all appearances, the calf is dead; but Joan feels a strong pulse, and knows it is alive. When the calf is half out, she pulls on its front legs, and it shoots out in a rush, wet and slippery in fluid and blood, dropping unceremoniously from a 101-degree cow interior to a 40-degree barn floor. Joan quickly cleans out the nose again, and urging "Come on, breathe!" slaps the calf smartly under the shoulder. And then it does.

A relieved thirty-six lurches to her feet and stares back at her calf in apparent amazement. Joan checks to make sure the umbilical-cord attachment isn't bleeding, then drags the calf by the front legs to the front of the stanchion, under its mother's head. The Holstein immediately begins to lick her calf, which is liberally decorated with hay and sawdust. She lays on with vigor, and the massive tongue sends the sitting calf sprawling on its back. It shortly rights itself, however, and once more submits to maternal ministrations. The calf will be up and looking for its first meal in several hours. Part of the placenta hangs from the new mother; if all goes well, she will expel it sometime in the course of the night. (Sometimes cows don't, leaving a vet the tricky task of going in after it.)

Cold and tired, Joan turns out the barn lights and starts across the barnyard and past Don and Irene's house for home. It is clear and cold—more a winter's night than an autumn one—and, noticing the brilliance of the stars, she turns off her flashlight and looks up at Cassiopeia and the North Star. She and Kevin are "sky nuts," she says. "We'll sit up some nights and watch the satellites go over, or I'll wake him up when there's a good display of northern lights. The rest of the family think we're crazy."

Joan pulls off her barn boots inside the front door of a warm house whose only sound is the voice of the alien, Alf, on the television. Alf is Becky's favorite, but tonight she lies—still bunny-suited and whiskered—sound asleep on the couch, her blue security blanket clutched firmly in one hand, a finger of the other in her mouth. Brian is dead to the world as well, curled up on the floor. Jeff is half awake on the other couch, a pile of trick-or-treat candy-bar wrappers on the floor beside him.

Shaking her head over her eldest's lapse into "sugar stupor," Joan proceeds into the kitchen, where she fixes and eats a fried-egg sandwich. She is thinking about getting the younger children to bed and retiring herself when the phone rings. Dick is at Porter Hospital in Middlebury. A security guard at the college has had a seizure, and the Porter doctors fear an embolus may be headed for the brain. Dick will shortly have to drive him to the big hospital in Burlington. Can Joan pick up Kevin at ten o'clock? She can. And Dick, who, alone among the family, has done no Halloweening at all, will have the longest Halloween of all.

## 7

MID-NOVEMBER APPROACHES. DICK STANDS ON the west side of the barn running haylage into the bunk and contemplating problems. Behind him is a silo full of chopped corn he can't feed, a piece of the unloader blower housing having broken out, shutting the whole system down. A replacement housing was not available at area farm-equipment dealers, and one has been ordered. Dick hopes it will arrive today. In the meantime, he has no option but to feed straight haylage, already in short supply.

Although cows prefer corn, they have no objection to this sweet third-cut hay. Many are lined up at the bunk, chewing enthusiastically as the tracked elevator passes by, dumping feed on their heads. More cows approach up the runway from the south end of the barn, pacing with slow dignity through a deep layer of dung pounded to the consistency of freshly poured cement. And that's another problem. Off the east end of the bunk, the organic sludge creeps steadily downhill toward the road. "We should have poured a platform on the end when we put in the bunk," Dick says, "so we could scrape manure into a spreader; but at the time we didn't have the money to do it." Now they will have to wait until the brown cement hardens some through freezing, then scrape it up with the bucket loader for dumping into the open-bed spreader.

Don drives up on a tractor to remind Dick of another problem. He has found several missing heifers mixed up with his nephew Charley's at the south end of the farm. "They'll never be easier to drive back," he says. "If you can give me some help, we'll do it now, and then check fences down there." Dick picks up the barn phone and calls the house, asking Kevin and Brian— home by virtue of an in-service school holiday—to drive down on the ATV, and the four start south, Don on a Deere (fencing tools and materials in the bucket loader), Dick in the Jeep, and the boys on the three-wheeler. Dick breaks away from the caravan, driving cross-lots down the middle of a corn piece which, he rightly figures, is no stickier than the road and unrutted. Here, too, he has corn stubble for traction, but the Renegade still side-slips on the gentle grade, and would be hopelessly mired without four-wheel drive.

Having arrived at the south boundary, Dick and the boys circle around behind the wary heifers, walking those with yellow ear tags toward the gate, which Don guards against Charley's animals. One at a time the escapees are driven through the gate, until all five are back on the north side of the fence. And then

Dick finds a sixth. "We must have miscounted the others," he muses. The gate closed—its end post inserted, bottom first, into two restraining wire loops—Dick and his father walk the line, trying to locate the porous spot(s). They find a couple of likely candidates, driving a new cedar post here, splicing in new wire there.

The bright sun of early morning has long since been lost in a gray, glowery day, and Kevin, complaining of the cold, hops into the Jeep. "You can drive the ATV back," he says to Brian, and the boys and Dick start for home, leaving Don to drive the field perimeters, looking for more fence problems. Halfway back, Brian's three-wheeler slips into a water-filled pothole the size of a bomb crater, his spinning balloon tires throwing back arcs of muddy water. Dick climbs out, and together they push the ATV out and proceed home. "Go fix lunch," Dick hollers as the boys run for the house. He backs the Jeep up to the farm gas tank, inserts the rubber nozzle, and drives the rotary pump handle around and around to fill up the Renegade. Buying gas and diesel fuel in bulk used to save farmers money. It doesn't any more, but, as Dick says, it's handy having it available on the farm.

Back at the house, half the family is missing. Jeff is off on a great adventure in Kansas City, attending a Future Farmers of America–sponsored agricultural convention, a prize in recognition of his outstanding work in the technical program at his high school. "He's the first member of the family to reach the Mississippi," Dick says. "Their plane flew in low over the river. He called and told us about it. He was pretty excited." Joan has taken Becky to school and proceeded to town to serve her rescue-squad shift, leaving a casserole in the oven.

Kevin dishes up the pasta casserole while Brian mixes himself a sandwich filling of tuna and mayonnaise. The sight of people eating seems to energize the two house cats in the room. Rocky, apparently asleep on the dust cover of the stereo's turntable, rises, stretches, pads over to and climbs upon the aquarium. Splaying her front feet to gain purchases on kitty-corners, she leans far down into the half-empty tank and drinks. Mosey, the other cat, decides to lunch. He stands tall at the side of the plastic pail containing dry cat-food pellets, one front paw resting on its rim. The other foreleg is lowered into the pail, then carefully raised, the leg straight and stiff, and paw cupped, supporting pellets. Several spill onto the floor. Mosey first eats those still on his paw, then cleans up the drops. "Why doesn't he just knock over the pail?" Dick wonders.

What Dick wants to be doing today is plowing a corn piece, and after lunch he decides to have a try. He has plowed a couple of sections of meadow to replace corn tracts being retired this year, and even on grass it has been slow going. It would be pointless to try to plow a bare cornfield without chains, and he now recruits Kevin and Brian to help put a pair on the Allis. The chains lie in a heap in one of the open bays of the machine shed. Dick leans over the pile and sets patiently to work separating one from the other. That takes twenty minutes, and another half-hour to straighten one set out on the ground. Meanwhile, the boys horseplay among the hay bales, Brian threatening to let Kevin's rabbit out of its cage, Kevin encouraging Brian to roll off the stacks of bales, which he does, nearly breaking his neck.

Disentangled and straightened out, a set of chains presents two parallel rows of heavy iron links, from which short link spurs jut inward, holding between them Frisbee-sized round iron pieces with cleats projecting from one face. Dick hammers on and closes a couple of replacements for missing links, makes certain all round irons are cleat side up, and calls for help. Brian climbs into the tractor cab and leans out the window on the near side, while Dick and Kevin struggle over with the chain and, straining, lift the draped central sections up over their heads to the top of the rear tire, where Brian grabs hold and helps wrestle it into place over the treads.

Dick tugs and straightens and centers the chain while Don, summoned from his house, inches the tractor forward until the loose ends are at the back top of the massive tire, where Dick hauls at them while Don backs and forwards until they can be fastened, inside chain first, with the terminal hooks. Dick got these chains a couple of years back as payment for plowing another farmer's fields, and he considers himself well paid. "A set of these chains cost between five and seven hundred bucks," he says; "they're a pain to work with, but you can't get along without them."

Disentangled and laid out like the first, the second chain is discovered to lack a fastening hook on one side, and the family disperse to sheds and barns to search for a replacement. No one can find anything remotely similar, leaving Dick little choice but to improvise. Using hammer and chisel, he takes the hook unit off an old set of chains and puts it on the new. The crew lift the second set, struggle around the tractor, slipping in the muddy ruts, and maneuver it into place. The replacement hooking mechanism is shorter than the original, and Dick has the devil's own time tightening the chain enough to fasten it, but finally he succeeds.

The wind has turned into the north, and the temperature has dropped since morning. Everybody wears a field coat except Dick, who wears a one-piece coverall over a flannel shirt. Like his father, he works without gloves, getting a better feel of the work with bare hands, which are now caked with mud. He walks down to the milkhouse to wash up, and then he picks up the barn phone to resolve another issue that's been weighing on his mind since halfway through morning milking, when it was discovered that someone had by mistake put a milker on a dry cow.

How much milk had she given, and had there been enough dry-off medicine left in her system to contaminate the milk? Milking over, Dick took a sample from his bulk tank, and Joan has delivered it to the milk plant for a quick test. If the test finds dry treatment, the Treadways will have to dump two milkings— about 2,700 pounds of milk—down the milkroom drain. Well, they wouldn't *have* to. "Farmers have been known to ship milk they knew had stuff in it," Dick says; "but the pickup drivers take samples at every farm, and if the stuff shows up in the plant test and is traced to you, you've bought a whole tanker load of milk." The voice on the phone checks and reports, and the relief on Dick's face leaves no doubt about the test results.

He emerges from the barn with good news, but it will have to wait, as the boys have disappeared into a warm house for another round of video games. Dick climbs into the cab of the Allis and pulls a four-bottom plow down to the nearest cornfield. "This tractor could pull five bottoms in loam," he says, "but in this clay we sometimes can't pull more than three." A fair amount of corn—some shelled, some on the cob—remains on the ground. Plenty of goose food; but the Canadas haven't been flying for several weeks, and it looks as if the birds will miss out here this year.

Dick lines up with the long axis of the field, drops his four bottoms, and hauls. A sharp-edged disk—the colter—leads the way on each unit. Its job is to cut sod; on fall corn ground it merely draws a neat, irrelevant line in the mud. Behind the colter comes the "point," the narrow leading part of the plowshare itself. The point digs into the earth, sending a ridge of soil back to the moldboard, the cupped and curved flank of the plowshare, which lifts, turns over, and lays down the ridge of earth. Each bottom unit is topped by a thirty-inch-long arched leaf spring, and when a point hits a boulder, the whole bottom, pivoting around its single-bolt attachment to the plow frame, jumps out of the ground, in theory, at least, preventing point and moldboard damage.

Plow—and especially plowshare—design differs from manufacturer to manufacturer. This is a Scandinavian implement (a Kvernelands), and the Treadways like it. "It works better in clay than the American plows," Don says. "It's got these long points and moldboards, like the old horse plows we used to have. Then the American manufacturers went to shorter moldboards, and they don't lay over the furrows as good. And they wonder why farmers buy foreign."

Long moldboards or no, plowing in wet clay is murder. Four furrows appear behind the plow, but the Allis is having a tough time even with chains, whose outsized cleats shortly disappear under caked mud. The tractor's front wheels double in size, and the wheel at the end of the diagonal row of bottoms packs solid and ceases to turn, becoming a further drag on the tractor. Dick backs the rig up, temporarily dislodging enough of the mudpack to enable the plow wheel to turn again. The second pass is a bit easier, as he can lay one rear tractor tire in the outside furrow, where there is a little more traction on the ground surface; so that the top-of-ground wheel races, throwing muck, while the in-furrow wheel labors slowly, hesitantly, carrying the whole load.

After three sweeps, Dick is ready to give it up. Don drives up in a Deere with the unwelcome news that the unloader housing didn't come in, and won't now be available until after the week-end. "Don't look like you're getting anywhere," he says, nodding back at the plow. "Just can't do it," Dick replies. "We may have to wait until it freezes some." Some years heavy snowfall comes before the ground can dry out or freeze, and plowing has to be put off until spring. But fall plowing is much preferable. "The freezing and thawing and heaving through the winter help break the ground up if it's plowed," Dick says; "then it's easier to work in spring. When it's plowed in the fall, we just harrow once or twice come spring. But after spring plowing, you might have to harrow four or five times, and even then it may not break up good. This ground is just like pottery clay, and if the sun bakes it somewhere along the line, you can't break it up with anything."

IT IS A GRAY, DRIZZLY DAY A WEEK LATER, AND it, too, begins with heifer problems. The Fish and Game warden who lives on the next road south calls during morning milking. A Treadway heifer has wandered into his front yard, and, being in heat, has prompted the warden's steer to crash through a combination barbed wire and electric fence to join her. Dick loads the trunk of his father's car with fencing equipment and a bucket of grain, and Don drives Dick and Joan the several miles to the warden's place, where the steer stands protectively over his new love interest.

Dick takes down a section of rail fence bordering the road ("You might have asked," Joan objects, though the two families have known each other for years), and uses the bucket of grain to lure the heifer out of the yard, down the road, and into her pasture, where Don is looking for weak sections of fence. Joan and the warden undertake the tougher task of driving the love-sick steer back into his pasture, haling and hazing the fleet-footed animal uphill and down before succeeding. Pastured once again, the steer rushes down the road-bordering fence to a position opposite the heifer and fills the air with urgent, stentorian bellows, his head held low on a stretched neck, like a rutting bull elk. "It's all in his head," the warden says, mildly disgusted; "he can't do anything about it. But he'll probably break out again before you get home."

Dick and the warden set about fixing the latter's fence, splicing in new electric wire, replacing a shattered insulator, driving new staples, and replacing a post broken in two by the steer's reckless charge. An impressively large man dressed in a red-and-black-check wool coat and a Day-Glo-orange hunter's cap, the warden may have been out all night attempting to monitor his section of the state during this sixteen-day madness known as deer-hunting season, when locals and out-of-staters alike drive the roads and hoof it through the woods bearing high-powered rifles, looking for sport.

Probably the warden has heard enough deer hunter stories already, but Don entertains him with another. "I almost had a wreck with some hunters," he says. "I was driving along slow looking for bad fence, and these four fat fellas in red coats were driving slow in a car watching the fields for deer. We didn't either of us see the other, and damn near run into each other! Then"—a chuckle building in his voice—"two hours later on the other side of the farm, damned if the same thing didn't happen again! I got to know those hunters pretty good." (Next week Don's daughter, Diane, will have her own hunting story to tell.

Hearing rifle fire down by the barn behind her house just after dawn, she will confront two hunters and ask what they are shooting at. "We aren't sure," one will reply; "either a fox or a cat.")

After lunch, Dick climbs onto the hood of the Allis, pops off the cab roof, and hauls into place the cab heater, another recurrent problem. The heater unit is essentially a small radiator, a heat-fin-sprouting tube doubling back on itself. Hot fluid from the tractor's radiator is pumped through the heater unit, and a fan blows hot air radiating from it down into the cab. A particular elbow in the tube on this unit has broken a couple of times, and now it has been welded once again. (A broken tube in a tractor-cab heater is not a problem that hides and festers. You know about it right now, as hot fluid pours down on your head while you are working away. It is, Dick says, quite a surprise the first time it happens.)

Dick is reinstalling the heater when the UPS truck pulls into the barnyard. "That'll be one of my gears," Dick says. The International Harvester has been having trouble backing up, and the problem has been traced to broken teeth on two gears. The larger of the two, Dick was horrified to learn, costs $400, the smaller $200, and so he initiated a search through a used-tractor-part network. One has been found and sent, and Dick climbs down off the Allis and writes a check for $98. "I hope that's the larger gear," he says, "but probably it's the smaller." (Dick's worry is not academic. Shoreham town taxes have been paid without borrowing, but Whiting taxes—a fraction of the farm lies in that township—and fire insurance come due shortly, and the farm's checking account is perilously low.)

Joan, once again folding laundry on the kitchen table, has set these worries aside to ponder a more urgent one. Becky has an appointment later this afternoon to get her hair cut short. Becky made the style decision, and her mother is having trouble with it. "She's my only daughter," she moans melodramatically. "My idea of her is an angel with long hair. I'm sorry." The family, always eager to be helpful, tease her about it whenever the subject comes up.

Luckily, Joan has happy news to think about as well, and as soon as the laundry is done, she says to Brian—home from school today complaining of neck pains—"Let's watch Jeff on TV again." Jeff has returned from the ag convention in Kansas City, excited not only about having toured a truck factory and seen the monster truck Bigfoot and attended a rodeo, but having tied for second place among more than 100 entrants in the machinery and power division of the agricultural-mechanics competition. Joan has taped the television interview with the returned Vermont delegates, which she now rolls. Jeff appears several times in the segment, retiring and self-conscious before the camera. The interviewer has no luck at all trying to get Jeff to elaborate on his successful competition, but his journalistic hide is saved by another convention delegate, a friend of Jeff's who sums him up in the mike as "a helluva mechanic and an all-round good guy," to which Joan, fist raised high, cheers in assent.

There is other good news on the farm. The silo-unloader housing has come in and been installed, and the cows are getting chopped corn mixed with their haylage once again. Best of all, the plowing is done. Fearing snow might arrive before the ground hardened much, Dick picked up the plow's fourth bottom with the bucket loader, fastened it cocked in the air, and he and Jeff gritted their teeth and muscled their way through the viscous clay until all the corn acreage was turned. Whatever the weather does, or tries to do, to the farm this winter, it will, here, at least, be working for the Treadways, helping to break up the corn ground.

## 8

THE DAYS CONTINUE TO SHORTEN, AND IT is nearly dark at 4:30 when Joan comes down from the house to join Dick, Jeff, and Kevin for evening chores. Things are noticeably brighter in the barn, however, particularly on the west side, whose fluorescent bulbs have been taken down and washed, and whose reflector shields have been repainted. Dick is at the moment filing away at the contact prongs of a sub-par east-side bulb, which, replaced, still delivers a dim, flickering light. He shrugs, and walks away.

"Everybody ready?" he inquires, and Joan tugs on the big south-end rolling door to let the cows in. It doesn't budge. Jeff and Kevin laugh and urge their mother to a more muscular performance. Dick joins her. He bangs on the door as if asking the cows to open it from their side, then wedges the door open just enough to stick his head out. Sure enough; a cow is lying down against the door. More banging and some shouting, and the cow finally moves. Dick shoves the door open, and the throng surges forward. The usual chaos ensues, with Dick trying to pick out dry cows and shouting the information to Kevin, who attempts to turn them with his cane into south-end stanchions. Milkers continue up the aisle, some cooperatively entering stanchions, some wedging in around them, all starting to work on hay.

A telephone call after morning milking informed the Treadways that they would be milk-testing this evening, and so, while Dick grains the cows and Kevin hauls and dumps piles of fresh sawdust along the central aisle, Joan and Jeff install their five rented milk meters on milking machines via hoses. These milk meters, two-foot-long double-tube devices made in New Zealand, are bypass units through which all milk passes on its way to the milk line. As the milk flows through the first tube, a carefully metered percentage is diverted into a second, parallel tube, where it accumulates through a particular milking.

Julie—a solid young woman with curly, carrot-colored hair, the latest in a series of milk testers to work in this barn—arrives and sets up her work station on a wheelbarrow, and milking begins. (Kevin is released to the house to do homework with the understanding that he will return in an hour. Jeff declares the arrangement patently unfair; *he* has homework as well.) As the first cow nears the end of its milk, Dick massages the bag, testing all four quarters. When the cow is finished, he pulls the teat cups off, hangs them on the milker, and calls out the cow's barn number.

Julie moves directly to the milk meter, which she straightens, then reads and memorizes the poundage figure from the calibrated tube, being careful to find the liquid line under perhaps an inch of foam. She then opens a valve which injects air into the collecting tube, converting it into a mini-blender, and then she draws off a sample of the stirred milk into a small plastic bag. She returns to her portable work station twirling the bag around its twisty top to seal it, bends the twisty ends back, and places the identified sample in a compartmentalized tray. The samples will be tested for butterfat content, and the point of the air-powered mixing is to blend in the cream. (Fat content figures from these tests, however, are consistently lower than those derived from milk-plant tests, and the Treadways think that either the milk meters don't stir adequately or the milk testers don't stir long enough before taking samples.) Finally, she notes on her form the poundage figure after the number of the appropriate cow.

In-the-barn milk-testing is key to the work of the Dairy Herd Improvement Association, which sends Julie to this and other member farms ten or eleven times a year, alternating morning and evening milkings. DHIA has, essentially, lifted from mem-

ber farmers' shoulders—for a fee, of course—the responsibility
of tracking the history of their herds. This requires considerable
data, and, between reading milk meters and twirling sample
bags, Julie brings her records up to date from Dick's jotted
notes. She enters each cow's current rations—grain, hay, haylage, and corn silage. She records appropriate reproductive data:
insemination dates, drying-off dates, freshening dates. She notes
the sex and fate of each calf born since her last visit, indicating
which were sold and which are being raised (and she ear-tags
four of the latter).

Finally, she officially closes her books on two milkers, sold via
commission sales during the past month. One failed, for some
reason, to become pregnant after repeated inseminations, and
the other was a marginal milker. Some cows are milked for
fifteen or more years, but the majority don't live half that long.
For any number of reasons—lagging milk production, impreg-
nation failure, difficult births, a hard-luck injury, a personality
problem (Joan was kicked in the shin at the start of milking this
evening, and will remember that cow's number)—cows become
expendable and are sold—there's no other market—for beef.
The very essence of herd improvement is, of course, the culling
of problem or underproductive animals in favor of promising
heifers; but it's a part of the business neither Dick nor Joan
much cares for.

What the DHIA computer-printout records out of Raleigh,
North Carolina, do is lay out in summary form all the factors
involved in each cow's reproductive history and return of milk
on feed, helping Dick make important herd decisions concerning
not only which cows to sell but which heifer calves to keep, and
which of a long list of bulls to use to inseminate a particular cow
in hopes of an improved daughter. Clearly, herd improvement
works. Twenty years ago the Treadway's average milk production per cow was 10,375 pounds a year. That figure is now
17,150 pounds—compared to the national average of 14,400
pounds—an improvement largely attributable to better feed in

combination with a more knowledgeable use of better bulls for artificial insemination.

During the testing, Jeff, who is alternately washing udders and loafing, makes an important discovery: he is out of Life Savers. Kevin is due back at the barn anyway, so Jeff calls home and tells him to bring a pack with him. Kevin shortly appears, pretending to have forgotten the Life Savers, which prompts a chase down a side aisle, which prompts Kevin to fork over the candy to save his skin. Dick pointedly suggests that Jeff share his booty, and the latter agrees to accept requests for any flavor except pineapple.

Sucking candy rings raises food issues in several minds, and conversation turns to the question of who in the family has been eating the doughnuts. Julie, who is mostly all business, chews her gum and attends the protracted debate with an air of faint amusement. "Dick and I didn't wake up the kids on Sunday morning," Joan says. "We came down and milked alone. You miss the help, but it was *so* quiet without all the bickering."

As milking nears an end, one of Jeff's favorite cows and one of Kevin's happen to have meter-rigged milkers on them at the same time, and the boys immediately stage a contest for milking champ of the barn. "Go to it, Pork Chop!" Jeff shouts. "Come on, you can do it," Kevin pleads, rubbing Blue just beside the root of her tail to encourage better flow. Each denigrates the performance of the competition. "Look, you haven't even got thirty pounds yet; I've got thirty-five!" "Naaa, yours is all foam!"

In the end, Pork Chop proves the better producer; best, in fact, of the herd. Julie has mostly entered poundages in the twenties and thirties, but Pork Chop milks out at 50.5 pounds. Since the morning-to-evening milking interval is somewhat shorter than the evening-to-morning interval, this test will extrapolate to a day's milk production of about 110 pounds, or almost 14 gallons. Or, as Dick puts it, 220 half-pint cartons, more than enough to supply the daily snack and lunch needs of the 130-pupil Shoreham elementary school. Inconsolable over Blue's defeat, Kevin manufactures a strident wail, his grief unbroken until Dick reminds him that Blue's butterfat content will almost certainly be higher than Pork Chop's.

Milking done, Julie packs up her equipment, her forms, and two trays of milk samples, and heads for home. Joan and Jeff disassemble the milk meters ("You don't want to drop one of those," Dick reminds them; "they cost two hundred and twenty bucks apiece") and haul them and the milkers into the milkroom, where Joan will start the washing process. Kevin, meanwhile, has climbed a ladder to the mow, whence he throws down bales of hay into each side aisle. Coming down after them, he hauls them up and down both aisles, one bale for each three cows. Grabbing a bale by one twine, he lifts and pumps it up and down, until the bale bellies out below and he can jerk his string free. Then he works the other string free, kicks the bale's contents under three noses, and moves on to the next bale.

Jeff, meanwhile, is bedding the cows down, broadcasting by shovel from the sawdust piles in the central aisle. Dick has left for his emergency-squad class, Joan for home and supper. Jeff notices that Kevin's task is nearly finished, and, not wanting to be last out of the barn, he literally runs through his last section, slinging as much sawdust on the cows as under them. The boys finish up bang-bang, and race for the light switch at the north end of the barn, leaving in the dark nine half-sized chickens roosting two and three a rung on the hay-mow ladder, and two long lines of stanchioned Holsteins munching fresh hay.

## 9

"THERE'S ALWAYS A DISASTER ON THANKS-
giving," Joan says the afternoon before as she lays out her baking things. This year the emergencies and minor catastrophes are
either starting early or, perhaps, getting out of the way before-
hand. Just after lunch, the water quit, which it does from time to
time. Most country water is pumped from private wells, but
Shoreham and two neighboring towns are exceptions. Farm
wells were running dry during arid summers back in the late
fifties and early sixties, and a three-town plant was built to
pump and pipe water from Lake Champlain. The quality of the
water is nothing like that of well water, but farmers have ap-
preciated the reliability of the resource. Interruptions occur,
however, and the story at the moment is either that the water
people have shut the system down to look for a leak or that the
big-money new farm southwest of the Treadways is temporarily
monopolizing the supply to back-flush its barn, a cleaning technology requiring more water than the four-inch pipe on the back
side of Shoreham can spare.

There is no good time to be without water, and Joan has been
left with a half-washed load of laundry and a sink and counter
full of dirty pots and pans to bake around. But it's pie time, and
she sits down to a box of apples bought at the local apple co-op.
She peels them first, working round and round from the stem
end down with a vegetable peeler. Then she quarters and cores
them, dumps them into a mixing bowl, and coats them with
sugar and cinnamon. She finds a bit of counter space on which
to roll out pie crust, cutting into the folded top two pine trees
and a star, as her grandmother had always done.

With the apple pie ready for the oven, Joan turns her attention to pumpkin. (Kevin had lobbied hard for a coconut "impossible pie"—a fast one-mix recipe so named because the Bisquick magically "migrates" out of the mix while baking and coalesces to form a crumb crust—but the motion had died for lack of a second.) She dumps a can of pumpkin—"Mother is making one from scratch" to bring—into a bowl and hunts a cupboard carousel for spices. Becky and Brian arrive home on the school bus, and Becky picks up the whisk to stir up the pie-filling ingredients. Joan cracks two eggs over the bowl, and soon the pumpkin custard is a sticky, glistening yellow-brown mass, which Brian and Becky agree is "gross." Becky continues to whisk through the condensed milk and spices and salt, however, and both pies are soon popped into the oven along with a small pan of cookies, which Becky has cut (two stars, two hearts, and two cows) from leftover pie dough.

Joan and Becky are just getting started on the date-nut bread when the uninterrupted ring of a fire call comes in. Joan takes the information and hurries out to put the red light on top of the van. Dick runs up from the machine shed and climbs into his fire gear. "It's a chimney fire," Joan says, naming a farm a good ten miles away on the far side of Shoreham. Dick makes a circle around the front yard and pulls out onto Cutting Hill Road. Most country gravel roads are three-track roads. Vehicles pretty much stick to their own side of the road, but their inside wheels share a path down the middle. Cutting Hill, like other very lightly traveled roads, is a two-track road, essentially a one-way road going both ways. When friends pass on Cutting Hill Road, they look in the rear-view mirror for brake lights, which means the other party has something to discuss. One backs up alongside the other, they turn the engines off, roll down the windows, and chat for ten or fifteen minutes.

Dick speeds north up the middle of Cutting Hill, easing some at hill crests for fear a two-vehicle conversation may be in progress over the rise. He pulls onto South Bingham—a three-track road—and turns the siren on as he approaches Highway

74. Then it's 65 mph down a stretch of highway and off on a cut-through road to Highway 22A and across and on west, Dick switching the siren from "wail" to the more urgent "yelp" as he approaches blind intersections. The cream van is the second vehicle on the scene, but no tanker has yet arrived; so Dick and two other firemen stand about with farm personnel watching smoke puff out near the top of the chimney and black ash decorate a gray slate roof.

Don Treadway is next to arrive, and then the first of three tankers, bearing unneeded water—cold water dumped down a hot chimney simply cracks it—and needed ladders. The men hook up a double ladder to reach the roof, drag up a third, which hooks over the ridge, and then a fourth, which they stand up against the chimney on the top side. One man steadies the ladder, Dick pays up cable, and a third man works the cable up and down and around the chimney's interior, its terminal knot of chain scraping down the chimney walls. Meanwhile, a second party works inside, cleaning out the base of the chimney. For an hour they chat and work, the chimney belching smoke all the while, and then, the majority of creosote-gunk cleaned away, they take down the ladders, pack up, and depart, leaving the fire to burn itself harmlessly out.

It has been an undramatic and, if there is such a thing, a comfortable fire to work on, a decent-weather, daylight fire in a good, solid chimney. "It's different," Dick says, "when it's three A.M. and below zero and a howling wind and the chimney your ladder's propped up against is crumbling. That's when you wonder what you're doing out there." Dick takes another route home, and begins to point out homes and farms where he remembers fire calls over the two decades he's been with the department. It seems as if every third property has been involved, a chimney fire here, a barn fire there, a bed fire up on the hill.

"There used to be a trailer right there," Dick says, pointing off the road. "One afternoon the boy was there alone, and something he was working with rolled under the couch. The kid was sixteen or seventeen, and should have known better; but he used a cigarette lighter to look for the thing. Once the couch got going, he didn't have a chance to put it out. These trailers are murder. The whole thing went up; sides melt right out of them. There was nothing left when we got there. Some people said the boy's father was pretty tough on him, and a couple of men stayed so the kid wouldn't be alone when his father got home."

Dick's mind skips to a nighttime house fire in Cornwall earlier this year. "It's funny what the human mind will do under the stress of emergency." The firemen had arrived to find a woman huddled outside the burning bedroom wing of her house with her "fresh-air" child—one of a number of inner-city New York kids placed for the summer in Vermont homes—whom she had snatched out of bed as she fled the house. "We were working on the fire and she was standing behind us holding the child and watching her house burn when all of a sudden she lets out this awful scream." Under the press of panic and the overriding concern for the welfare of her "borrowed" child, the woman had entirely forgotten her own child, who was also sleeping in the burning wing. Unlike some, that fire story had a happy ending, as the second child was rescued as well.

"One thing these fires do, they make you thankful for what you've got. You feel happy to go home and do chores." That, as it happens, is what Dick has ahead of him now, and he is putting on his barn boots and recruiting help inside the front door when the phone rings. "I'll tell him," Joan says; "it'll make his day." And Dick looks up, knowing by the tone of her voice that it's his father with bad news. A longer water shutoff would, it turns out, have been welcomed, at least as far as the barn is concerned. A number of water cups have been overflowing since morning milking. The gutters are full, the barn awash. "C'mon," he says to the boys, "we've got a mess to clean up."

"I'll be down in a while," Joan says; "I've got to be here to take the date-nut bread out of the oven." And she has a decision to make in the meantime: where to secrete the pies? She can't leave them out; the cats would get into them. "I could just put them back in the oven. That would save them from the cats. But Dick and the boys know about that hiding place."

THE OPTIMISTIC READING OF YESTERDAY'S disasters proves to be the correct one, and Thanksgiving goes off with scarcely a hitch. (Two uneventful days in a row would be too much to hope for. Fortunately, Joan cannot now know that she and a colleague will spend a sad afternoon in the woods tomorrow doing CPR on a deer hunter, dead of a heart attack, waiting for a defibrillator unit that will arrive much too late.)

Grandmother and Grandfather Pelletier have arrived from the south along with Aunt Shirley. Aldore, a large, bluff man comfortably attired in a brown check shirt and rainbow-striped suspenders, has made himself at home in the living room easy chair, half-heartedly watching football on TV. His wife, Elsie, a woman with kindly eyes and a winning smile, and quiet, diminutive Shirley offer to help every few minutes from their seats at a kitchen table crowded with china, wine glasses, and candles. The sideboard is decorated today with several of Irene's intricately elegant crocheted doilies, which Joan treasures.

It is just past noon, and Dick is busy carving a golden-brown twenty-two-pound turkey while Joan fills a row of serving bowls with mounds of mashed potatoes, stuffing, squash, mixed vegetables, two salads (pineapple whip, a favorite of the kids, and a fruit Jell-O), three cranberry sauces, rolls, date-nut bread, and pickles. Finally, she tackles the gravy ("What," she asks, "would Thanksgiving be without Mom's lumpy gravy?"), and the family is called to the table. Brian has chosen to have Thanksgiving dinner with Don and Irene and Aunt Diane, but the rest of the family is here. The children get the first plates, Becky and Kevin sitting at a tiny table set up in the kitchen doorway, Jeff retreating to the living room.

The adults seat themselves around the kitchen table, and relish that prefeast pause when hands are rubbed, nostrils flare, and expressions of relief and anticipation counterpoint across the platters and bowls of steaming, brightly colored food. There are no preliminaries, and no one stands on ceremony. Everyone picks up the nearest dish, serves himself, passes it on ("Which way are we going?"), and receives another. Helping follows helping, and soon, despairing of finding plate room for more, the families set to eating in earnest just as Becky returns with an empty plate for seconds on pineapple whip and pickles.

Gradually, the pace of attack slows around the table, and the feasters find time for bits of conversation. Joan and her mother, particularly, have questions about family and friends in their respective parts of the state. Dick kids his father-in-law about his courtship days, egging him on to a retelling. "I first took Elsie out on a bet," Aldore obliges. "A guy bet me a beer she wouldn't go out with me. I got a free beer out of that." "Yah," says Dick, who in fact is fond of his mother-in-law, "but you've been paying for it ever since!" Platters and bowls make the rounds again, but there are few takers now—though Becky manages thirds on pickles—and soon the adults are lamenting the discrepancy between desire and capacity.

The kids finish first. Uncharacteristically, Becky retires to her room and naps, while Jeff and Kevin don boots and coats and head out for a ride on the three-wheeler. One by one the adults put down their knives and forks as well, declaring their intention to leave off eating permanently. This does not deter Joan, who removes the serving dishes and replaces them with four pies and French vanilla ice cream. Good intentions are abandoned— "well, maybe just a small piece of apple (pumpkin, mince)"— and dessert is underway.

The Pelletiers want to know about Dick and Joan's ongoing rescue-squad classes and work, and Joan talks about the old people they find living alone. "Sometimes they don't eat or get attention. It's so sad. Often they have relatives living in the area, but they haven't looked in that week or the old folks don't want to bother them." That reminds her of another case, and of an attitude toward elderly parents she simply can't understand. Her team were loading a gray-haired woman with an irregular heart-beat into the ambulance when a family member took one of the squad aside and requested that she not be revived should she have a heart attack. "I held her hand all the way to the hospital," Joan remembers. "She was so sweet. She kept saying she didn't want to be a trouble to anyone."

That story reminds Dick of a similar case with a twist. A woman had married several elderly men, whose property she inherited at their deaths. When her current spouse had an attack, she rode along with him to the hospital, and asked the emergency-room doctor not to use extraordinary means to try to save him. At which point, the grizzled old husband, whom she had thought unconscious, opens one eye and, "By Jesus," he says to the doctor, "you'd *better* try to save me!"

Joan's father has brought his deer rifle with him, and has talked of doing some hunting. Dessert over, Dick reminds him of the fact: "Al, I thought you were going to take your gun out in the woods." "Well, I've been thinking about it," he replies, but retires instead to the easy chair in the living room, where Dick joins him to watch the hapless Detroit Lions embarrass themselves against the Minnesota Vikings while the women work in the kitchen.

The second holiday NFL game has begun when Elsie appears and announces that it will soon be time to do chores back home. Aldore is happy where he is ("Pick me up about next Wednesday"), but they and Aunt Shirley are eventually on their way, just in time to miss a Treadway family altercation. Jeff and Kevin return from their ATV adventure with their barn overalls covered with mud, which upsets their mother. But when Joan discovers, suiting up for chores, that Kevin had by mistake worn one of her barn boots, and that it is now muddy inside as well as out, she announces her intention to do bodily harm to both Kevin and Jeff, who make themselves scarce.

Evening milking goes smoothly, however, and then the aromas of dinner are reprised as plates of turkey and fixings and glasses of soda and a different kind of pie are consumed in the living room through *Wheel of Fortune* and *Cheers* and *Jeopardy*. And then chins begin to droop and eyes to close, and one by one pajamas are donned, teeth are brushed, and the children pad down their respective halls for bed, not long in advance of their parents. It has been, Brian says, a "pretty good Thanksgiving."

# WINTER

WHAT HAS PIQUED DICK'S CURIOSITY ENOUGH to prompt him to clean up after morning chores and head south on Highway 30 is a green leaflet that arrived at the farm in early November, announcing an "All Day Informational Meeting for Farmers Who Want to Know More About Producing Better Quality Crops at Much Lower Cost by Using a More Natural Approach in Farming," a meeting scheduled for December 1 at the Sudbury town hall. Dick arrives at 10:30, half an hour after the leaflet's declared start-up time for Presentations and Discussion. No one is presenting or discussing, however, perhaps because only a half-dozen farmers are present in the cavernous town hall, and Joe Choma, a local ag consultant and organizer of the meeting, nervously watches the door.

Dick, who has had no breakfast, picks up a doughnut and a cup of coffee at the refreshment table and asks his friend Mead Murphy, a local dairy farmer and seed dealer, what cover crop he can plant in the fall to loosen up some hard corn ground. Murphy recommends triticale (he pronounces it to rhyme with "palely"), a cross between rye and durum wheat. It's got a big root system, he says, which would help loosen the ground as well as add organic material. "I want to get corn back in in the spring," Dick says; "would you plow the triticale under?" "It'd be better to leave it through a year's cycle," Murphy replies; "but you could plow it under, or you could graze it off or chop it: it's comparable to corn in protein."

At eleven o'clock the meeting is called to order, with perhaps ten farms represented. Mead Murphy reports on the seed-corn situation for next spring. Corn is short because of the drought, he says, but it will be available; "just don't count on getting your first choice of varieties." And kernel size will be down, another result of the summer's drought.

Joe Choma introduces the day's featured speaker, Carroll Montgomery, of Dexter, Missouri. A graduate of a college ag program, Montgomery was a mainstream chemical farmer until he saw that establishment solutions weren't solving his problems, and he began to experiment with "natural biological nutrient programs." The experiments proved successful, and the Montgomery family founded the Christian Agriculture Stewardship Institute, in part to spread the word.

Which is what Carroll Montgomery is doing today in Sudbury, Vermont. He is a small man, ramrod-straight and field-tough, dressed in jeans, cowboy boots, and a western shirt. He jumps immediately into the question of soils in a rich south Missouri accent, and it is some time before the audience realizes he is talking soil, because he pronounces it "soul," and at first it gives one a start to be told that "We have to purge our 'souls' of chemical residues." There is a certain appropriateness about this momentary confusion, however; the CASI literature is replete with biblical messages (a "Praise the Lord" motif concludes many a page, and a question about fertilizers is referred to 1 Corinthians 3:18–20 and Proverbs 3:5), and the soil is, for Montgomery, the soul of agriculture.

Farmers have got to get their soil analyzed and then get it in balance. "The American farmer has been sold a bill of goods," Montgomery says; unproductive land cannot be "fixed" by dumping yet more nitrogen, phosphorus, and potassium on it. He talks "cations," positively charged soil nutrients that attract negatively charged particles and flow to negatively charged plant roots. Get your major soil cations—calcium, magnesium, potash, sodium, and hydrogen—in balance, he urges, or the fertilizers can't be properly utilized by the plants. Most commercial fertilizers aren't solutions; they're part of the problem. Potash fertilizers, for example, are high in chlorine and salt, elements that kill soil life and interfere with nutrient uptake.

"Lemme make this point," Montgomery continues. "You guys are mostly dairy farmers. You're using a lot of manure. You've got to watch that stuff. You're building sodium and nitrogen levels with that stuff, and you're going to have to counteract them with sulfur if you want to take quality into the barn."

Joe Choma calls a halt for lunch, and the sparse audience chews over cations and manure salts while helping themselves to plates of fried chicken, meatballs and pasta, bread and rolls, cole slaw, milk, coffee, and cake. There has been—and will be—no talk of "organic" farming here. Organic farming to this audience means raising specialty crops in a special (and difficult) way for a high-priced specialty market, and there is no call, in any case, for "organic" milk. But much of the thrust is the same, and Louis Bromfield and Robert Rodale and Wendell Berry would underwrite most of CASI's goals.

In the afternoon session, Montgomery and two other presenters tackle other issues. The importance of organic matter in the soil. ("You guys are lucky; up here they tell me you've got four percent or better OM; down home we're lucky to have two percent.") The technique of neutralizing ammonia in the manure pit with lime, which both lessens odor and protects soil life. About earthworms, major soil good guys which are killed by the abuse of fertilizers and pesticides. The technique of using citric acid to lower the pH of water in which herbicides are dispensed, making the herbicides more effective and so allowing the farmer to reduce the dosage.

Carroll Montgomery talks about foliar feeding, whereby plants—in particular, for this audience, alfalfa—are fed via spray through the leaves rather than through the roots. And Bill Campbell, a deliberate, slow-talking North Carolinian, describes his own foliar feed, a "biological" (here an adjective used as a noun, the counterpart of "chemical") containing aerobic bacteria, amino acids, micronutrients, and growth stimulants. Campbell's blend, which involves kelp and blackstrap molasses, feeds the soil as well as plants, and that's the key. Campbell and Mont-

gomery agree: clean up, balance, and enrich your soil, then see
what your crops do. "Build sugars in your crop," Montgomery
says, "and disease and insect problems drop off."

Mostly, Montgomery talks agricultural science as he understands it. On occasion, however, an Armageddonish note breaks
through, as when, late in the session, he refers to well-water
studies made in nine states. The findings have long been complete, he says, but buried in Washington by the politicians. But
recently the *Des Moines Register* got hold of some of the results
and published them. Just wait, he says, until the American
housewife finds out the extent to which our drinking water has
been polluted through establishment-approved farming prac-
tices. Other states, he predicts, will follow California, which is
now banning over 100 agricultural chemicals. "You'd better
find out what you're doing," he warns the audience pointedly,
"and get off chemicals before you have to, and still have time to
work out an alternative."

The meeting shortly breaks up, and it is impossible to read in
the faces of the men and women leaving the town hall a verdict
on the CASI mix of hard science and back-to-nature agriculture
flavored with tent evangelism and rural populism. Dick Treadway, for one, is not ready to dismiss the message; a lot of it, he
feels, makes sense. Still, he doubts that the "more natural approach" to farming will catch on like wildfire. His guess is that
Joe Choma, as area point man for these methods and materials,
is going to have to put in some free time at first, to get a local
farm or two to test them out and find out how they work and
what they cost.

If there is an abundant element of go-slow in the local attitude, it would hardly be surprising. Farmers understand the
system as it now operates. And even if they don't understand the
details, it doesn't much matter; industry and university extension experts will tell them what to do. (The fact that the experts
are interested parties—that the soil tests are taken and analyzed
by chemical fertilizer outfits, which then tell the farmer what he
needs to buy from them, and that corn and silage analysis is

done by the grain dealers—is itself significant, of course, and it is a situation that bothers the Treadways and others.) Farmers do not, most of them, understand this talk about cations and combating bugs through building high sugar in crop juices, much less measuring that sugar content in brixes with a refractometer. There are practical concerns as well. Dick points out that repeated foliar spraying costs money, perhaps $10 an acre per visit just for the truck. And he wonders about what "withdrawal" problems might follow the jump off the chemical bandwagon. Would not a switch to "natural" systems mean a couple of bad crops while one's soil was being purged and balanced and enriched? And how many farmers in these parts could afford that?

The Treadways will think about it, will talk about switching a couple of fields, perhaps, to see how it works out. "Can you afford to farm this way?" Dick wonders; "or maybe, in the long run, can you afford not to?"

2

THROUGH SPRING, SUMMER, AND FALL, THE Treadways work straight through morning chores, returning to the house at nine o'clock or so for breakfast. Chores take longer in winter, however, and the family usually breaks after milking, returning for another session in the barn after breakfast. Ten o'clock this chill morning finds Don and Dick cleaning up. Don is talking about last night's fire call. A barn near a mansion south of Orwell had somehow caught fire. "Jeff and I went down, and I never saw such a gathering of trucks and cars. There were trucks and tankers from Bridport and Orwell and Whiting and Shoreham and Benson and I don't know where all. It looked like Chicago: a line of blue and red lights a mile up the

road." The crews saved some of the barn, and, more impor-
tantly, prevented the fire from spreading.

Most of the herd are lying down now, the very picture of
contented cows. Don walks behind them, poking them in the
hindquarters with his scraper tool. "Come on!" he hollers; "get
up!" (Probably Don is missing the absent Thorson, whose one
skill with cattle is the raising of prone animals. "Get 'em up!"
someone will shout, pointing at the target cow, and Thor will
rush up and bite the base of the beast's tail, occasioning a quick
and undignified rise.) Don opens the stanchions and starts the
cows out of the barn. While Dick scrapes fresh manure into the
gutters, his father climbs over the high sill out the east-facing
door and opens up the manure chute, dragging the heavy cover
to one side and lifting the trap door. He has brought with him
a stout crowbar, which he now takes to one of the myriad small
problems winter brings to a farm. The same cold that has mercifully solidified the barnyard clay has also frozen yesterday's
manure spill into solid blocks wedged under the chain which
operates the gutter cleaner. Don—working bare-handed, as
usual—drives the crowbar repeatedly under the chain, breaking
out chunks of dung-hay mortar.

When the chain is free, Don switches on the gutter cleaner,
which begins its slow clanking march around the barn. The men
shovel out the calf pens, and parcel the accumulated manure
into the gutter where the load is light. Dick drives the pickup
over to the machine shed, puts on a load of hay, and drives it to
the north barn door. There he loads a wagon from which he
distributes bales along both side aisles; he breaks the bales and
kicks hay under the water cups. More hay is chucked into the
calf pens, the gutter scraper is switched off, the off-load chute
closed, and morning chores are done.

It is nearly lunch time, but Dick pauses in the milkroom to
check the dipstick in his bulk tank. Yesterday's milk pickup was
6,966 pounds, and tank capacity is 7,050 pounds. The herd's
production is rapidly peaking, and Dick fears he'll have too
much milk for tomorrow's pickup. There is a stop charge for

milk pickup, and he wants to delay as long as possible the switch
from every-other-day to every-day pickup. The family will get
up earlier than usual tomorrow and milk early, hoping to cut
herd production just enough to stay under tank capacity. "If we
don't," he muses, "we'll be drinking an awful lot of cocoa
around here tomorrow."

In front of the house, Thorson, driven, as he occasionally is,
to great exertion, carries on an athletic feud with his dog dish,
the cut-off bottom third of a five-gallon plastic jug. He rushes up
and down the yard, now holding the vessel aloft, now dribbling
it ahead of him with astonishing dexterity, growling menacingly
all the while.

Inside, Becky is playing as well, the object of her attention a
new brown and white teddy bear sporting a red Santa hat. The
bear sings Christmas carols when you squeeze its paw, and
Becky has named it Sing. "I'm six!" she says brightly, and indeed
Becky is among those unfortunate children whose birthday lights
pale under the overwhelming glow of Christmas. If Becky re-
sents a winter-solstice birthday, however, she doesn't show it.
Besides Sing, she has a new Barbie doll and a Ken doll, and a
custom carrying case with drawers to hold their wardrobes and
accessories. Her friend Erin, who lives up the road, has a different Barbie, matched with a different boyfriend, and prospects
for new combinations of doll play are bright.

Dick, Joan, and the kids—school is just out for holiday
vacation—sit down to a lunch of hot dogs and beans. "We were
supposed to have cole slaw with this," Joan announces, "but
Brian's guinea pig ate it." "I'll pay for the cabbage," Brian says
morosely. "You don't have to pay for the cabbage," his mother
responds, her tone softened. Lunch conversation turns to Christmas, and Joan can't figure out how everything's going to get
worked in. The family will get up early and open stockings; then
straight to the barn for morning chores; then a quick cleanup
and church, whence directly south to Joan's parents' place for
the traditional dinner; then the rush home for evening milking,
immediately after which Dick leaves for ambulance duty. "So

when do we open the real presents?" Joan wonders, then adds: "I've got a headache." "I've got a solution for that," Dick replies. "I know, a walk in the fresh air."

That is exactly what Dick has in mind. This is the day, he has decided, to put the heifers in the barn for the winter. Despite repeated driving and fence-fixing, two heifers are back running with Charley's on the next farm, and the first order of business is to chase them back onto the farm and, with luck, up toward the barn. Dick, Joan, and Jeff climb into Don's car, and Don drops them off down Cutting Hill Road near where Charley's heifers are believed to be. He heads back to the barn, where he and Kevin will move the new calves to assigned winter stations.

The heifer hunters climb the fence and hike cross-lots to the east, dressed in barn coveralls, jackets, gloves, and ski hats. The weather this early winter (the calendar calls it late autumn) has been a mix of warm and cold periods, with overnight temperature swings of 50 degrees not uncommon. What has been largely absent is snow, and the season's two or three decent snowfalls have all succumbed to subsequent warm spells. This would be a typical Christmas-week day—15 degrees and a nippy wind from the north—except that the land is quite bare, the plowed fields dulled to brown, the close-cropped meadows glowing tawny-buff in the low sun. Jeff makes a detour to stomp on an iced-over stream, then treks upstream a short way and stomps again. Dick looks on, shaking his head. "You trying to find a place to fall through?"

Charley's heifers are soon discovered, and two animals with yellow ear tags among them. The family cut these out and walk them northeast, toward a gate opening onto their farm. The two animals amble along, periodically looking back over their shoulders. They are nearing the gate when one breaks into a run east along the fence, and it is as much as Jeff can do to keep up with it and turn it back. But as he does so the second heifer breaks through between Dick and Joan, and the first quickly follows.

One problem here is that the two can't see the Treadways' other fourteen heifers, pasturing well to the north, and, seeing no alternative company, choose to remain with the old. Dick suggests a new strategy: moving the whole group together, pushing their own animals through the gate—while attempting to hold Charley's back—at the last minute. As Dick scouts ahead, searching for a new route, Jeff spots a red fox in the fencerow ahead of his father. Dick is unaware of the fox, which is watching him. "Hey, Dad!" Jeff shouts, pointing beyond him; "fox!" "What?" Dick calls back, and the fox breaks and runs up the fencerow, bushy tail flying straight behind.

The family push a dozen heifers up along a creek, losing an animal now and again as they proceed. Most have filtered through the loose cordon by the time they approach the gate, and then they lose their own animals as well. A third drive also ends up dry, and a frustrated Dick calls a halt. "We'll wait till there's some snow on the ground," he says, "and maybe they won't be so frisky."

The three begin the long walk home, easing through the barbed-wire fence and starting north. As they emerge from the farm's southernmost corn piece, Jeff again spots the red fox slipping into the woods. "Diane and I found a mangy little fox when we were kids," Dick remembers. "Poor thing was half dead. We took it home, which delighted Mother no end." "It probably had rabies," Jeff conjectures, "which explains a lot about Dad," and indeed Dick promptly falls into a Frankensteinish fit marked by a lurching gait, subhuman expressions, and gurgling vocalizations, which brings a broad grin to Jeff's face and a "what next?" look to Joan's.

Halfway back to the farmstead, the hikers come upon the other fourteen heifers, and Joan calls them in that curious nasal sing-song that sounds like the ceremonial chant of some obscure Mongolian tribe. These animals, caught in a surprisingly cooperative mood, follow the Treadways north toward the barn. Dick leaves them at the last fence, hoping they'll stay, and gathers the family at the barn. (Becky and Brian have been required to stay home—Becky happily, Brian unhappily—for fear of injury in the coming barn melee.)

The new calves having been tied in the side aisles for their own safety, the last preliminary business is to get the cows in and stanchioned. (The heifers will have to come in the south door, and should that be opened with the cows out, some would enter with the heifers, compounding problems.) The cows aren't used to entering the barn at this early-afternoon hour, and some have to be driven in. Eventually, however, all are in and accounted for, and Joan heads down to the fence to let the heifers through. Don, Dick, Jeff, and Kevin scatter to strategic positions around the south end of the barn, where sixteen stanchions remain empty, as Joan brings the heifers—several now pregnant with first calves—up the ledgy path.

Not surprisingly, the early-winter putting in of heifers is very like the spring letting out of heifers, the same film run in reverse. Some charge right into the barn. Others enter timidly. Still others don't want any part of four walls. The gutter, once again, proves a major obstacle. Some fly across, but others roll their eyes and shy away as if it were electrified. A couple of animals quickly clear both end and side gutters and begin to attack the hay while carefully avoiding stanchions. Two of the family address themselves to each such heifer, one blocking the body in while the other attempts to ease its head into a stanchion. These animals are tremendously strong and notoriously resistant to direction, but from time to time the sudden clank of a closed stanchion signals a victory of man over beast.

As always, there are particular—and unpredictable—problems. One of the larger heifers shies left on entering the barn and climbs onto the elevated walkway behind the feeding manger of the southwest corner calf pen. Hemmed in by the manger and unable to turn around, it rears up against a chicken nest box at the end of the line and looks wildly about, now and again plunging with its raised forequarters, threatening to break the manger or a window or a calf's head. "Get *out* of there!" Don shouts in his gravelly angry voice, an order the animal would be hard-pressed to obey even if it wanted to.

Kevin, meanwhile, is chasing down a heifer that has bolted to

the north end of the barn, and Jeff and Dick attempt to deal with
one trying to escape a stanchion by wedging itself under the neck
of the heifer locked in the next stanchion. It forces more and
more of its bulk under its unfortunate barn-mate, pressing the
latter's trapped head to the top of its stanchion, all but stran-
gling it. "Back up!" Dick shouts at the hiding heifer, while Jeff
cuffs it on the face from the other side.

One by one, the heifers are solved and stanchioned, until a
single animal which *will* not cross the first gutter remains.
"Come on; get over," Don urges; "be brave; you're a big girl."
She is a big girl, but shame will not move her, nor do shouts and
imprecations and cane blows rained on her hindquarters. Finally, Dick halters her, and when the animal realizes that the
push-and-pull trick is tipping her toward the abhorred gutter,
she simply collapses into it, preferring to lie sprawled over and
in it rather than step over it.

Even this animal is eventually stanchioned—where it immediately begins to chew its hay, apparently bearing no grudges—
and Dick, leaning against a post, says, "Somebody count the
house." A check shows 115 animals—cows, heifers, and
calves—in the barn, and two empty stanchions for the two heifers still running on the next farm. Two more milkers were sold
last week to make room for this throng—"we're probably keeping too many calves," Dick says—and clearly the barn will be
tight this winter.

Bushed from chasing and wrestling cattle, the family retreat to
their two homes to rest up until milking time. One by one, the
kids drift off to the kitchen, returning with bowls of cold cereal
to the living room, where another TV video game—this one
involving a small boxer, controlled by the player, who fights a
succession of big, mean, and ugly braggadocios—absorbs their
attention.

As dusk falls, Dick climbs into his barn clothes and tries to get
Jeff and Kevin started for the barn again. The boys—Kevin
playing the video game, Jeff napping on the couch—are perfectly
happy where they are, and, like the heifers, drag their feet.

"Let's go!" Dick finally barks. "You go on ahead," Kevin responds; "we'll be down in a little while." "That's what you said yesterday, but you stayed up here an hour." "We had to," Kevin explains, "we were doing science." "I remember," Dick replies dryly; "you rubbed balloons on your heads and had to stay put to see whose came down first off the ceiling."

## 3

IT IS 9:40 WHEN DICK AND JOAN RETURN TO the house from morning milking, and while Joan cooks oatmeal, Dick tackles the big Ashley woodstove in the boys' dormitory extension. He repeatedly shakes the grate to fill the ash pan, and the smoke takes advantage of the open door to send small exploratory parties off for the far reaches of the house. Dick casts a baleful eye on the glistening brown creosote oozing around the collar at the ceiling and tracking down the stovepipe like thickened tobacco juice. "Problem is, we don't open the stove up enough. But nobody's here most of the day, and I don't like to leave it hot. This afternoon I'll open it up and cook the creosote so we can brush it out." He carts the large pan outside, strews the silver-gray ashes on the iced-over driveway, and returns to sit down to breakfast with Joan and Becky.

Back in the barn, Dick gets busy with a scraper while Don starts the cows out of their stanchions. "It was a damn short Indian summer," Don quips, and indeed it turned bitter again just after New Year's. By comparison to yesterday, when the wind chill registered 45 below, this morning is all but balmy. The mercury has recovered to zero, there is much less wind, and a strong sun is beginning to coax drops from the tips of icicles lining the roof edge on the south side of the barn. The frigid weather has caused immediate problems. Don and Irene's pipes are frozen. Jeff's car required a new battery, and the pickup has died, perhaps permanently. Dick has begun to worry about the two heifers still running on the next farm, and, because there is still no snow cover, the specter of meadow winter kill looms as well.

There are, as usual, animal problems on the farm, and a two-man vet team arrives to work on three cows. A urine test on number seventy-nine has shown a buildup of ketones, confirming the suspected ketosis, a nutritional disease marked by lowered blood sugar. This cow has been fresh about a month, and it is not uncommon for an animal in heavy milk production to outproduce its feed. When that happens, it starts to metabolize body fat (and the by-product ketones build in the urine); it then goes off its grain, causing it to metabolize more body fat, and a vicious circle has begun.

"Cows aren't meant to give a hundred pounds of milk a day," the vet remarks, "but about fifteen pounds for a calf." ("And fifteen pounds used to be enough," says Don, passing by with the sawdust wheelbarrow, remembering when he and Irene milked fourteen or fifteen cows by hand, putting the milk out on Cutting Hill Road in eighty-pound-capacity cans.) Agricultural science has engineered the cow to be a milk-producing machine, and ketosis is one result. This case has been caught early, and the cure should be quick and easy. The vet will attempt to break the cycle by megadosing the animal with dextrose, getting the blood sugar level back up and the cow back on grain, in the hope that it will be able to catch up with its milk production.

The vet's helper halters number seventy-nine, pulls her head to one side, and hitches it tight. The vet jams an inch-long needle into her neck three times before blood spurts out. Then he secures the hose hanging from a bottle of dextrose to the needle, and begins to dose her. Tied though she is, the cow manages to throw the needle, uncoupling the rig, and the exploratory needle-jabbing begins once again. This time the needle holds, and the sugar solution slowly drains into the animal. "Go easy on her grain at first," the vet advises Dick, "or she might twist a stomach."

The vet washes up in his scrub bucket and turns his attention to cow number eighty-six, on the other side of the aisle. She has an ugly swelling in a hind ankle, perhaps a migrated foot infection. Her rear leg hoisted with block and tackle, the cow plunges desperately. Either the straining or a knock on a post causes the swelling to break, and a pencil-thick rope of cream-white pus shoots from the leg. When she calms down, the vet examines the leg. "This is too high for a foot problem," he suggests; "she must have got a puncture up here somehow."

He probes the infected area with a forceps and squeezes out more pus, now reddening as it mixes with blood. He then uses a small scalpel to cut through the hide about three inches to one side of the rupture, and drives his forceps into the original rupture and under the hide until they appear out the new incision. He next fills a large syringe with iodine and flushes the ankle interior, forcing the liquid in through the incision, whence it leaks out through the original break. "You don't want to wrap this," he says to Dick, who is distributing hay; "leave it open so it can keep draining. If she'll tolerate it," he adds, "flush more iodine through in a day or two." The vet's helper drops the leg, and the cow, in obvious pain, holds the trembling hoof just off the floor.

The vet washes up again and proceeds to cow number thirty, which had been treated earlier in the week for a sore foot. He unwraps the cheesecloth-like bandage and examines the foot. It seems to be coming along, and so he simply repacks it with a pink foot medicine the consistency of grease and wraps it up in a new bandage. "I think this will do O.K.," he says to Dick; "I don't think we'll have to block it." ("Blocking" a foot involves gluing a block of wood to the base of the healthy half of the hoof; the result is a sort of half-hoof elevator shoe which holds the infected half off the ground, keeping it out of the filth and relieving it of pressure, thereby aiding its healing.) The vet's helper packs up their barn kit—a kind of oversized tackle box—hauls it out to the truck, and the team is on its way.

It's 1:15 when morning chores are completed. Dick checks the feed bunk, turns off the silo unloaders, and he and his father head for home, Don to contemplate his frozen pipes, Dick to contemplate lunch and baking creosote. He and Joan sit down to fish sticks, peas, and rice, and, as it often does, their talk turns to their emergency-squad work. Ski season is now under way, which means injury calls from the Snow Bowl in the Green Mountains to the east, and volunteer emergency people have difficulty feeling charitable about some of those calls. A couple of days ago, a squad had responded to a Code 2 call from the Snow Bowl. They tore up the mountain to find the victim sitting on a chair. He "thought" he had hurt his shoulder. "All he needed, if he wanted to check it out, was a ride to the hospital," Joan says. "His family was with him, and could have taken him, but they didn't want to miss out on their skiing. So he makes free use of an ambulance and crew, and not so much as a 'thank you' at the end of the trip."

Most emergency calls are serious, of course, and Dick is wondering whether the eleven-month-old baby he drove to the Burlington hospital earlier in the week lived or died. "It was having awful convulsions. They had IVs hanging from it and everything, but they couldn't stop the convulsions." It had been the day after New Year's, and Dick had not been on call. But the on-duty crew was on its way north to the Burlington hospital, and the backup crew was out of commission when the call came in; Dick dropped what he was doing and ran.

(What had sent one crew north and incapacitated the second was a car accident earlier in the day. The car had hit a patch of ice on Highway 22A in Orwell and had slid off the road, striking the corner of a barn. On arrival, the on-duty crew quickly determined that the young woman in the passenger seat was, in rescue-squad terminology, "unsalvageable," and they worked to free the seriously injured young driver and get him to the hospital. This left to the backup crew the unpleasant task of extricating the

young woman. Her head injuries and crushed side were bad
enough, but when they finally pulled her from the wreck, both
legs separated from her torso. The grisly work completed, the
shaken crew went home, called headquarters to remove their
names from the duty roster, and poured themselves stiff drinks.)

Halfway through lunch, Joan experiences a medical problem
of her own, an attack of back spasms, unpredictable bouts of
which have recurred in recent weeks, perhaps related to the
downstairs woodpile. Somehow mold has gotten into this winter's wood supply, and since both Dick and Jeff are allergic to
mold, Joan has been loading the great chunks of wood into the
cellar stove. Whatever the cause, the spasms are painful and
debilitating, and she now rises slowly from the table, arms
braced for support, and eases out of the kitchen, one hand
pressed in the small of her back.

When the spasms quiet down, she will ask her doctor to call
in a prescription for Valium, then ask someone to drive her to
town to pick it up, after which she will get a pill in her and
struggle through a grocery shop. Then home before dark while
Dick and Jeff—one parked by the upstairs stove, the other on
the roof—brush out the stovepipe before milking time. Then she
will put on an easy dinner and wrap up in a blanket and rest,
happy in the mild Valium high, not even minding when the kids
say, "You're all right, Mom; you just don't want to milk."

## 4

MORNING CHORES ARE FINISHED, AND DON
reminds Dick that they ought to do something about the loose
piece of tin on the peak of the sugarhouse roof. He finds a
three-by-four-foot piece of aluminum lying about, and Dick

climbs onto the roof at the uphill end to see about patching. He laps the aluminum over the loose tin and attempts to nail it down. A couple of nails find secure anchorage along one margin, but at the other side he finds nothing but tin roofing to nail to. "Well, this might hold," he concludes doubtfully, and climbs down.

Dick stops at the head of his driveway to pick up the mail, then pauses in the dooryard to admire the new family vehicle. He has concluded a deal with an area veterinarian team for their Ford F250 ¾-ton pickup for $3,500. Vets do a lot of driving, and this three-year-old truck has 99,100 miles on it. Still, the cool maroon body is, for the most part, in good shape (the mysterious two-inch-long, quarter-inch-wide scrapes here and there are the result of equine clients at a nearby Morgan horse farm chewing on the vehicle), and Dick thinks it will be a good truck for their purposes. Jeff, a longtime Ford fanatic, was transported by the purchase. He hugged his mother and forgave both parents all previous trespasses. He plans to drive the truck to school on Monday.

It is a calm, sunny winter day, heading for 40 degrees for the second day running. Back roads are wet, barnyards threatening to return to mud, not from melting snow—of which there is next to none in the valley—but from frost coming out of the ground. In an ordinary winter, this would be called "the January thaw"; this winter, it is simply another warm spell. Dick drops into a chair on the patio to look at the mail. "Wish I had time to do this in the summer," he says ruefully. A red-tailed hawk drifts over, takes a turn, and sails on.

Joan returns from taking Becky to school, and the two sit down to a lunch of submarine sandwiches and potato chips, after which Dick puts the chain saw in the back of the new pickup, and they drive north up the road past Diane's house and jounce across a meadow west into a white pine woods where Dick started making sugar wood yesterday and means to make more today. The pine here are too thick for a sun-loving species, and many small-to-medium-sized trees are dead and dying. Pine burns quick and hot, not the sort of fire you want in a wood-stove, but ideal for sugar making, where a slow cook will drop your syrup a grade.

Dick, in sweatshirt, cords, and sneakers, oils and gasses his saw and sets to work felling trees a foot and smaller at the butt. Joan, in coveralls and boots, limbs the downed trees with an axe and then begins the slow work of carrying out to the tractor road the forty-inch logs into which Dick converts the trees. The carry isn't long, but it's not easy, either. Cows haven't been in this woods for some years, and the sapling growth—some hemlock and witch hazel, but mostly hardhack, all of it hung with tan pine-shed five-needle bundles, apex up like miniature tepee foundations—is heavy, so that, threading his way howsoever carefully he may, the face of the arm-filled log carrier sustains a repetition of minor insults on the way through what Joan calls the puckerbrush.

Joan's back has been better of late, but she still feels some tightness in it, and Dick stops sawing from time to time to carry out the heavier logs. Pausing between trees, Joan, blinking a newly switched eye, passes the time with a perfunctory complaint about the work, prompting Dick to wax lyrical: "Why, Joan," he says in mock amazement, "lots of people would *pay* to be out here in the fresh air, at one with the rhythms of Nature, 'finding' themselves in the Great Outdoors!" "Put a lid on it," Joan replies. Then, thinking somewhat better of her lot: "I wish I had some Hershey's kisses; then this would be O.K."

At about three o'clock, Joan drives the truck back to the house to make a snack. She returns shortly with Brian and Becky, home on the bus, and the family gathers for what, on a typical January day in the North Country, would be most unusual outdoor refreshment: ice cream bars and cold soda. The family head back into the woods to work wood. Brian and Becky haul out a few logs, but their interest soon flags. Brian's request for a ride home having been denied, he sets off on foot, thinking about more food, while Becky amuses herself sliding on an eight-foot-long patch of ice in a tractor-road rut near a pile of logs.

Dick sizes up a pair of same-sized pines leaning over in mutual support. He cuts them, and, as he expected, they do not come down. He cuts a couple of sections off the two butts, then picks them up a butt at a time and drags them down. Joan limbs and carries, Dick saws and carries, and in time the second log pile of the afternoon is enlarged in the amount of two trees. Dick already has his eye on more trees, but Joan talks him into closing up shop for the day. "We've got chores and you've got rescue class tonight." Dick loads the chain saw in the truck and they head out, leaving axe, gas can, and oil in the woods.

They stop at the house to see who's available for chores. Jeff and Brian are apparently in the barn already, and Joan and Kevin are soon straggling down as well. Dick comes out of the house last, calling after them: "I left my boots in the woods; this is awful!" This winter evening he will grain and milk in sneakers.

ON THE FOLLOWING SATURDAY, THE LAST OF the month, the male Treadways are back in the pine woods for another of many afternoons of work. Kevin and Brian ride down in the red pickup with Dick, while Jeff drives the International Harvester and Don pulls the open-wagon manure spreader with a Deere.

Dick wants to take out a wagon load today, and sets to work on the first pile of logs. Anything less than six inches in diameter will be burned as is. He simply chucks the smaller sticks over toward Brian, who picks them up and hands them to his grandfather, who starts the first of three tiers that will fill the wagon, first setting a stand-up stick at each end of the row, so that they can pile higher than the wagon's sides.

Most of these logs must be split, however, and split by hand, since forty-inch logs are much too long for the power splitter to accommodate. Hand-splitting wood—especially pieces of this length—is painstaking work, and it is made more difficult now by the lack of snow cover. Whether pounding on a wedge or striking with the axe blade, Dick must balance the stick on the uneven ground before each blow, which means moving the down end six or eight times, a half-inch this way, a half-inch that, until it stands. The pine splits pretty well—although pieces this long often have to be split from both ends, or a split completed while the log lies on the ground—but some of this pile is hemlock, which is miserable stuff to work. Dick drives in a wedge, and succeeds only in breaking off a foot-long piece. He knows he could work for fifteen minutes on this one stick, and would end up with a pile of useless shards. "We'll just have to burn this hemlock as is, no matter how big," he says, heaving the log in Brian's direction.

From time to time, Jeff's red-and-black plaid outer shirt has been visible down the tractor road as he jockeys cut trees into place with the small International Harvester. Now he putts up the road to complain about his co-worker's behavior: "Hey, Dad!" he shouts, "tell Kevin to smarten up. I'm trying to chain a log out and he's sitting on it!" "Better get him some Preparation H," Don hollers back, "in case you hit a bump!"

A grumbling Jeff returns to work with his unrepentant brother, whose cheeks and ears, despite coveralls and a ski hat, are nearly as pink as his shirt on this chilly day. Jeff and Kevin's job is to cut and snake out more dead trees, and at the moment they are looking at a sugar-wood goldmine. Three two-tree blowdowns, but twelve or fifteen yards between pairs, lie before them, their gnarled roots displaying large clotted samples of the valley's clay and rock soil mix. All three pairs of trees point southeast, perhaps victims of a single storm out of the north-west. These are fair-sized trees, almost more than Jeff's small chain saw can manage; but there is a lot of sugar wood here if they can get them out of the woods.

Kevin limbs with an axe while Jeff backs the tractor off the road into the woods margin, then snakes his chains back to the first pair, trying to pick a path where the dragged log will do minimal damage to living trees. Thorson keeps a dubious eye on these proceedings, and on Kevin as he loops the end of the third chain around the first tree's bole and hooks it. "O.K.!" Kevin shouts to his brother, who is back on the tractor, "tighten her up." Jeff eases forward, and Kevin stands by the tree, watching the long chain come taut off the ground. "Looks all right," he calls; "haul her out." Then, *"Wait!"* he screams, turning and dashing for cover, suddenly remembering repeated warnings concerning the unexpected (and regrettable) things a snapped logging chain can do to the human body.

Jeff drags the forty-foot log out to the tractor road, demolishing an old stump on the way and leaving a trail of brown conifer-woods duff behind. He then removes his extension chains, hooks the log chain to his tractor, and pulls the tree out into a clearing where the woods give way to meadow. He takes off the last chain and jockeys the tree into position against another, shoving it along with the tractor's front tires. He backs the tractor into position once again, and hauls his chains into the woods for another tree. This one is easily over fifty feet long, and the boys hope for a new personal logging record, but it disappoints them, breaking off in the middle at the start of the pull.

Back up the road, Dick is about "split out," and he conscripts Jeff to take a turn with the axe. But the second tier nears completion in the spreader wagon, and by chores time the Treadways will have a first load of wood to drop off at the sugarhouse.

## 5

JOSEPH WOOD KRUTCH, DRAMA CRITIC AND commentator on the American scene, left his native Northeast for the Southwest, saying: "The most serious charge which can be brought against New England is not Puritanism but February." Certainly February starts off in memorable fashion this year, and not only for New England. A massive arctic air mass organized itself over Alaska in late January, punishing that state for a week with temperatures of 60 to 70 degrees below zero and wind chills of −100 degrees, numbing cold that cracked and flattened truck tires, preventing the transportation of food and other essentials to outlying villages.

Finally, the frigid air mass moved southeast through western Canada and overspread virtually the whole of the United States. The leading edge of that enormous cold front reached western New England on February 2, and any woodchuck unlucky enough to peek out of a Vermont burrow on this particular Groundhog Day would have been instantly blinded, its eyes glazed over with cold sleet. Jeff's vocational-tech class was to have graduated this evening, but high school officials took a look at the impassable roads and reluctantly called the ceremony off.

Nobody has much lamented the postponement on the Treadway farm, where February has not started well. A virus picked up by Becky has spread first to Jeff and then to Joan. This has left Dick doing chores with a half-crew while trying to look after the other half vomiting up at the house. ("He's been a saint," Joan confides to friends.) Then, at an evening milking, he noticed that two cows were ignoring their grain, and Joan, dragging around the barn trying to help, took their temperatures. In each case, the thermometer read 105 degrees. There were no signs of mastitis, and, fearing something bad, Dick called the vet. The vet came by late that night, and their fears were confirmed. They had pneumonia in the barn.

Ordinarily, the herd is vaccinated for pneumonia in the autumn. Last fall, a new vaccine had been promised, then delayed. Dick put off the vaccination, and it simply hadn't been done. The vet now treats the two cows with a new drug, and the two-man team returns in the morning to vaccinate the rest of the cows and the heifers. The Treadways aren't sure how, but cows know that vets are visiting even before they enter the barn. (Jeff thinks the tipoff is the metallic rattling of their oversized equipment box.) Any cows lying down immediately get to their feet. Cows associate vets with unpleasant experiences, and news of the impending vaccination is quickly communicated through the barn. Pausing at regular intervals to reload their multidose caulk-gun–like vaccination tools and occasionally to replace bent needles, the two vets move down two lines of bellowing, eye-rolling cows, driving their needles into both sides of each rump, often a moving target.

Pneumonia in cows is often curable; sometimes not. At best, the Treadways will lose several days' milk production from two cows; then again, they may lose two cows. But there is a further worry. Pneumonia is highly contagious. (Pulmonary disease is an important reason why the Treadways' fan-powered barn ventilation system runs even in the coldest winter weather, when the cow pies smoke along the gutters like rows of winter chimneys along a village street. Cold won't hurt the cows, but "old" air will, laden as it is with urine- and dung-generated ammonia fumes, which can weaken a cow's resistance to pneumonia and other respiratory diseases, and with pulmonary-disease organisms expelled by any infected animal.) How many more cows will contract the disease during the lag time before the vaccinations provide protection? Until yesterday, Joan was worried only about future victims of her family's flu virus. Now there is a second "other shoe" waiting to drop.

THE HIGH SCHOOL'S SECOND ATTEMPT TO graduate the vo-tech class meets with better weather and goes off without a hitch before an audience of families and friends (including a number of vocal babies and youngsters) in the school auditorium. The speaker, a state hospital administrator, talks about ethics in the marketplace, quoting polls suggesting a majority of Americans believe that people cheat on their income taxes and that workers steal merchandise and tools from their employers. Integrity, he tells the students, is their most valued asset. There are, he warns, no shortcuts to advancement. Hard work is the key. He advises the graduates to be aware of technological change, keep their job skills up to date, and, if necessary, be prepared to learn new skills and change jobs.

The speech is no less well received for its brevity, and then the Outstanding Student awards are presented in various disciplines, from Human Services, Secretarial Office Practice, and Photo Offset Program, to Horticulture, Forestry, Agricultural Mechanics, Agribusiness Management, and Building Trades. The Agricultural Mechanics teacher introduces a young man who "takes challenges in stride," whose projects included putting new head gaskets in a fire truck, and who did the high school proud at the Kansas City competition. Jeff climbs onto the stage, shakes hands with his teacher, gets his certificate, and exits behind the back curtain for a brief photo session.

It is diploma time, and those students in attendance—many live a fair distance away, and some haven't made the trip—parade across the stage as names are read by discipline. Most of the young women are dressed as if for a dinner date. Like the audience, the young men vary widely in dress. Most, including Jeff, wear carefully laundered jeans and shirts; a few wear coats and ties. Flashbulbs flare now and again as proud parents stand briefly and attempt to catch the diploma transfer, with Joan Treadway, seated front and center in an elegant black sheath setting off a fringed white shawl, among them. The whole ceremony has lasted but an hour, and Joan talks Jeff into putting in at least a token appearance at the reception in the vocational-ed building, where the adults socialize over coffee while the students mostly stand around the room's periphery, as if leery of the fancy food laid out on trays on the long central table.

The Treadways have their own celebration ready at home, and Jeff ushers his mother out into a cold, starlit night and into the new truck. ("Why didn't you take your car?" Dick will ask. "I couldn't get it out where it was parked," Jeff will reply, a sheepish grin giving the show away.) The family gathers in the kitchen to see the cutting of Jeff's cake. The cake is a huge one-layer affair, down the center of whose white frosting runs a blue highway complete with yellow no-passing lines. An over-turned tanker truck lies off a curve near two spruce trees, its skid marks evident on the blue highway, and a wrecker is backing into position to render service.

Joan cuts the cake and lifts the first piece onto a paper plate, a move greeted by exclamations as it is discovered that the three-inch-thick cake is exactly half frosting. "There's more frosting on that cake than we've got snow on the ground," Dick says. The children attribute the unusual proportions to a novice cake-maker who couldn't locate the stop switch on the frosting machine. This much commercial frosting is too much even for Brian, Becky, and Kevin, who pass up cake in favor of ice cream. The rest of the family loyally eat cake, wondering from time to time what animals on the farm might be willing to eat what's left.

If the spirit of this celebratory gathering is a bit subdued, more than a disappointing cake is involved. The February blues have continued, and this has been an especially hard day on the farm. Joan has spent the middle of the day at the hospital with her younger sons. Kevin mashed a hand in the barn, and Brian managed to snap a finger doing handstands in the house. The X-rays proved negative in Kevin's case, but Brian has indeed broken a middle finger at the top-knuckle growth plate, for which he has been fitted with a metal finger cast.

Meanwhile, the unloader in the hay silo quit during morning chores. Chores finished, Dick had just started to climb into the silo to check out the problem when a fire call came through, and he spent much of the day fighting a house fire in the village. He had planned to attend Jeff's graduation, but with a late start to afternoon chores and Kevin and Brian banged up and Joan and Jeff leaving for town, he couldn't get away from the barn. Now he sits on a kitchen chair dead tired, the light gone out of his eyes, thinking, perhaps, of the third cow now down with pneu-monia, perhaps wondering what else this February may have in store.

# 6

THE MASSIVE ARCTIC HIGH HAS GRIPPED THE country for a week, bringing frigid temperatures straight down to the Gulf of Mexico. A snowstorm closed freeways leading into Los Angeles this morning, and across the country sixty-one deaths have already been attributed to this weather system. The brunt of the air mass is passing to the southwest of New England, but a couple of modest snows have finally enabled Vermont's lower-elevation cross-country ski trails to open, and it looks as if Shoreham will be white for the remainder of the winter.

It is a clear, sunny day on Cutting Hill Road. The thermometer on the north end of the barn reads 12 degrees, and a blustery south wind makes it feel colder. Leaving morning chores on hold immediately after milking, Joan and Dick walk up to the house for breakfast, joking about needing something strong to drink to get up courage for the silo job.

The day after the unloader breakdown, Dick had climbed into the silo and found that a bearing in the auger shaft had frozen up and gradually worn through the shaft until the auger mechanism simply collapsed. "You'd think they'd have a bolt-on shaft in these things," says Dick; but no such luck. He had to order a whole new auger assembly at something like $600. When it came, he and Jeff had the very devil of a time getting it into the silo, hauling it up the outside by pulley and then maneuvering the heavy ten-foot-long assembly through the on-load door at the top.

It is now ten o'clock of the sixth day since the unloader failed, and Dick is anxious to get haylage back into the feeding program. "We've got to get started," he says to Joan, who, lingering over her coffee, puts on the voice of a whiny child: "Do we *have* to?" And then she starts at a sudden crash from the living room, and her startled look changes to one of vexation as she realizes that one of the house cats has smashed into the plate-glass window, once again determined to snatch a chickadee or downy woodpecker dining at the feeder hanging outside.

They stop at the barn to put new teeth on the "chipper wheel," which, attached to the end of the auger, theoretically prevents the buildup of frozen silage on the silo's inner wall. (The chipper wheel is seldom entirely effective, and in most winters someone has to climb into the silos perhaps once a week to chip off frozen silage with a crowbarlike ice fisherman's pick. The intermittent warm periods this winter—which Dick thinks may have contributed to his pneumonia problem—have so far at least prevented the frozen silage problem.)

Dick and Joan work on the barn "table," a hunk of plywood on a wheelbarrow that sits under the Heat Expectancy Chart & Freshening List on the wall. Dick bolts four-inch-wide teeth on the wheel while Joan loads tools into a grain bucket. A black cat sits among the tools on the table as well, calmly eating cat food out of a dish. Another cat—a large white one with black blotches, a stray that visits the barn from time to time—lies in the other wheelbarrow, now parked in the central aisle.

Dick climbs up the chute—some of the bracketed foothold bars are stuffed with silage, making progress tricky—and drops a rope. Joan ties on the tool bucket and follows it up the chute. Climbing through an off-load door into the silo is like walking from daylight into a movie theater. Soft light from the plastic skylight illuminates the upper silo, but it is dark down toward the bottom, and it is some time before one's eyes become accustomed to the point where one can see one's breath. Outside it is cold and windy, inside cold and still, the rank smell of haylage calmer in the cold air.

Dick and Joan roll the new auger into position under the shield "roof" of the unloader arm, lift the outside end up and through the hole in the support bracket, then together lift the other end to see if the hollow end of the auger shaft can be fitted over the short "male" shaft protruding from the engine assembly. As Dick had guessed, the two shaft ends overlap. Working by flashlight while kneeling on sawdust bags, they take the auger down and then remove the support bracket, during which process a bolt head twists off. Dick calls down the chute to Don for a replacement bolt, but Don is off on other business.

Dick and Joan lift the auger into place once again, and try to work it onto the male shaft, but it won't go on far enough to match bolt holes. "Try to twist it and shove at the same time," Dick says, lying on a bag and tugging at his end, but Joan is struggling just to keep the awkward and heavy assembly aloft, and the wickedly sharp teeth projecting from the curving flange prevent her from resting it on her upper leg. (A glance at the old auger shows just how hard cold-packed winter silage is; in about five years the 1½-inch triangular steel teeth that dig up the silage have been reduced to dull-edged, rounded nubbins.)

They work the auger back off, and Dick files on the connector shaft for ten minutes. This time up it slides all the way onto the power shaft, and they are able to line up the holes and pound the bolts into place. Dick now brings the tool bucket down to help support Joan's end while he reattaches the support bracket. While moving one hand to make way for the bucket, Joan sings out, having cut a finger on a tooth. She examines the finger and grimly announces: "I am losing my sense of humor."

Dick now discovers that the good bracket bolt he had dropped down the chute to his father was not returned with its match, and, as Don has left to drive Becky to school, Dick has to climb down and hunt the shop for the original. Abandoned in the cold silo, Joan remembers the silage situation during her first years on the farm. "There was a wooden silo here then, with no top and no unloader. We'd climb up every morning and fork silage down. Of course, when it had snowed a foot, you'd have to shovel out a foot of snow before you could get at the silage." Then, contemplating the tools scattered about the disabled unloader arm: "At least then you knew how long it would take to feed the cows."

Dick returns in due course, but the support bracket, weighted down by the auger assembly, will not line up with its anchor holes, despite heaving and hammering and grunting. Eventually, they start the bolt on one side, then work to hammer and muscle the other side into position, hoping the bracket isn't being sprung in the process. Dick and Joan lie on sacks tightening nuts at either end of the auger assembly, after which Dick sets the locking collar around the bearing wheel with an allen wrench. Finally, they carefully lift the heavy chipper wheel into place and secure it.

The people who engineered unloader augers didn't worry about questions such as how one is to be gotten out of a silo. The Treadways have already tried the relatively easy—and almost only—solution, namely tipping it out an off-load door and lowering it down the chute. But door and chute proved too restrictive to accommodate the ten-foot-long assembly. Dick thinks of an alternative to a reverse replay of the nightmare new auger trip. He ties a rope around one end and stands the auger upon the other. Joan balances it while he climbs up to the middle of the silo. She throws him the coiled rope, which he catches on the third try. He hauls the assembly up and hitches it to an open door, leaving it to hang out of the way until the silo is emptied next summer. Then it will be lowered and run out through the bottom off-load door, the only door unguarded by the chute.

Dick and Joan lower the tools in the bucket, throw down the sawdust sacks, and climb down from the silo. Trying to walk, they remember that cold silage is hard on more than auger teeth, and they stamp feet and lower legs drained of heat and feeling. In the barn, they find Don talking with a man from a local farm-supply business, out to check on the hot water heater. The barn inspector has complained that the pipeline and milkhouse equipment are not cleaning up properly, and they suspect that the wash water simply isn't hot enough.

Dick and Joan limp up to the house and put some fish patties into the microwave. It's past noon now, and morning chores are still half undone. "Look at it this way," Dick says, justifying the ways of do-it-yourself to his wife. "We could have had somebody come out to replace that auger, but it would have cost thirty bucks for the visit and twenty-five an hour for a couple of men; so we probably saved something like two hundred dollars. And," he adds, the would-be deadpan face betrayed by double crow's-feet sweeps, "we had the fun of fixing it ourselves." Joan has been searching for a couple of clean plates in the midst of two days' worth of dirty dishes stacked high on counters and in the sink. "Shut up," she replies dispassionately.

Lunch is barely over when the phone rings. Don is on the barn phone; he could use some help with chores, and there has been another machine failure, about which he declines to be specific. Dick and Joan pull on their coveralls and barn boots and walk to the barn, where they find the silage-feeding system shut down once again. The problem is not, at least, at the unloader end. "The new auger was kicking haylage down like crazy," Don says; but something at the feed bunk end had begun an awful clanking, and had ground to a halt before he could reach the switch.

Dick soon locates the problem at the barn end of the feed bunk. The end drum roll—which looks like an elongated bird cage with jail-house–sized bars—around which the silage-carrying conveyor belt runs, had apparently broken a weld at the central shaft. The resulting play in the drum roll has resulted in one bar breaking out completely and the other fifteen snapping at one end plate. Dick and Joan set to work with socket wrenches, and soon have the drum roll out. He hauls it off to the shop to see if some welding can save it.

Don, who has been watching the operation, is off to Diane's place to feed two of her new triplet lambs, the third being off to school with Diane. ("I hope the kids like lambs better'n I do," he complains.) It's 2:30 now, and Joan is alone in the barn, whose gutters are full of dung, whose sawdust is unspread, and whose hay has yet to be distributed. She starts to work on the hay when the phone rings. It is Becky's kindergarten teacher. Could Joan make some heart-shaped cookies for the school valentine party? "Sure," she replies; "how many do you need?"

Home from school, Jeff starts up the gutter scraper and feeds the calves. Don, home from lamb duty, scatters sawdust starting with the side aisles, each sideways sweep of the oversized shovel laying down a ten-foot-long arc between pairs of barn support posts. Dick has been working for an hour up at the shop and hasn't got to step two. The drum roll's end plate simply won't seat properly, making it impossible to line up and weld the rod ends. He turns the plate on the shaft and taps it with a small hammer, turns and taps, turns and taps. Finally, he finds the single place where the broken weld on the shaft will fit together, and the plate seats properly.

None of the shop's vises will accommodate the drum roll, and Dick is off to the house to get a larger woodworking vise. That doesn't work either, and he ends up balancing it on the ground while welding the sixteen rods and the break at the shaft. He then smooths the rod ends with a power grinder, examines the drum roll, and carries it back to the bunk.

Joan and Dick reassemble the drum roll and snug the belt up to it, surrounded by an audience of cows. Having cleaned up every flake from the aborted silage run, most merely stand around, the very picture of terminal boredom. A few are curious about the mechanical work. One sniffs the tool bucket, another the WD-40 can, while a third snakes out its tongue to taste a pant leg. Fred stalks down the conveyor trough from the silo and climbs into the silage hopper over the bunk belt, much to Jeff's delight, who wonders aloud if the cat intends suicide.

Fred having been chased off, Don throws the switch while Dick watches to see if the belt is straight. He makes a final adjustment, and the automatic silage-feeder system once again roars to life. The cows know that racket well enough, and all move into position, pressing their heads down into the bunk, waiting expectantly for the silage dump to begin.

It is nearly 4 P.M. and time to start evening chores. But the cows can use a half-hour to eat, and none of the Treadways seems to be in a hurry to start dirtying a just-cleaned barn. "Let's go up to the house and have something hot to drink," Dick says, "and then we'll let the cows in." The family has, at least, the satisfaction of knowing that the herd is healthy once again. The pneumonia scare has passed, and all three victims have recovered and gone back on line.

# 7

THE ANNUAL DISTRICT EASTERN INSEMINATION Association dinner meeting rolls around on a foggy Wednesday evening. Joan and Dick have decided to take a break after some years of regular attendance, and besides Joan has spent the afternoon on emergency-squad duty and in the emergency room at the hospital, and Dick will be driving the ambulance tonight; so Jeff finds himself driving alone to his first Eastern meeting, the trip north to the Eagles building in Vergennes taking an hour at 40 mph in the low-beam fog.

There are perhaps fifty farmers—mostly husbands and wives—in the meeting room when Jeff arrives, and during the next fifteen minutes a hundred more appear, hanging coats and taking seats at long tables featuring the Eastern I.A. Daughter Gallery placemats, a gallery of twelve photos of prime milking cows sired by Eastern bulls. (Daughter Gallery captions are composed of number and letter codes. Under the picture of Likabul's daughter, for example, one finds: 3-02 2X 316D 21,412M 3.1% 671F, which means that in a 316-day lactation beginning in the second month of her third year, she was milked twice a day and gave 21,412 pounds of milk, whose butterfat content was 3.1 percent, or 671 pounds).

There are farm couples—and some singles—in their twenties, and a few in their seventies. A very few are attired in dresses and jackets and ties, but most are in "town clothes," sweaters and slacks, plaid shirts and casual pants. Some, especially among the middle-aged men, would be taken for farmers anywhere, their unruly hair greased and combed back over lightened brow lines and open, weathered faces; others, in particular some of the younger couples, could pass for Wall Street yuppies.

What the annual Eastern dinner meeting is mostly about is dinner, and the men and women serving it go about their business. They distribute paper cups and pitchers of milk and plastic cups of cole slaw to the tables. Men carry huge pans of hot food to a central table, and the lines begin to form. It doesn't seem to occur to anyone that the spread before them invites a *choice* of entrees. Jeff, like most of these diners, piles his plate up with scalloped potatoes and ham, beef, turkey, ham, *and* meatballs, with baked beans and rolls and butter on the side. He sits down and applies himself to the business at hand, occasionally exchanging remarks with a friend up the table.

Across the table from Jeff, a fiftyish couple are eating quietly when a young man—who must still be in his teens, and who would look at home on a surfboard—recognizes old friends while passing through with his plate. He sits down beside them, and the three catch up on the news while eating. The young man talks about his young daughter, now getting into the cupboards. How does she do in the barn, the older couple want to know, their thick accent placing them among the area's Dutch farmers, remembering when their own daughter had slipped into the gutter, breaking an arm.

They talk about the corn shortage, exchanging information on where corn can be bought cheapest and the problems of keeping it in bulk. The younger man is going to try feeding cornmeal, and see how that works out. The subject of the drought comes up, and the older man shakes his head and complains that once again poor farming paid off when it came to collecting government relief. They move to the issue of the new state tax-rebate program for farmers. The young man has applied, the older man has not, a decision he emphasizes by waving in dismissal of all such offers of dubious government largesse a typical farmer's hand, the enormous fingers sprouting from a great palm whose cuts and cracks are permanently traced as brown lines on the scrubbed surface.

Jeff's plate has long since been empty, and he heads back for seconds. Across the table, the conversation runs nearly nonstop, obviously a source of pleasure to all parties. Both farms have had good success with breeding this year, and seem pleased with Eastern's work. It's a different story with the young man's eczema. He pushes up a sleeve to reveal an afflicted forearm, and admits that it's "driving me nuts." The woman has the problem as well, and blames it on contact with the acids in barn wash water. "I'll tell you what will stop the itch," the young man says. "Straight Clorox. But it sure does hurt."

The young farmer is breaking in a new hired man, a subject rich in interest for farmers. The older man wonders where the man has come from and what he did before, where he will be housed and how good he is with animals. "He doesn't see real good," his friend replies, "but he seems like a good worker." They pass on to the subject of slaughtering beef, and the older farmer has had good luck with a local man who cuts and wraps meat. "I wish I'd known about him last fall," the young farmer responds. "Two of us butchered seven steers, and it was the first time for either of us." "Did you drop them with one shot?" his friend asks, a twinkle in his eye. "That was no problem, but one of them kicked me after he was down. I thought the sucker was dead. He got me right in the belly. Must have knocked me back twenty feet. And my wife was standing back laughing!" The Dutch couple laugh as well.

Milk-pitcher refills and strawberry shortcake follow the main course, and then, the dishes cleared away, the meeting begins. The emcee, a humorist and a popular figure on the local dairy scene, introduces the area Eastern "technicians," those men who visit the barns and do the actual insemination. His ploy is to

embarrass each technician with what purports to be a biograph-
ical story, and he hits home with a heavyset and bashful young
man who, the emcee says, showed up last summer clutching his
throat, barely able to speak. Asked what was wrong, he had
replied: "Golf."

His companion naturally wondered what golf could have to
do with his throat, and slowly, with much miming and gasping
on the part of the emcee, the story comes out. It seems the young
technician had been golfing, and had driven a ball out of the
fairway into a pasture. A pretty "young chick" does the same,
and the two strangers go off hunting the pasture for their balls.
They have no luck until the young man notices a white spot
under a cow's tail. He checks the markings on what is, indeed,
a golf ball, and it isn't his. So, turning to the young woman—
and the technician himself has now turned his face toward the
wall in agony—he lifts the cow's tail and says: "Does this look
like yours?" Howls and peals of laughter fill the room, drowning
out the triumphant emcee as he delivers the last line about the
woman hitting the young man in the neck with her golf club.

The technicians thank their farmer clients for their business
and pass out certificates to several who have managed dramatic
increases in milk production. A brief talk follows, an Eastern
official telling the crowd that their co-op is in good shape, but
that insemination fees are going to remain high, in large part
because Eastern's lease on the Ithaca, New York, property where
its bulls are housed runs out in 1999, after which they will have
to spend several million dollars to build new barns elsewhere.

The emcee takes the floor and announces that the evening's
entertainment will be "short and sweet," a three-and-a-half
minute slide show that "will make you feel good about yourself
and your farm and your country." Someone hits the lights, and
the room falls quiet as slide after slide of Americana flashes
rapid-fire onto the screen while a male country-and-western vo-
calist sings about hitting the road, visiting America; his chorus:
"America, I'm still holding the dream."

Image follows image, mostly small-town and rural, of landscapes and faces, of Americans at work and play and on the road, of country stores and wheat fields and barber shops, of American flags and children playing on swings and old men leaning on farm fences. The show hurries to its conclusion, and the song with it:

> Then it hit me like a freight train
> That a mile from the fast lane,
> America is still staying the same.

The lights come up, and the spirit of jocular good fellowship gradually returns to the crowded room as door prizes are claimed, and then the emcee says: "Unless somebody's got something to say, we'll go home." No one claims the floor, and the meeting breaks up just under two hours after its commencement. Jeff joins a quickly forming line of men and women working their way to the coat rack, whence he and they swing through the meeting hall door and out into a cold and foggy night.

A FEW DAYS LATER, EASTERN'S AREA TECH-nician arrives at the Treadway farm to breed two cows. Popular with the family, Ed strolls into the barn in jeans, barn boots, and a denim vest over an ample check shirt, and begins to joke with the children. He addresses Kevin, who hasn't said a word, in a severe tone: "No, I'm *not* taking you with me today so you can get out of chores." Kevin grins through a spreading blush.

Having double-checked with Dick on the identity of the ordered semen, Ed returns to his car, more particularly to the milk-can–sized stainless steel canister resting on the back seat, a canister containing something like two thousand doses of semen worth $4 to $40 a shot. He extracts two doses in six-inch-long, brightly colored "straws"—they look like cocktail straws—from the –320-degree liquid nitrogen bath, in which semen will remain viable for several decades. He wraps the two straws in a paper towel and puts the package into his shirt pocket, where his body heat will thaw the semen in minutes. He then inserts the straws into larger straws called sheaths, loads those into the barrels of stainless steel breeding guns, and prepares to breed.

Having donned a shoulder-length plastic glove, he works his arm up inside the first cow, feeling through the rectal wall for the uterus' cervix, which he describes as "like the neck of a dead chicken." He inserts the gun into the birth canal, positioning the end of the tube in front of the two "horns" which communicate between uterus and fallopian tubes, and pushes the plunger to discharge the semen. The actual insemination takes perhaps thirty seconds, and he now moves to the second cow, using the second breeding gun.

Having completed his $38.50 call ($30 for two shots of semen plus service fees of $5.25 for the first cow and $3.25 for the second), Ed turns the feces-coated glove inside out around the sheaths and straws for disposal, waves to the kids, and heads out for another job.

## 8

ALREADY, IN THE DARK OF EARLY MORNING, a few vehicles—many of them pickups—are headed up and down the Champlain Valley on Highway 7. Some pull off into the huge parking lot of the Standard Register plant to start the early shift, while others make for other jobs in and around Middlebury, where this morning the lighted time-and-temperature sign in front of the bank registers −10 degrees, which is, as usual, optimistic. A bitter wind leans in from the northwest, driving frozen spray from the Otter Creek falls up and over the bridge on the main street in town.

The eastern sky lightens just enough to show the peaks of the

Green Mountains, then turns deep purple and then rose and then orange, and then a cold sun rises on a cold world. Driving south and west down highways 30 and 74 and then out Doolittle Road, one passes houses whose smoke streaks sideways from chimney tops while the "grass-skirt" fronds of their dooryard weeping willows lift at forty-five-degree angles from the vertical.

At the end of Doolittle Road, on Highway 22A, a hanging sign—similarly defying gravity—announces the Halfway House, an eatery catering to truckers and the agricultural trades. In the entryway, a rack offers a stack of bright green bumper stickers: "Don't Complain About Farmers With Your Mouth Full." Inside, a couple of tables already have customers—most wearing that year-round badge, the long-billed, ventilated headgear called a seed cap in some regions—who talk and drink coffee while addressing themselves to plates of bacon and eggs and hash browns and toast. Visible in the pass-through window behind the counter, a woman washes dishes; a cigarette hangs limply from her lips, the base of its alarmingly long ash reddening momentarily from time to time.

Having finished his breakfast, Pete Paige drives south down 22A to the Shoreham Service Center, where he lounges in the store out front smoking an honest-to-God corncob pipe and talking with a couple of other milk-truck drivers. Perhaps forty, Pete is, like his truck, sizable and solid. He sports a full beard and a pair of intense gray-green eyes. Today, he wears a pair of rubber and leather pacs and a two-piece blue work suit, the jacket unbuttoned over a red-and-black-check shirt unbuttoned over a blue-and-white-striped shirt partially buttoned over long-johns. An ex-Navy man and ex-logger, he now hauls milk, and, at 7:30 sharp, he knocks the ash from his pipe, picks up his clipboard and forms, climbs up into the cab of his idling truck, adjusts the pneumatically controlled seat behind the huge, nearly horizontal steering wheel, and heads for his first pickup, a farm out the Shoreham-Whiting road.

Using four outside-mounted rearview mirrors, Pete backs his "tandem" (silver stainless steel tank by Walker on a deep blue cab and chassis by Mack) into position close up to the milk-house door. He opens the doors to two compartments at the back of the tank, where he hooks up the electric line to power his pump and connects the milk hose, breaking ice out of the fittings with a massive wrench. He then inserts the free ends of electric cord and milk hose—the latter looks like a triple-sized vacuum-cleaner hose—through the small flappered door into the milkhouse, whence he follows them.

He lifts the hinged lid on the bulk tank, and gives its contents, which look like a thin, off-white milkshake, a quick check by eye and by nose. He then measures the contents with the tank's calibrated dipstick—which is periodically checked for accuracy—and converts the depth figure into pounds from a chart, noting that figure on his forms. He next switches on the bulk tank's agitator, whose paddles stir the milk, thoroughly mixing its good stuff (butterfat) and bad stuff (bacteria). Now Pete takes two samples from deep in the blending brew, retriev-ing them with a small, long-handled ladle and pouring them into numbered, sterilized plastic snap-capped tubes. He then takes the milk's temperature with a quick-registering thermometer, noting the result on his forms.

Pete plugs his electric cord into the milkhouse outlet, un-screws the plug from the outflow pipe at the base of the bulk tank, threads on his milk hose, and throws the lever to open the valve. Now ready to pump milk, he first checks the pulley ten-sion on his pump's motor, and, not surprisingly, finds it frozen up. He returns to the milkhouse for a bucket of hot water, which he sloshes over the motor housing to free up the rubber impeller within. He turns on the pump, only to find the hose leaking into his tank compartment. He shuts down the motor, loosens and tightens the giant stainless steel nuts on the hose system, and tries again. Again milk leaks into the left compartment.

"Sometimes the first stop of the day takes awhile," Pete says, considering his problem. Finally, he disassembles the hose-attachment system and finds a misseated rubber gasket. "Who-ever drove this truck yesterday was in a hurry when he quit." He soaks the gasket in hot water and reshapes it with his fingers. He hooks the system back up, and this time there is no leak, and his first load is pumped from bulk tank to truck tank. When the transfer is complete, he rinses down the inside of the bulk tank with a hose and closes it up. He detaches his milk hose and electric cord, replaces the tank's plug nut, lowers his milk samples into a plastic ice chest, stores hose and cord in their compartments, and hits the road again.

Pete hasn't run this particular route for some time, but he knows all the farmers, and talks with those who show up in the milkhouses. The farmer at the second stop is "down in the dumps," as Pete puts it. "His wife's dying of cancer, and getting real bad now. He's going to sell out; says he'll be gone by June." Most of the talk this morning is about the weather. "You're looking at a damn fool," a sixtyish farmer confides, on his way to a freeze-up problem somewhere with a pickaxe; "I should be in Florida." "What could you do in Florida you can't do here?" asks Pete, incredulous. "Survive!" the farmer retorts, and slams the door. A young farmer at the next stop bursts into the milkhouse with: "God*damn* it's cold! The neighbor over here took a load of shit out this morning and it froze before he got to the field." "It was sixteen below at my place," Pete replies; "all my pipes are froze."

Pete's blue cap—like the blue door of his truck—announces: "E. Pomainville Inc." Pomainville, an independent trucking outfit, operates thirteen rigs—all but one tandems and the larger tankers—out of Shoreham Service Center, where a huge shop keeps them running. Contracted by Agri-Mark, these trucks haul milk from 200-plus farms in a large area from central Vermont and neighboring New York, most of it off-loaded at the Agri-Mark receiving station outside Middlebury. (When there is an excess of milk there, tankers drive it south to larger Massachusetts receiving stations in Springfield and Boston.) Some of Pomainville's routes entail long-distance hauling, but the route Pete is running today is close in, involving farms in the three adjacent towns of Shoreham, Cornwall, and Whiting.

Pete is scheduled to pick up seven farms this morning, and they show some remarkable contrasts. One farm clearly has money behind it. The owner, Pete says, is into real estate and other business ventures as well as farming, and doesn't do much of the actual farm work now. ("He don't leave much sweat in the barn," is how Pete puts it.) Another farm is a classic "end-of-the-road" operation. Pete can't get through the milkhouse door, which, having hiked around through the barn and shoved a wheelbarrow from out in front of the other door, he finds propped closed by a two-by-four anchored under an old motor. Doors are sprung and window panes broken, and the milkhouse temperature is below zero. Both lids are up on the small bulk tank, leaving the milk vulnerable to contamination, and the compressor isn't running. Apparently the farmer is hoping to warm the milkhouse with the milk while cooling the milk with milkhouse air. It isn't working in either direction. The milk, which is supposed to be cooled immediately to under 40 degrees, registers 55. Pete doesn't like the looks of it. He agitates the milk, takes a sample, and leaves. "I'll have them run this through at the plant while they're checking my load. If it's O.K., I'll come back this afternoon and pick it up."

This kind of farm gives milk handlers fits, and there are still a number of them around. A check of the pickup sheet in this milkhouse shows radically varying numbers, which means that the farmer milks only when he feels like it, and he doesn't make much milk when he does. "We lose money on these two-hundred-pound producers," Pete says, "but we have to pick them up so long as the milk is good quality. Some of these old-time farmers were milking two hundred pounds twenty years ago, and they're still milking two hundred pounds. They don't buy any animals—raise their own replacements—and probably don't feed no grain to their animals, so they don't need a lot of money. After hauling and stop charges, they may make twenty-five bucks for two days' milking, but they hang on farming and will until they can't move."

With six of his scheduled seven morning loads aboard, the seventh on hold, Pete adds his dipstick conversion numbers and finds that his tandem (tank capacity, 4,000 gallons, or 35,000 pounds) is respectably loaded with 28,921 pounds of milk. It is 10:30, and he heads the rig east for the receiving station, passing farmsteads where pickups with jumper cables are still trying to start tractors. He slows to a crawl on the big hill on Highway 125 west of town, checking the exhaust-gas temperature of the laboring truck on his dashboard pyrometer. It registers 9,000 degrees, high but not dangerously high.

Both receiving bays are busy when Pete pulls around back of the plant. He parks in front of a bay door and immediately delivers his rack of sample tubes through a sliding-glass door to the lab, where a twenty-minute preliminary test will be completed before he will be allowed to off-load. That test completed and a bay free, Pete pulls his truck inside. A man on an overhead catwalk hoses down the tank's porthole area and then opens its cover to prevent a vacuum during off-loading that might collapse the truck's tank. A huge hose is threaded into place, connecting the truck tank to the plant's pipeline, and Pete's load is transferred to one of four "small" (capacity 84,000 pounds each) silos, where it will be held pending the results of a lengthier and more sophisticated lab test for bacteria and penicillin. From there, the milk is pumped into larger silos, whence it is sent on its last (as liquid) short trip, via overhead pipes to vats in the next-door Kraft plant, where, each week, just under five million pounds of Vermont- and New York–farmer-produced, Pomainville-collected-and-hauled (most of it), and Agri-Mark–handled milk is converted to cheese, the whey and excess cream coming back via return pipes to be loaded on trucks and hauled to other plants in other states to be processed into cream cheese and other foods.

This particular plant specializes in Swiss cheese. Its nearly twenty million pounds of Swiss—which constitutes a third of

Kraft's Swiss production and nearly 9 percent of the nation's annual Swiss consumption—leave Middlebury in 180-pound blocks for cutting and packaging plants in Pennsylvania and Missouri and Illinois and Wisconsin. In addition to Swiss, the plant makes some Gouda and is currently test-marketing a new product called "baby Swiss," a smooth, mild-flavored, higher-fat snacking cheese which is "real good," says plant manager Doug Marsten with a great-expectations light in his eye.

(Depending as it does on a continuously huge flow of milk to make its products, the cheese industry largely controls the price of raw milk in America, bidding it down in times of perceived abundance, bidding it up when near-future shortages are feared. If there is resentment in some quarters at the cheese tail wagging the milk dog, it should also be noted that strong consumption growth in cheese [and Swiss is a leader], yogurt, and nonfat dry milk—much of the latter for export—is "carrying" the dairy industry into the nineties, offsetting declining sales of whole milk, butter, and cottage cheese.)

Pete loafs, sneaks a plug of chewing tobacco, and talks with other drivers and plant personnel while his truck is unloaded. He is back on the road before noon for his second run, which includes an out-of-the-way trip back to the dilapidated farm for a small load of what the lab test has shown is good milk. (Pete is amazed. "How can that milk be good?" Things work the other way as well. "Occasionally you take a good-looking load from a spic-and-span barn that turns out to be bad stuff.") He heads back into Cornwall for another stop, and chats with a great bear of a red-bearded farmer, outside the barn surveying his frozen domain. Pete sets to work, and, not liking to find animals in the milkhouse, casts a baleful glance over seven gray cats huddled in patches of sunlight on floor, counters, and windowsills.

His next-to-last stop is the Treadway farm near the top of Cutting Hill Road, where the barn thermometer reads −10 degrees, but a slackening wind has brought the wind chill well up, to −35 degrees or so. No one is about, and Pete carries on in silence, threading and unthreading nuts, hitching and unhitching hoses, reading dipsticks, agitating, taking samples, taking temperatures, writing down figures, moving milk with a cold and reluctant pump.

Everything goes well until he switches on the automatic bulk-tank cleaner mounted on the north wall of the milkhouse. A hose immediately explodes off a fitting, spraying liquid about. Pete guesses the line is frozen up somewhere. He plays with the hoses, and tries the cleaner twice more, with identical results. He gives up and writes Dick a note describing the problem on a paper towel, leaving it on top of the bulk tank.

His route completed, Pete trucks back to the plant with 20,820 pounds of milk sloshing in the tank behind him. He arrives at 2:40, this time for a longer stay. The same off-load procedures are repeated, after which the truck's tank is hooked up to the plant's automatic wash system for its daily internal cleaning. During off-load, Pete wanders into the plant's cafeteria room, where, having, as usual, eaten nothing since breakfast, he lifts the lid of an abandoned pizza box and consumes a large piece of the leftovers within. When his truck moves up from the off-load station to the cleaning station, he returns for another daily chore, disassembling, cleaning, coating with Vaseline ("It's about the only lubricant that won't contaminate milk"), and reassembling his pump mechanism.

Pete Paige is out of the plant and heading back for Shoreham shortly before 4 P.M. At the Service Center he will gas up the truck, park it, plug in the overnight engine-heater, complete and turn in his paper work, and, at 4:30, he will call it a day and start for home to see what, if any, progress his pipes are making.

IN DUE COURSE, THE TREADWAYS' TWICE-monthly milk check—covering Pete Paige's pickup and fourteen others—arrives in the mails from Agri-Mark headquarters in

Lawrence, Massachusetts. The detailed information sheet attached to the check indicates that member farm #001156 has
shipped to zone 19's plant #930 a total of 57,739 pounds of milk
during the two-week period. At a blend price of $13.08 per
hundredweight—the basic unit of measurement for raw milk—
this milk has a basic value to the farmer of $7,552.26. The but-
terfat content of this milk is listed at 3.71 percent. Agri-Mark is
paying a premium of 15.1 cents a hundredweight per point of
butterfat above the standard 3.5 percent, which adds $183.16 to
this milk check. Production-incentive premiums add another 46
cents per hundredweight, all of which raise the milk price to
$13.83.

Chalked up against the milk on the debit side are organiza-
tional dues, a 15-cents-per-hundredweight assessment to support the dairy industry's ad campaign to encourage milk-
drinking, a stop charge of $4.50 per pickup, and a haul charge
of 21.4 cents per hundredweight, all of which reduce the actual
pay price of this Treadway milk to $13.03. In addition, the
family's health and accident insurance premiums are deducted
automatically from milk check to milk check. The bottom line
for this particular check is $7,519.17.

# 9

IT IS THE THIRD WEEK IN FEBRUARY, THE
time each year when the Treadways, as Joan puts it, "get crazy."
First it's income taxes—a farmer's are due March 1—and then
the month-long madness of sugaring. This year things seem even
crazier than usual. Every time Dick sits down at the kitchen
table to close out the farm books and work on taxes, an emergency call intervenes.

On Wednesday, it's a seventy-year-old farmer living near Lake Champlain who may have had a minor heart attack. He lies on his couch surrounded by Joan and Diane and other squad members, including his own daughter, while Dick drives the ambulance out from Middlebury, and the black farm dog in the corner lowers and growls at the strangers.

On Thursday, it's a head-on collision on Doolittle Road, and Dick and Joan arrive to find two gray Chevrolets, one on the road and one off, their smashed front ends presiding over great patches of radiator-coolant–colored snow, one bright yellow, the other a sickly green. Joan works on the young woman, who is a nurse, and who thinks she may have a broken neck, and no rig with a backboard has yet arrived ("Get me a door; get me *some*thing," Joan says); while others attend to the logy young man, who was not wearing a seatbelt and who has somehow ended up in the back seat after having used his face to break out his windshield.

Friday afternoon, it's a 2½-year-old boy who has fallen through the ice into the Lemon Fair on the Richville Dam Road, his mother out of the house in pajamas and bare feet trying to flag down cars. Luckily, the child fell in face up and his coat floated him, and when Dick and Jeff arrive, their neighbor and friend, Donna, is checking vital signs and trying to keep awake a cold, ghostly-white boy while awaiting the ambulance.

On Saturday, a depressing week came to an end with a call to a house on the next road, where a fifteen-year-old boy, a year ahead of Kevin in school, lay unconscious. Joan and a colleague immediately began CPR and started an IV to keep a vein open. They worked steadily on the lad until the Middlebury ambulance arrived. The new crew worked on him all the way to the hospital, where he was pronounced dead. Rescue-squad members seldom learn the fate of the people they treat, nor do they always know the causes of death for those who don't survive. Unless the autopsy report for their distant neighbor is made public, the Treadways won't know whether Reye's syndrome or a drug overdose—the early suspects—or something else was responsible for the teenager's death.

The tax deadline is fast approaching when Dick finally closes out the farm accounts book and sits down with his table-top adding machine and the official IRS instructions—an eighty-nine-page document called the *Farmer's Tax Guide*—to complete his 1040 form, while Joan pays bills out of the business-size checkbook.

Farms' gross incomes are typically impressive. During the recently completed year, the Treadways shipped 1,040,322 pounds of milk, for which their gross return was $130,605. Cumulative milk-check deductions take a sizable bite out of that figure. The year's bill for stop charges was $794, for haul charges, $2,224. Their share of the industry's milk-promotion campaign was $1,560, plus deductions for co-op dues and equity investment in Agri-Mark and support for the federal government's Whole Herd Buyout program. The family's health insurance premium totaled $2,548.

Livestock sales added to the farm's income, with receipts of $4,525 for ten cows and $3,773 for forty-five calves. Last year's maple syrup crop grossed $4,594, and, in addition to several small additional sources, the family received a $2,377 payment from the Regional Co-operative Marketing Association, an umbrella organization to which Agri-Mark farms belong, and which, having made some lucrative deals with big milk buyers during the relatively milk-short year, has passed premiums along to member farms. Dick adds up the numbers and puts down the figure $141,952 on the Gross Farm Income line of his 1040 form.

If a farm's income is encouraging, its expenses are likely to astonish those who work for wages or on salary. Dick copies them one at a time out of the farm ledger. Garbage and telephone he divides arbitrarily in half, assigning half to the house, half to the barn; farm shares are $124 and $428, respectively. Vet fees and medicines total $2,888, and Eastern's breeding fees add another $2,509. The Dairy Herd Improvement Association collected $1,042 for milk-testing; Tri-Town Water, $918 to water the cows. Cows need food as well as water, and purchased feed—nearly all of it the high-protein grain mix—last year cost $33,017. Most of their feed, of course, the family grows, which means more expenses: fertilizers and lime ($7,678), chemical sprays ($502), and seed ($641). You need land on which to grow the food, and property taxes ($3,036) and rent for a couple of fields on the farm's periphery ($1,329) are added in.

Repair bills ($5,172) for work on tractors and other equipment are deductible, as is the cost of the gas, diesel, and oil ($3,122) required to run them. The farm part of automobile gas and insurance Dick figures at $1,553, while the insurance premium on the farm itself adds another $1,585. General farm supplies total $4,455, and maple syrup supplies, $1,387. The year's sawdust bill comes in at $1,308. The farmstead's electrical energy consumption—the silo unloaders, feed-bunk belt mechanism, and bulk-tank compressor are especially heavy users—has been billed at $4,836.

The farm is able to deduct, in addition, token wages ($7,186) paid to Don and the three older children, wages apportioned to roughly reflect the amount of work accomplished. Interest on loans and mortgages totals just over $11,000, most of it associated with Dick and Joan's continuing purchase of the farm from his parents. Finally, depreciation on structures, machinery, and equipment—everything from the tedder to fence material and manure-pit construction costs—amounts to $17,893.

Dick totes up the numbers and finds that his farm deductions total $112,278. Calculating his way down the form, he comes up with a preliminary net farm income of $37,321, including wages paid to Joan of $2,448. He then figures the deduction for six family members and plugs in itemized deductions (helpful because of the family's high medical expenses) figured previously. This leaves a taxable income of $21,453, for which income and self-employment taxes would amount to $6,698.

Dick has been working with these figures off and on for a week, and he knew that he was headed for a higher tax figure than the family was accustomed to paying. Partly this is due to a gradually strengthening milk price through the year, adding to the farm's gross income. Mostly, however, it has to do with lost deductions. A longstanding tax break on machinery and equipment called "investment credit" allowed farmers to take 10 percent off the top of their tax bill. The allowance was canceled a couple of years ago, and that has hurt. Beyond that, the Treadways' depreciation deduction has fallen dramatically for last year, simply because much of their machinery and equipment had exhausted its amortized depreciation allowance the year before. "You've got to keep buying equipment to keep your depreciation up," Dick laments, "but then you have to figure out how to pay for it."

The options for juggling are limited this year, and they reside mainly with the new mower. In his original calculations, Dick figured to depreciate the mower over the full seven-year amortization period. Now he refigures the whole business on the basis of taking the full depreciation allowed in a one-year bundle. This option, he finds, would shave about $2,300 off the tax bill, which is cause enough for Joan to arise from her seat and open a bottle of sparkling white zinfandel. Ignoring the glass set in front of him (Joan complains, on occasion, that her husband has a "drinking problem," by which she means that he can seldom be persuaded to touch anything alcoholic), Dick punches in more numbers, and determines that—assuming fairly stable milk production and milk prices—this immediate savings would cost them about $400 over the next six years. Do they want to save money now, or save later? He will sit on the question for a couple of days before deciding.

(Dick's final decision is to throw the whole mower at this

year's taxes. This brings the farm's deductions total up to $120,748, reducing net farm profit to $21,204, taxable income to $12,983, and total federal taxes to $4,318.)

Neither the "net farm profit" figure nor any other figure listed on these forms represents, in any case, what the family actually has available to spend during the year. Playing with the numbers once again, Dick figures that the family's usable income for the preceding year was roughly $27,000. "Just for fun," Joan says, "divide that figure into two fourteen-hour-a-day wages and see what you get." Dick obliges, and announces that the two of them are farming for $2.64 an hour—"less, if you count the kids' work."

(A last year's study of 523 farms of all sizes in the Northeast found that the average farm's net earnings after living expenses and taxes was $5,564, and no one would be surprised if a Presidential commission appointed to examine the "farm problem" should conclude that "agriculture is not commercially as profitable as it is entitled to be for the labor and energy that the farmer expends and the risks that he assumes." A Presidential commission *did* conclude that. It was appointed in 1908 by Theodore Roosevelt, and it included such notables as Liberty Hyde Bailey, Henry Wallace, Sr., and Gifford Pinchot. Roosevelt was worried about, among other things, the fact that Americans working the land had dropped under 50 percent of the population as unheard-of wages beckoned from the cities. Well-meaning commissions notwithstanding, the farm population erosion has continued unchecked. Today, 2 percent of Americans live on farms, with just over half of those supported by primary incomes off the farm.)

At present, the financial health of the Treadway farm is good, even if no one is getting rich working it. The family's debt burden comes to only about a third of the farm's credit limit of $35,000, and they are proud of having borrowed nothing at all during the last two years. Barring unforeseen misfortune, they hope to have the farm debt-free—aside from the mortgage with Dick's parents—a few years down the road.

## 10

IT IS THE LAST SUNDAY IN FEBRUARY. THE sugaring season is due to begin any time now, and Dick wants to get a start "spreading" buckets while the children are available to help. Sap buckets nest nearly to the rim, so that the open-wagon manure spreader can easily carry 500 laid out as five horizontal "columns," three bottom columns supporting two more. The family loads the spreader bed's periphery with stacks of covers—the curved shields that will guard the bucket tops once tapping is under way—and Dick pulls the spreader with the small tractor south to the farm's main sugar bush, a mixed woods of maple, oak, ash, beech, hickory, hardhack, and hemlock lying on the rock-ledge hillside rising to the east of Cutting Hill Road.

The snow drought has continued in the Northeast. Indeed, last week's full moon—the Snow Moon—brought another spell of warm rain, destroying most of the Champlain Valley's sparse snow cover. The return of cold weather has left bare ground with accents of frozen snow and ice in low and protected places. Long strips of crusted snow mark the furrows of plowed corn land, and from a distance the meadows look like giant heads of butch-cut strawberry blonde hair with alarming cases of dandruff. The Treadways marvel at the openness of the sugar woods, remembering all those late Februarys spreading buckets in two feet of snow. One year the tractor couldn't manage the knee-deep "road" through the

sugar bush even with chains, and they had had to work out of
a sled pulled behind the three-wheeler, taking forever to get
the buckets out.

Joan takes over the driving, and Dick carries a stack of a
dozen or so buckets into the first section of open woods. (These
galvanized tin buckets are much heavier than their predecessors,
and hence a chore to haul. But they do not rust out quickly like
the old tin buckets, nor do they dent easily like the aluminum
ones that replaced them. Buckets and covers are also expensive—
about $4 a set—making it less costly for new sugar makers to
start up with plastic-tubing pipeline systems, which are also
great labor savers, especially if you don't count the labor involved keeping pipeline tight and flowing and replacing squirrel-
chewed sections.) Dick quickly checks the girth and top health
of each sugar maple before plunking down one, two, or three
buckets beside it, calling out the appropriate number as he heads
for the next tree, and the trailing "cover man" drops the same
number of covers beside them.

Dick and the children march through the woods while Joan
maneuvers tractor and spreader along an often invisible path
that winds back and forth along the rough terraces of the hillside, occasionally missing her way. Spreading buckets on the
relatively flat benches is child's play, but trucking up and down
the steep hillside is another matter, and there is just enough
snow and ice in these woods to make the slopes treacherous.
Brian, overloaded by at least a factor of two, takes a tumble, and
his covers clatter and scatter on the ground. Upslope of him,
Becky collapses in turn, but is immediately up and chasing her
downhill-slithering covers.

Soon Becky and Brian discover a ready-made skating rink—
much of it a rich brown in color—in a swale down near the
road, and they are off to slide. "Stay on your feet," Joan calls
after them; "that's frozen feed-bunk slurry!" But her two youngest are already flat on their backs sliding and laughing; Joan
shakes her head and drives on. Kevin takes over as major dis-
tributor of covers, while Jeff follows his father with a stack of

buckets over his shoulder. Thor, who has been off exploring the woods, appears with a whitened cow bone in his mouth, which he worries like a cat with a catnip mouse, while Mindy, the black and white sheepdog mix, stands stock-still upslope, her head down a woodchuck hole.

A couple of the switchbacks along the tractor path are steep, and Dick orders Becky and Brian—returned to the party to pass out covers from the wagon—out of the spreader while Jeff negotiates a particularly precipitous one. What with little snow and no ice, it proves no problem this year. Kevin, walking downhill behind the spreader, lies down and rolls the last stretch of the incline, wiping out Becky in the process. Brian, watching from the top of the hill, commences to follow suit, intending to roll the whole way. What he has neglected to consider, however, is the question of steering, and after fifteen or twenty rapid revolutions the blithely unaware dervish leaves the open path and sails off into the woods, crashing to a halt against a pointed sapling stump, which gouges his mouth. His mother, looking on in suspense from the tractor seat at the bottom of the hill, doesn't bother to inquire about injuries: *"Brian! Get up* and get your body into this wagon!"* Which he does, limping and rubbing his mouth.

It is approaching chore time, and the spreader's supply of buckets is nearly exhausted. "Let's not be late starting chores," Joan pleads, but Dick ("He doesn't know how not to work," she complains on occasion) sends Kevin and Jeff back to the farmstead for another hundred buckets. They have been out of sight for some time when Dick asks Joan to turn off the tractor. "Jeff!" he hollers. No reply. "Hey, *Jeff!*" "What?" comes a faint reply. "Make it a hundred and fifty!" Dick shouts, while Joan, slumping over her steering wheel, strikes the heel of her hand to her forehead in the classic posture of despair.

ON THE FOLLOWING SATURDAY, AFTER TWO more days spent spreading buckets, Dick decides they'd better get to tapping. It's not a good idea to tap much before the first sap run, which may not be imminent; but it's already well into the first week in March, and sap flow can't be far off. Morning chores completed, the male Treadways, along with a school friend of Kevin's, start out to tap a wooded ridge on the east boundary of the farm. It is a dull, cold, leaden day, the sky the color of the heavy cast-iron spouts Kevin and Jeff carry in leather apron pouches around their waists.

Dick parks the Jeep, Jeff the small pickup, and Dick gasses up his portable Tanaka tapping drill, a trim red rig costing about $300. Dick starts up the drill, which sounds like a small chain saw, and gets to work, penetrating the trunks an inch and a half, at a slightly upward angle, with his 7/16-inch bit. (Don Treadway vividly recalls as a young man tapping a large sugar bush on the home farm with "breast" drills—hand drills with back-projecting rods ending in small plates, enabling the user literally to lean into his work. "We'd do nine hundred taps the first day, and the next morning you couldn't raise your crankin' arm above your waist.") Dick drills most of his taps into south-facing halves of trunks, since these ordinarily run better than north-facing ones.

Jeff and Kevin follow the drill, locating taps—if they aren't immediately evident, the boys look on the ground for the curled wood plugs shed by the extracted drill bit—into which they seat their spouts, driving them in with hammers. After the spout men come Kevin's friend and Brian, who hang buckets from the hooks suspended under the spouts and slide on the covers, whose side flanges catch and hook under the lips of the buckets.

The crew works north along the upper woods, then turns and comes back south, tapping a second wooded strip along the lower side of the pasture. "Aren't you tapping kind of low?" Kevin asks, noticing that he is seating some spouts at waist level. Dick is trying to stay well away from last year's taps, having puzzled over the fact that some of them haven't healed over at all well. "We'll be O.K.," he replies, "unless we get a big snow," which would mean gathering some sap on one's knees. They have had the opposite problem in some years past, tapping with a heavy snow cover which subsequently melted, leaving them to wrestle with buckets suddenly at head level.

The drill is shut down for refueling halfway through morning tapping when Jeff says "Listen!" Everyone pauses and quiets down, and it takes a few moments to track the mysterious sound to a thin sleet pattering the dry leaf litter. "It sounds like a giant bed of Rice Krispies," Jeff says, smiling embarrassedly at having created a simile. The frozen rain makes the cold day seem colder, and the boys are more than ready to caravan when Dick announces a halt for lunch.

The family started tapping yesterday, and two or three day sessions will remain before this year's complement of 1,050 buckets is in place. Often sap is running when the Treadways tap, literally following the drill bit out of the tree. Dick laughs, remembering Becky and Brian running from tree to tree holding a finger over the end of the spouts, not wanting to waste any sap. No drop will be wasted today, and no run is yet in sight.

THE CLATTER OF BUCKETS AND THE INCESsant racket of the drill have ceased, and quiet returns to the deserted hillside woods south of the peaked, mint green Treadway farmhouse. The quiet contact notes of a chickadee flock sound upslope, while a couple of crows express urgent displeasure in the distance. A hairy woodpecker taps nearby, and from up the road comes the sudden derisive laughter of a pileated woodpecker followed by the bird itself, the great black-and-white wings propelling it in shallow scallops along the fenceline and into a dead elm down the hill.

Driven to cover earlier by the bustle and noise of spreading and tapping, the gray squirrels are now back in command of these woods. The seasonal mating chases are on, and at the moment four grays rocket through the canopy, hurtling through the open spaces between trees, tails flung out for balance, now in full chase of one another, now racing frantically apart, as if someone had mentioned a frightful and highly contagious squirrel disease. One squirrel races its private course, up a shagbark hickory trunk and out a main limb to the margin, where it casts off for a neighboring ash, and, whipping through the crown of that tree, leaps for the outermost twigs of an oak, and thence to a maple, where it plunges headlong halfway down the trunk and disappears into a knothole.

Clearly this slightly-below-freezing weather has gray squirrel hormones in good flow. Meanwhile, at the base of this squirrel's den tree hang two buckets, empty and silent, waiting for ten degrees more of mercury and another kind of late-winter flow.

## 11

"THIS WEATHER'S ALMOST OVERDOING IT," Dick says, slogging through six-inch-deep mud in the tractor road above the barn. It warmed suddenly yesterday, and this morning it is in the low 50s, with a rip-roaring wind expected out of the south. A honey bee—out early and far from its home hive—prospects around the sawdust pile, which is (and will long remain, whatever the weather does) frozen into balled chunks.

Yesterday's warming finally started the first sap run, an unprecedented and distressing twelve days after tapping had begun, at what would ordinarily be the midpoint of the sugaring season. Dick checked the nearest buckets—just across the road in the heifer pasture—immediately after finishing chores, and was disappointed to find that the hoped-for continuation of the run through the warm night hasn't happened, and the run so far today isn't particularly strong. Cold weather is supposed to return later today for another spell, however, and Dick decides to gather what sap there is.

He hitches the 200-gallon gathering tank to the International Harvester, and mushes the chained tractor up to the shop to add oil. A tire under the gathering tank is nearly flat, and Jeff is hard at work on the air compressor, just returned from the shop after motor work. The problem now is to remount the motor, which requires new bolts. Because of limited space, the ends must be cut off the new bolts, and because cutoff bolts don't thread easily, and because the nuts must be held with a needle-nose pliers, Jeff works and works to secure the four motor mounts. Eventually he succeeds, but the plugged-in compressor doesn't "take off." Don, Dick, and Jeff study the situation, and decide to reverse two wires and try it again. This time it comes to life.

The tanker-wagon tire is soon inflated, and Dick, Jeff, and Julie, a family friend, chug across the road to the closest sugar bush to get started on a load before noon, while Joan takes Becky to school and gets lunch. Jeff eases the tractor along while Dick and Julie make bee-lines from maple to maple—or as near bee-lines as the rough topography will allow—pulling buckets off spouts and pouring the clear liquid contents into five-gallon gathering pails. When a gatherer's pail nears full, it is carried to the gathering tank and, the square wooden plug-type cover removed, lifted to shoulder height and dumped in.

Tractor and gatherers work north across the high heifer pasture, around Diane's place, up a fenceline, and down behind a hemlock woods. It is soon clear that this first run is a spotty one. Some trees—no pattern is evident—have run yesterday and are running today, a fact immediately apparent in the considerable heft of the first bucket pulled off the spout hook; and the sap oozes down the spout trough and is wicked away from the tip a drop at a time by the wind while a gallon (or even two) of sap is dumped from bucket to pail. Most trees, however, have had a modest run, showing but a couple of inches of sap in their buckets, and some trees haven't run at all.

Julie and Dick hop aboard the tailgate of the tanker wagon for the ride home, their feet now dragging in the mud, now suspended aloft as tractor and wagon hump and dip over the bumps and ruts. Back in the kitchen, Dick, Joan, and Julie, along with a mostly silent Jeff, eat Joan's popular lasagna, left over from last evening's dinner party, among whose guests were Julie and Rick (Dick's longtime partner in the fire department), recently moved to Kentucky and back now for a week's visit. Julie had helped sugar last year, and the three of them now laugh over their misadventure in Montreal, where they had gone to celebrate the conclusion of sugaring season.

They had no more than sat down to what they assumed would be an elegant dinner in a revolving restaurant at the top of a fancy hotel when a massive blackout darkened the whole of southern Quebec, and the restaurant threw in the towel. Someone in the party copped a candle, so they could see their way around back at the motel; and, finding no food available anywhere in Montreal, they returned to their room, where they hovered around the candle and consumed what they had—a sack of M & Ms and two bottles of warm champagne—vowing to get together at the end of every future March for a ritual lighting of the stolen candle and the sharing of (preferably cold) champagne.

After lunch, the group, now including Joan, goes back to work south down the west side of the road, slipping and slopping along a woodland slope the consistency of a fresh cow pie. With that area gathered, Dick drives the tractor a couple of miles down Cutting Hill Road past Stone Bridge Flats to the foot of Money Hole Hill, where, by invitation, they have set more taps on the Norman Treadway farm. (This recent extension of the operation brings their tap total to about 1,350, "which," Joan explains, "is Dick's idea of 'cutting back' from last year's twelve hundred fifty.")

Dick and Jeff are allergic to bee stings, and they leave the trees surrounding the very busy hives here to Joan, who puts up her collar and steps gingerly into the breach. Bees are everywhere, but no one is stung, and soon the operation moves along to the back side of the hill, where tractor and tank find rough going, and so do the gatherers, climbing the steep hillside to barberry-bush–guarded trees whose pails must be balanced against knees supported by insecure feet while buckets are dumped, and where the trip downslope is an adventurous boot-sledding on dry leaves over wet ground where a slip is likely to mean at least a sap-drenched leg.

Through the early afternoon the crew watch the load slowly build, the tank's sap level evident in the perforated "bucket"—it looks like an oversized bait bucket—set in the top well of the tank, through which the sap is poured to be filtered of leaves, twigs, insects, spiders, bark, and other items that circumvent the bucket covers. The first load is now complete, and Dick heads up Cutting Hill at road speed, the tailgate sitters remembering nervously that one wheel occasionally comes off the tank wagon. This is a long, mostly uphill haul, and Thorson, who trots alongside the wagon, stops now and again to cool off in ditch pools, then runs hard to catch up, his ears clapping rhythmically over his head while his limp, pink, spatulate tongue keeps the same beat, slapping his face just behind the right eye.

The last steep stretch proves too much for Thor, who stops dead, head hanging, in the middle of the road, while the tractor pulls into the barnyard to find storms brewing both to the north and to the southwest. Dick hurriedly backs the tank wagon down the mud-rutted tractor road to the sugarhouse, where he and Jeff pull out the holding tank's on-load pipe and lower the gathering tank's off-load hose pipe, and proceed to empty the load of sap while the rest of the crew ducks into the sugarhouse to wait out the rain.

After a brief shower, the bucket brigade is out once again, starting this load on the wooded ridge above the feed-bunk–slurry ice rink, now reduced to a brown mush. Here, as elsewhere today, some trees are running, but many are not. A brown creeper calls from overhead, its high note as thin as the sap run in the maple whose bark it explores. Some buckets, indeed, are bone-dry, and the gatherers lift each bucket bottom away from its tree with one hand, checking for extra weight, before taking it off the spout hook.

The Shoreham school bus must have arrived, for Brian comes charging down the slope, his barn boots slapping out little explosions of mud and water. Amazingly, he keeps his feet the whole way, and gallops up to join the crew. "Gathering's fun the first time or two," Joan says; "after that it's just more work." But Dick is wondering if there will be enough gathering ahead to turn it into work, or syrup. A sap run requires cold nights and warm days. The first half of March has seen cold nights and cold days; what if the second half follows suit, or changes to warm nights and warm days? Dick has noticed two things today that bother him. First, the row of mature maples on the north side of the hemlock woods was running; and second, every third bucket has had a medium-sized tan moth (or two or three) fluttering about upside down in the sap. Both normally signal the end of sugaring season.

The second load takes most of the afternoon to complete, and, as the tractor labors through the mucky clay along a corn piece back to the sugarhouse, a strident killdeer call rings out, and then Joan spots the bird flying over the meadow to the east. One early migrant, at least, has returned to the North Country, but the redwings, grackles, robins, and song sparrows are conspicuously late. The maple sap is not alone in sitting tight this cold sugar season.

As the second tankful is off-loaded, the crew take turns climbing up a short ladder to watch the fresh sap cascade into the holding tank, blocked up under the jutting roof at the west end of the sugarhouse. Gradually, a "soapy" froth spreads to cover the liquid's surface, as, even more gradually, the sap level rises to cover the curved bottom of the 1,000-gallon holding tank. The final third of the family's sugar bush remains to be gathered, and Dick sends his father and his three sons out to try to bring it in before dark, while he and Joan stay to do evening chores.

What Don and the boys will find this evening is what the

morning and afternoon crews found—a mediocre and uneven sap run. And they will find the same wildlife in the buckets: the odd spider, luckily no drowned mammal to add to the afternoon's single native mouse (the sodden corpses of gray squirrels particularly upset Joan), lots of tan "millers," and lots of a curious half-inch-long beetle—with glowing dark green elytra and orange parentheses enclosing a raised bulbous ridge on an oversized pronotum—an early *Ellychnia* beetle, one of the minority of nonflashing lightning bugs.

The Treadways will have another late supper tonight; and while they will have a start on collecting, they will be well short of enough sap to begin boiling, and more cold days ahead.

## 12

MARCH HAS CONTINUED COLD AND BLUSTERY in the Champlain Valley. Apparently despairing of improved weather, most early migrants have finally arrived. The first robins appeared, calling from fenceposts, tail-pumping for emphasis. On the sixteenth, a mixed blackbird flock of at least 100 birds—mostly redwings and grackles, but with a few cowbirds as well—hunted along a field-margin fenceline, redwings and cowbirds picking and walking, the grackles chucking wads of sodden leaves over their shoulders. To the northwest, on the Lemon Fair flats, the first clamorous Canada goose music sounded throughout the day and continued unabated well past midnight.

On the official first day of spring, it snowed in the North Country—a good snow by this winter's standards—but now, later that same week, a massive low-pressure rain system has pushed up from the Gulf of Mexico all the way into the

Ohio Valley and mid-Atlantic states, bringing hope to the precipitation-starved East, where New York City and other urban centers are already putting water-rationing programs into place. Warm air is rumored to be crowding in from the south and west behind this weather system, bringing hope for a major sap run.

It is not, this Friday, particularly balmy, and a chilly wind under heavy cloud cover makes 40 degrees feel like freezing. Some sap is running, however, and Dick wants to get gathering after chores. First he has to split and haul to the house a cut-up dead elm which had fallen across the sugar track west of the road. But the bucket tractor won't start, a problem traced to faltering battery spark. He pulls the battery cables, cleans the terminals, and reattaches the cables. There is too little wood even in a large single tree to make it worthwhile to set up the splitter, and Dick gets to the hard work of splitting elm by hand, chucking firewood logs into the tractor's bucket.

There is time to gather only one load of sap before lunch, and Dick, Joan, and Don find another mediocre, radically uneven run, a few buckets literally running over, many others bone dry. They are anxious to try out the new sap off-load system, 100 feet of 4-inch PVC sewer pipe Dick has rigged up from sugar-house to barnyard, so that sap loads won't have to be backed down the rutted track to the sugarhouse. The system works just fine, and will save time for the gathering crews.

In the afternoon, Joan leaves for emergency-squad duty in Middlebury, but the boys soon return from school, and the crew drives out to gather the sugar bush up against the east ridge. Out of the Jeep, Jeff and Kevin charge over to a patch of north-slope–protected snow and pelt each other with snowballs while Brian slides on the questionable ice covering a small pond. Here, too, the sap run is uneven. At one point Jeff finds a patch of maples running with spirit (a "two-drop-a-second run," he calls it), while other trees are completely shut down. Here and there dark-stained bark under a bucket indicates a leaking spout. Dick picks up a rock and pounds the spout in another quarter-inch, hoping to seal off the leak.

Back on the west side of Cutting Hill Road, Jeff drives the
Jeep in off the road, and Dick can't get it back out, the vehicle
repeatedly sliding on the muddy wrong-way-banked exit lane
into a log. He heads out across the pasture to the south, hoping
Charley's barnyard lane isn't blocked and that he can negotiate
it. He manages to get through the foot-deep ruts, barely, and
back on the road. The Treadways' own dooryard isn't in much
better shape; indeed, most town drivers would become hopelessly mired there. Dick laughs about it: "Every mud season we
talk about getting a load of crushed rock drawn in here, but it's
too soft to get a truck in. Then, when it dries up, we don't need
it any more!"

Two more loads of sap drain down the long pipe into the
holding tank, settling on top of a two-inch ice crust over the old
sap. (Sap shouldn't sit for any length of time, and this delay
since first gathering will probably cost the syrup a grade; at least
the ice has kept the sap cold, and hence fresher than it would
otherwise now be.) The question at the moment is whether the
run will continue overnight. Whatever happens tonight, Dick
decides they can't wait any longer. The family will finish gathering tomorrow and boil what sap they have.

BREAKFAST OVER AND MORNING CHORES
finished, the Treadways walk down behind the old horse barn to
the new sugarhouse to start making syrup, Dick moaning about
missing the NCAA basketball tournament playoff games this
afternoon. Jeff scrambles onto the top of the structure to start
the hinged roof sections around the chimney pipe opening as
Dick hauls on ropes inside. Dick opens a valve, and sap runs into
the evaporator's eight-by-four-foot drop-flue (or back) pan,
gradually covering the mazelike floor around raised flues, and
then working its way into the six-by-four-foot front pan. Dick
stokes the firebox at the end of the evaporator's foundation
structure, called the arch, from the woodpile at the east end of

the sugarhouse, and, when the sap level in the pans has reached about 1½ inches, he douses the logs with diesel fuel and, to encouraging shouts of "Light it!" and "Fire it up!" from his sons, he lights the fire, opens the draft, and the boiling season is—finally—under way.

Don, Joan, Jeff, Kevin, and Brian leave to gather sap, while Dick stays behind to tend the evaporator. The circular thermometer mounted on the end of the front pan rapidly rises through 60 and 80 degrees to 100 degrees, and now the brew is steaming and frothing. Soon it begins to boil, and Dick scoops brown froth off both pans with long-handled scoops and dumps it into a bucket placed on either side of the evaporator. A leak has developed on the far side of the base of the front pan, and Dick worries that they may have to "empty out" and do some soldering. After a time, however, the leak seals itself.

Dick restokes the firebox, and things are really cooking now. Through a crack where the two pans join over the arch, a four-foot-wide solid band of flame is visible rushing out of the firebox into the flues of the back pan. The whole surface of both pans is now in furious boil, fifty-six square feet of jumping and steaming egg-white soufflé. From time to time a section of one pan or the other builds to boil-over, and just before the sap runs over, Dick dumps eight or ten drops of milk from a shaker bottle onto the froth, and after a two-second pause the whole mass mysteriously collapses to the accompaniment of a wonderful momentary roar as of distant jet engines revving.

Last year, the whole sugarhouse dripped condensed sap, and it had been impossible to see ten feet. Dick has since suspended an open-topped wood-framed plastic hood over the evaporator, hoping to funnel the steam up and out. For the most part it seems to be working, and the family will be pleased at the prospect of working with better visibility and keeping fairly dry while boiling.

Last year had been this sugarhouse's first trial. The Treadways had been out of the sugaring business for several years, ever since the installation of the feed bunk had cut off access to the old sugarhouse south of the barn, a structure which had, in any case, fallen into disrepair. They decided to build a new house on the cement floor of the old, now collapsed cow barn. They designed (this one has windows, unlike the old, which makes daytime work much more pleasant), built, and wired the house. They retrieved the evaporator out of the old house, had the arch retinned, put in new angle irons, rebricked the arch with special 3,000-degree fire brick, and set up shop, putting themselves back in the sugaring business for under $5,000, a sum which wouldn't replace the evaporator alone in this operation.

The gatherers, returned with a load of sap, storm into the sugarhouse to ask how much syrup has been made. They are more than a little premature. The boil, in fact, has slowed a bit now and again, and Dick surmises that this wood is cut a bit large and perhaps isn't as dry as it might be. "We used to burn old fence rails, which made a good hot fire. Last year we burned the barn boards lying around outside; that wood had been drying for a hundred years!"

Joan brings a radio down from the house. If Dick can't watch basketball, at least he can listen to a spring exhibition baseball game. The noon news ends with a weather report, predicting temperatures in the 50s—maybe even 60—for the next several days, and in the 30s at night. Dick winces. Confident that he is the bearer of good news, the radio announcer concludes with relish: "Winter is at the end of the line!" "Then so is sugaring," Dick replies grimly.

The front-pan thermometer, which has held steady at 110 degrees for some time, now starts up once again, and Dick, dipping a scoop into the sap and holding it up to see if it is still dripping or beginning to sheet, declares that they're getting close. He and Joan and Jeff put three "felts" (wool straining bags) into the top frame of the syrup storage tank on the south wall while Don hooks up to a battery the Canadian-made automatic "draw-off," a temperature-sensitive unit that opens and closes the spigot to release syrup when ready. In a few minutes, the spigot opens, and the season's first syrup flows into the waiting bucket. Dick intercepts part of the flow to fill a tube, into which he drops a viscosity-measuring hydrometer to double-check the drawoff. The thermometer-like tool floats in the hot sap precisely to the "hot-test" line. The syrup is right.

Jeff pours the syrup into a felt, whence it will drain into the holding tank, and Dick and Kevin quickly restoke the fire. Boiling, which to this point has required mostly patience, now becomes a matter of watching everything at once and acting immediately on a variety of cues, a situation which gets on the nerves. Things are particularly dicey when the automatic drawoff releases a large quantity of syrup, because sometimes the sap in the flue pan doesn't "follow" into the front pan quickly enough to replace the expelled syrup. When this happens, part of the front pan may be briefly empty, in which case it will burn in a matter of seconds, ruining a $2,000 pan.

More syrup is drawing off now, and Dick is checking it with the hydrometer and playing with the float valve on the intake pipe, making sure new sap is flowing into the flue pan, while Joan stands by at the firebox end of the evaporator holding a bucket of cold sap, ready to dump it into the front pan should the level get dangerously low. It is at times like this, when everyone's attention is entirely occupied, that Joan worries about Brian and Becky being in the sugarhouse. Kids underfoot are tension-building, of course, but beyond that the evaporator and its contents are super-hot, and boiling syrup is sticky; once it gets on you, it burns and burns and burns. "Brian, you've got that 'I'm-going-to-do-something-dumb' look on your face," his mother warns, receiving an "I-can't-think-*how*-you-can-suspect-me" look of innocence in return. Becky chooses this moment to experiment with the spigot at the base of the syrup holding tank, making a mess while wasting hard-won syrup, and she draws sharp words, and cries.

"God*dammit,* Fred!" Jeff is busy canning the first hot syrup for early orders, drawing it out of the tank into official blue-and-white-and-yellow State of Vermont Pure Maple Syrup cans, setting the seals, and grading it, when Fred nimbly jumps into the middle of the action. The syrup is graded by pouring some into a small bottle and comparing it for color with pregraded samples in a rack held before a window. This first syrup is a shade too dark for Fancy; it will be designated Grade A, Medium Amber.

Joan brought sandwiches and chips and water when she came down to help sugar, and Dick eats when he gets a chance while watching the evaporator, including the leak on the north side of the front pan, which opens and seals, opens and seals through the afternoon. Brian tears in one side door and demands Jeff's canning job. Becky flies in the other door, back in smiling form. For some reason, the top of her new haircut sticks straight up, and she looks for the moment like a miniature British punk-rocker. She stoops to pull a wad of burdock burrs from her boot laces, then darts off to hunt up Brian.

Everyone except Dick and Brian leaves for a last gathering run, and Brian seizes the opportunity to try some canning. He painstakingly fills pint and quart cans right up into the necks, has his dad set the seals (which requires more force than he can muster), and lines up the hot cans on their sides to assure a good seal as the sap cools. The sugarhouse is quiet once again, and again one hears the continuous soft, sizzling hiss of the boiling sap punctuated by the emphatic pops and snaps of burning pine logs.

Dick turns the baseball game back on—it had been interrupted in the first inning when the milk-truck driver pulled the plug in the milkhouse—and watches the evaporator. It is the fourth inning, 2 to 1 Red Sox, and 5½ gallons of newly canned maple syrup line the picnic table with thirteen inches of sap left in the holding tank. Smoke rising from a sugarhouse tends to attract visitors, and now a spare, flinty old farmer stops by to see how sugaring's going. Dick turns off the radio to talk. They mull over possible reasons for the worst sap flow in anyone's memory. They touch on acid rain, which may be weakening the trees, and pear thrips, a tiny insect that has been defoliating maples in the southern part of the state, but which hasn't yet seemed to be a problem in this area. They ponder the current official explanation, which is that the ongoing drought is doubly to blame; that the dry summer left little moisture in the soil, and the winter drought, depriving the land of snow cover, has left the unprotected ground to freeze deeply, making what little moisture the ground does contain unavailable to the trees' roots.

The old man begins a story about a big syrup maker in the area who bought some fancy machine to take the excess water out of the sap—"a reverse osmosis machine," Dick contributes, knowing the man and the story and already smiling in anticipation of its conclusion—and who now says that if there are no more sap runs he'll have to sell his syrup at $1,200 a gallon to recoup his investment! Dick sympathizes, and adds: "Thank goodness we don't have to pay off the sugarhouse on this year's syrup." What he doesn't add is that last month he signed up for a new John Deere baler at $9,000 plus the old baler, with $4,000 down and the expectation that the upcoming syrup crop would about handle the remainder. It now seems doubtful that, after the cans (many of which won't be used this year) are paid for, this syrup crop will cover even the *taxes* on the new baler. Some syrup, however, they now have, and Dick will finish boiling out this evening while the rest of the family milk in the barn.

# 13

MILK PRODUCTION HAS HELD UP WELL through late winter, bringing the Treadways good milk checks despite a raw-milk price already falling in anticipation of the traditional nationwide increase in production called the "spring flush." At the same time, there has been a dispiriting run of bad luck in the barn. It started with the loss of a milker. The cow had been hurting for two days when the vet dosed her for ketosis and said she'd be all right. But a high fever followed, and more medicines were dispensed. The family found her down the next morning, her head lolling in the gutter. An outfit that buys "down" cows came to pick her up. They hoisted her in a sling, but she died on the way to the truck, so that, though she would be converted into pet food or some other commercial use, the Treadways would get nothing for her.

Joan, in particular, was "bummed out" about the cow. The fact that the animal had freshened just five days before she was stricken suggested to her that she had a twisted stomach—not uncommon after giving birth—and perhaps peritonitis as well. She thinks the vet missed the cow's real problem, or perhaps complications set in after he had treated her. Whatever the case, the family lost a producing Holstein for which they didn't get even a salvage fee.

Then one of the family made a costly mistake. The milk-pickup man switches off the bulk-tank compressor before he starts the automatic tank wash cycle just prior to leaving the farm. One of the milking crew turns that compressor back on at the start of evening chores. One evening no one did. Next morning they walked into the milkroom to find a load of stinking 90-degree milk. Dick ran the load down the drain and called Agri-Mark, whose policy it is to pay—but no more often than once a year—half the value of the dumped milk, thankful that the farmer hasn't tried to sneak a bad lot onto the truck.

And then came the mysterious case of the bad-luck heifer. The new milker had lost a quarter of her bag after a bout with mastitis, and, since she hadn't been bred, and since the barn was still crowded, Dick decided to sell her. He called the commission sales, and a truck arrived and loaded her up. Several days later the family opened an envelope from the commission sales to find, not the expected check for $400 or so, but a notification that the heifer had arrived at the sales barn dead. Dick called several days running, but the promised return calls never came. He doubts that the commission sales stole the heifer, but he knows that she was healthy when she boarded the truck. His guess is that the animal fell or was knocked down during the truck ride, breaking her neck, or perhaps, once down, she was smothered by larger cows. Whatever happened—and the commission sales didn't even bother to offer an explanation, let alone do an autopsy—neither trucker nor commission sales accepts responsibility for animals in transit, and, once off the property, neither does the farm's insurance, and so the Treadways will receive not one penny for the unfortunate heifer.

Emergency-squad work has served this late winter, as always, to put farm problems into perspective. A student at the local college somehow lost control of her car while driving home and hit a pole. When Dick's crew arrived in the ambulance, the young woman might have been peacefully napping. There was no blood, no cuts or scrapes, not even bruises. She had not been wearing her seatbelt, and had merely bumped her head. Dick drove her to the Burlington hospital unconscious, and several days later her parents requested that her life-support systems be turned off.

A week later, a local college boy with some beers in him dived into a mostly empty hot tub and broke his neck. On the way to the hospital with an immobilized patient, driving 70 mph on a 50-mph two-lane two-way highway, Dick found himself with two vehicles "drafting"—like race-car drivers hanging on rear bumpers to save fuel—in his wake. Ambulance drivers have enough to worry about without this kind of illegal and dangerous idiocy, and the squad member riding shotgun radioed ahead for a police intercept. The drafting continued for miles, and then idiot number one, driving a van, decided the pace was too slow. He passed the ambulance *on the right,* sped ahead, and turned off the highway short of the police trap, which netted the second drafter. Dick, generally a genial and forgiving sort of man, did not thereafter conceal his profound disappointment at the van idiot's having eluded retribution.

And now the local weekly newspaper arrives on Cutting Hill Road, and when Joan, working in the kitchen, sees the front-page banner—"Teen-ager's death ruled drug overdose"—she knows immediately that the subject is the distant neighbor boy on whom she had worked to no avail. She pauses, a dinner plate in one hand, and glances grim-faced through the story of a fifteen-year-old boy and an oral preparation of morphine. She shakes her head, puts the paper down on the table, and continues to load the dishwasher.

## 14

IT IS THE FIRST WEEK IN APRIL, AND SEA-sonal changes are apparent in the above-ground swimming pool below the yellow ranch house. The ice atop the undrained pool is now an island ringed by a narrow margin of water. The giant ice discus—three inches thick at the perimeter, but a foot or more thick through the interior—is unsound now and pocked wherever an entombed leaf has been absorbing solar energy. A huge black predacious diving beetle is rigid in the ice cake as well, while here and there a torpid water boatman hangs suspended in the surrounding icy water.

It is visiting day at the sugarhouse for the Shoreham kindergarten, and Joan leads ten of Becky's school friends up the lane in front of the older Treadway home, having shown them some bucketed trees across the road. One boy's boot gets stuck in the treacherous deep clay mud of the barnyard, and he is hopped across to firmer ground with one foot in the air while an adult hauls the boot out of the goo. The teacher remarks that parents have, at least, attended to the note requesting that children wear boots today. "We usually get a few

children showing up in patent leather shoes and white tights,"
she says.

The kids pile into the sugarhouse, where Dick is cleaning out
the flues under the back pan with a long-handled brush. He then
sets to work stoking the firebox, and the children are impressed
by the size of the logs. "That wouldn't go in *my* furnace!" says
one, and "That looks like the trunk of a tree to me!" says a
second. Dick fires up while Joan passes out small paper cups of
syrup to have with doughnuts the teacher has brought. The
group quiets down and eats, then by two's and three's they go
out to play, climbing up to peek through the windows, returning
when steam begins to rise from the pans. Some want to see into
the evaporator, and Dick holds them up one at a time, including
an excitable dark-haired boy with a drop of syrup square on the
bridge of his nose.

Soon the kindergartners are back outside, climbing about
over the rock-and-wood-rubble remains of the old barn, and
the teacher decides it's time to leave. The children are called
in to recite their thank-you's, and the class treks back up to
the barnyard. Surprisingly, half the cups on the picnic table
are unemptied. "Some people don't like maple syrup," Joan
says, dumping the contents of the cups back into the roiling
sap.

Noon approaches, and the first syrup of the season's third
boiling session comes off—it's pretty dark; "road tar," Joan
calls it—Dick working with the hydrometer while she holds a
bucket of raw sap at the ready. When things settle down, she
decants a can and pours some into a sample jar. She holds it
up to the window in the sample rack, and "It's C," she announces, "definitely C." "What a bummer," Dick responds; "I
don't know if it's worth risking the pans to boil out." He continues, however, knowing that this will be the last of the year's
syrup, and needing to make what they can out of a bad sugar
year. It's not that there's anything wrong with C syrup ("It's
fine for baked beans and stuff"), and last year the Treadways

sold ten gallons or so to the Natural Foods Co-op in town.
"The problem is that it takes the same work to make C as it
does Fancy, but you only get fifteen or twenty dollars a gallon
for C," about half the return for the higher grades. He scoops
up some brown froth from the back pan and checks the float
valve on the intake line. "Maybe it'll lighten up as we go
along, but I doubt it."

The syrup doesn't lighten up, and the sugar season comes to
a depressing close. Pipeline sugarers have done somewhat better than bucket people, probably because their tubing-sealed
spouts slowed the drying of the taps during the long interval
before the first run. And for the upmountain and far northern
sugarers, the season will continue for two more weeks, with
several good runs before the sap darkens. But for the Treadways and other valley sugarmen, it has been a disastrous season. Last year—a bad sugar year—the family made 150
gallons of Fancy alone. This year they manage to can
54 gallons total, 37 of A, 17 of C. The rule of thumb is that
it requires four taps to make a gallon of syrup. Last year, the
Treadways made a gallon for every six taps. And this year?
This year the tap-to-gallon ratio works out twenty-five to
one.

These numbers will make it difficult to extract much fun out
of the task of cleaning up the evaporator, or of pulling 1,350
spouts out of maple trees with claw hammers, or of gathering
and stacking 1,350 buckets and 1,350 covers in the sugar bush,
or of putting those stacks into the bucket loader and hauling
them back to the barn, or of washing the 1,350 buckets one at
a time in sinks moved outdoors from the milkhouse, or of packing them and the covers up the rickety stairs above the shop to
store them next to the wooden sap buckets of yesteryear. End-
of-season sugaring chores are not going to be among the happier
on record.

"I guess we'll *have* to sugar next year," Dick says ruefully;
"we've got the wood and the cans already."

## 15

APRIL PROVES, IF NOT A CRUEL MONTH, A mostly depressing one in the valley. Early on the weather story was off-again on-again cold rain, the newly arrived phoebes sitting disconsolate on low perches in an insect-barren world. Snow intervened on the night of the ninth, and furious snow squalls erupted the following day. The snow disappeared in more rain, and then it snowed again on the thirteenth, and then the rains returned. The amphibian mating season should have been in full swing, but the rains were too cold, though on the morning of the sixteenth a few wood frogs were quacking back in woodland ponds, and the first of the season's spotted sala- mander, red eft, and wood frog corpses could be found on area roads, females of the latter spewing gelatinous egg masses.

Midmonth brought more rain, and it snowed for the last time on the twenty-second, and then, while the Southwest and still drought-stricken and wind-eroding Plains states and then the Southeast were setting record high temperatures, the New En- gland weather finally cleared but remained cool under a persis- tent northerly air flow. It is on such a day during spring vacation week that a Hendy company pickup arrives towing the bright new green-and-yellow John Deere 328 baler. Don is conferring with the delivery man when the fire phone rings, and Dick, Don, and Jeff are off in the Ford truck for the village, leaving a sud- denly quiet farm.

There is little green in the landscape; indeed, if one misses the furry male catkins hanging from fencerow aspens and the vague rose blush of red maple flowers, a middle-distance view shows little in the way of vegetational advertisement for the coming season. A vesper sparrow picks in the now-dusty tractor road below the barn, then flies into a small dead elm and sings. A red-tailed hawk and then a sharp-shinned hawk ride a thermal overhead, gaining altitude before setting off to the north. An anomalous shape across a meadow swale resolves itself into a red fox. Observed, it trots southeast, stops and stares, walks, stops and stares, taking five minutes to traverse the fifty yards to a brush-lined fence. It lies low in tall grass by the fence and, come upon again, it scampers down to a stream and up the far ground-juniper-dotted pasture slope.

Leaf-out has yet to begin on 'Coon Ridge, but new growth is showing among the dead leaf litter. Mullein rosettes are blue-greening, the new pointed leaves soft and furry as makeup pads, and the mottled dull red-brown and soft green adder's tongue leaves are popping up here and there. Five-petaled Carolina spring beauties are blooming under the hardhacks, their soft lavender flowers veined with rose. Delicate, hairy-stemmed hepaticas are in bloom as well, in pink, purple, white, and baby blue.

A blue jay bugles; a kestrel cackles in the distance. The minor-key two-note chickadee song reiterates along the ridge. Tiny red mites patrol lichen-blotched rocks. A pile of deer pellets lies along a four-foot-high stone wall above 'Coon Ridge, and old scat spaced along the top of the wall shows that a fox has used the wall as a regular runway. Most of the dung crumbles to reveal chitinous remains of last summer and fall's meadow grasshoppers. The mellow tooting of a pileated woodpecker sounds from the woods on the farm's east boundary. The rock crevasses on 'Coon Ridge still have foot-thick ice floors, but above them, along the west-facing cliff, patches of multipetaled white bloodroot are in glorious bloom, each plant's leathery green leaf cupping the flower stem.

A pair of phoebes—uncharacteristically silent—work the back edge of the ridge, flying out or down for insects, then returning to branch or fence wire to pump their tails and watch. Silent, too, is the polished white skull of a striped skunk nestled among the crisp oak and hardhack leaves, the six incisors and two jutting canines of the upper jaw still in place. Here and there along the cliff edge of the ridge are great masses of different-aged dung—the farm coyotes' defecatoria—mostly on the roots of great tree boles, but also on flat logs and rock platforms. Tucked into rock-outcrop crannies side by side with coyote scat are newly blooming wild gingers, the curious bladder-shaped red-brown flowers hugging the rock between a pair of hairy-stemmed valentine-shaped leaves. At the north end of 'Coon Ridge, between two outflow streams below a tiny cattail pond, clumps of bright green marsh marigolds thrive among the hummocks, a few already showing lighter green knob-shaped flower buds.

The Treadway men have returned from a minor fire, and Dick appears on a meadow west of the ridge dispensing dry fertilizer from a commercial spreader. In a typical year, the family would now have finished sugaring chores and be at work fixing fences. But with next to no snow to melt, mud season ended abruptly in midmonth, and the farm is now bone dry, the clay already cracking in places. Dry and cold means no growth in the pastures, and so no hurry about fixing fences. Dry land also means the Treadways can get an early start on field work, and the stacks of unwashed sap buckets wait next to the corn head above the shop while the family scrambles to order lime and seed while getting on with harrowing and fertilizing. It's supposed to rain on Sunday, and Dick would like to get some crops in first.

Jeff, who had been at the shop fixing the old manure spreader's beater when the fire call came in, is now below the feed bunk, loading the spreader with the bucket loader, whence he shuttles back and forth to the corn pieces east of the farmstead. He interrupts the routine to spread—and harrow in—part of a load on his grandfather's garden. Don doesn't sound particularly enthusiastic about getting into planting, but serious considerations are pushing him in that direction. "My pickles are getting pretty scarce," he says. "Potatoes, too."

It's past 4 P.M. now. Clouds have been building all afternoon, and the overcast is now nearly complete. The wind is chill out of the northwest. Crows caw. The cows have collected at the south gate of the barn. Dick and Don have gathered at the new baler, lifting lids, cranking cranks, wondering about fluid capacities and how the timing mechanism works and what will break first. Kevin charges up on his bike, Brian right behind with his baseball glove. The boys climb about on the baler exploring. Dick and Kevin wonder how far the platform kicker on this rig would catapult a boy about Brian's size. Brian isn't at all cowed by the idea, but he's got to get to baseball practice, and Don leaves to drive him to the village. Dick has a bone to pick with Kevin's new hamster, which immediately figured out the exercise wheel in its cage. "He played on it all night," Dick says; "trouble is, it squeaks."

Joan, who has been taking clothes off the backyard lines, now strolls into sight in her barn clothes. "Go find Jeff," Dick says to Kevin; "it's time we got to chores."

SUNDAY COMES, AND A HUMID, OVERCAST morning seems to promise the predicted rain. It does not rain, and in the early afternoon the cloud cover vanishes into thin air, the sun pushes the mercury into the mid-60s, and just like that— on the last day of spring vacation, which happens also to be the last day of April—it feels for the first time this year like spring.

At the north end of the new meadow below the hill west of the road, a big porcupine grazes on new clover. The near-sighted animal chatters its teeth at closely approaching humans, munches more clover when they back off, then waddles off into the white pine woods, carefully lifting and placing each leather-covered footpad. There isn't much clover showing on this meadow, or anything else for that matter. A bit of grass here and there, but very little alfalfa. "We'll just have to wait and see," Dick says; "maybe something will come up."

On the warm, west-facing hillside below the meadow, the

woodland floor is thick with adder's tongue leaves, promising a
sea of yellow blooms for May. Flower buds on the earliest violets are a couple of warm days short of opening, leaving the
show at present to the elegant white bloodroot and the low-
profile wild ginger. There is more insect life about now—in the
air, on plants, on the ground—and ten miles to the east in the
mixed woods below Mount Moosalamoo on the western flank
of the Green Mountains, the first red-eyed and solitary vireos are
in song, competing with a multitude of ruby-crowned kinglet
lisps and the hoarse-cat *yeowws* of yellow-bellied sapsuckers.
Next week, fern fiddleheads will be lifting above the duff in
Shoreham woodlots, and early shad will burst into delicate
bloom along the fencerows. Next week, yellow-rumps will be
flitting about the hemlock groves, and barn swallows will be
chattering about the Treadway houses and barns, back at the
farm in time to find robins and grackles and song sparrows
already building nests and incubating eggs.

Daffodils and forsythia have been making a show for some
time in town, where favored lawns already sport scattered stands
of short-stemmed dandelions, but things are generally slower on
the farm. Tulip leaves, at least, are well along in Joan's flower
box bordering the front patio, and patches of flat spiked leaves
in front of the older home's stone porch foundation mark the
return of Irene's wonderful iris. Tiny green leaves decorate the
farmstead's lilacs, and the swimming pool is iceless at last, two
water striders stalking the surface of the green, leaf-strewn
water.

It is evening when the family finish milking, but still full light,
and Dick, Jeff, and Kevin leave the barn to the young stock and
a sore-footed cow and Spooky's litter of five blind kittens, and
join Becky, Brian, and Brian's friend Ben in batting and (sometimes) catching balls in the meadow above the house. After a
time the game thins out again. Dick leaves for town and his
seven-to-midnight ambulance shift, while Jeff, apparently thirst-
ing for headier entertainment, takes the three-wheeler for a roaring spin up and down the road. The landscape slowly darkens,

the valley to the east dimming first, and when Joan calls the children in for supper, only the farm's east ridge and two silver silo domes still catch the sun.

Sandwiches and chips are consumed at the kitchen table in anticipation of a rented video, and immediately afterward Joan and the children flop down in the living room to watch Rodney Dangerfield get shut of an execrable wife and make a shambles of his son's college. The film over and the kids beginning to wander in the direction of bed, Joan steps out the front door into a warm, still night, checking the high, black, star-dotted sky. It is perfectly quiet on Cutting Hill Road, except that, from the brook at the bottom of the hill to the north, she can hear—a full month late this tardy season—the first tentative spring peeper calls, which she knows will swell to full chorus after the next warm rain. She smiles. "What with the frogs carrying on all night and the robins starting up before first light, it's tough sometimes to get a decent sleep around here."

She leans over the stoop railing into the warm night, preoccupied now with her own thoughts. Perhaps she is wondering how Dick's emergency shift is going, or perhaps she is thinking ahead to the upcoming state FFA meeting, to which Jeff has been invited as district representative in the Outstanding Future Farmer competition, and which she and Dick plan to attend as well, hiring someone to do chores for the day. Perhaps her thoughts carry ahead to autumn, when Jeff will begin a two-year course in diesel mechanics at the State University of New York's Cobleskill campus, and to the question of whether, with $15-an-hour jobs already waiting in several diesel shops, her eldest son will make any kind of future farmer at all. She may be thinking about the school experiences in store for her other children, wondering how Kevin will take to high school and Becky to a full day of first grade, and whether Brian will manage to conclude his elementary school career without more broken bones.

Perhaps she is thinking about the farm, wondering about the extent of winter kill on alfalfa ("We're going to be awful short on hay," Don says, "unless the Lord is kinder to us than I think He's going to be"), or wondering how the farm work will get done with Jeff off to college, or worrying for the thousandth time about this summer's silo-jacking. She may once again be rehearsing the arguments—which currently fill the newspapers and dairy magazines—over the new industry controversy, BST (bovine somatotropin), a soon-to-be-available synthesized growth hormone for cows, which its chemical company producers tout as a sure bet to increase milk yield, while skeptics in farm circles wonder how much it will cost, how big an increase in grain rations will be required to support that increased yield, whether treated cows will "burn out" early, whether increased yields may not—by triggering cuts in government price supports—actually lower farmers' incomes, and whether American consumers will embrace milk from BST-treated cows.

Joan may be contemplating the future of the farm on Cutting Hill Road. There are financial questions, of course, as there must be for the operator of any business whose economics are, like those of dairy farming, marginal. There are personal considerations as well. There is the continuing family concern for Irene, of course. ("She was in the hospital with a bad spell a year ago," Joan has said, "and the farmhouse seemed deserted without her.") There is the troublesome cartilage problem in her own knees. ("The doctor says that deep knee bends are bad for you; and when you milk cows, you're doing fourteen protracted sessions of deep knee bends every week.") Most of all, she worries that Dick may not be able to finish out the nineties on the farm. "Farmer's lung"—an allergic reaction to the infinitely small dust particles and mold spores that farmers breathe in while working hay and silage—attacks and scars deep lung tissue, and, after repeated exposure, becomes untreatable. The threat of farmer's lung hangs over every farmer, but it is doubly dangerous to an asthmatic like Dick. ("Especially a stubborn one," Joan will say, "who won't wear his mask half the time.") What would the future hold for the family, should farming become impossible?

And even if she and Dick are able to stick it out, will any one of the children want to carry on with the farm when they retire?

The look of preoccupation fades, and Joan finds herself once again in a quiet early-spring night on firm, familiar ground. She takes a last look and smell of the rich warm darkness before retiring. "The bats will be back in the barn any night now," she says; "it's time we thought about getting the heifers out to pasture."

## A Note About the Author

ALAN PISTORIUS is a writer and naturalist living
in Leicester, Vermont. He received his A.B. from the
State University of Iowa and his M.A. and Ph.D.
from the University of California, Berkeley. He is the
author of *The Country Journal Book of Birding and
Bird Attraction,* co-author of several books, and co-
editor of *Treasury of North American Birdlore.* He
is also the author of numerous magazine articles and
reviews.